PIONEERS

OF

INTERPERSONAL

PSYCHOANALYSIS

ABOUT THE EDITORS

Donnel B. Stern, Ph.D. is a Supervising Analyst and member of the Faculty at the William Alanson White Institute, the Manhattan Institute of Psychoanalysis, and the Institute for Contemporary Psychotherapy. He is on the Editorial Boards of *Contemporary Psychoanalysis* and *Psychoanalytic Dialogues*.

Carola H. Mann, Ph.D. is a Training and Supervising Analyst, Fellow, member of the Faculty, and Director of Continuing Professional Education at the William Alanson White Institute. She is also a member of the Faculty and Supervisor at the Westchester Center for the Study of Psychoanalysis and Psychotherapy.

Stuart Kantor, Ph.D. is a member of the Teaching Faculty, Supervisor of Psychotherapy, a Supervising Analyst, and Director of Adolescent Treatment Service at the William Alanson White Institute. He is also an Adjunct Assistant Professor of Psychology and Education at Teachers College, Columbia University.

Gary Schlesinger, Ph.D. is a member of the Faculty at the William Alanson White Institute and is an Adjunct Assistant Professor of Psychology at New York University.

Lib

er

PIONEERS

OF

INTERPERSONAL

PSYCHOANALYSIS

edited by

DONNEL B. STERN

CAROLA H. MANN

STUART KANTOR

GARY SCHLESINGER

THE ANALYTIC PRESS

1995   Hillsdale, NJ   London

Published by
The Analytic Press, Inc.
Hillsdale, New Jersey 07642

Typeset by AeroType, Inc.

Library of Congress Cataloging-in-Publication Data

Pioneers of interpersonal psychoanalysis / Donnel Stern ... [et al.].
    p.   cm.
    Includes bibliographical references and index.
    ISBN 0-88163-177-9 (hardcover). — ISBN 0-88163-216-3 (paperback)
    1. Psychoanalysis.   2. Interpersonal relations.   3. Psychotherapist and patient.   I. Stern, Donnel.
RC506.P564   1995
616.89′17—DC20   95-30973
                                                                      CIP

Printed in the United States of America
10 9 8 7 6 5 4 3 2 1

CONTENTS

PREFACE

Interpersonal psychoanalysis as we know it today is rooted in the thinking of Harry Stack Sullivan and Erich Fromm. Starting in the 1930s, these men, along with Frieda Fromm-Reichmann, Clara Thompson, Karen Horney, Janet Rioch Bard, David MacKenzie Rioch, and others, worked out a new psychoanalytic way of understanding, one based in interpersonal relations, not drive. In 1943, this same group (minus Fromm-Reichmann, who was based at Chestnut Lodge in Massachusetts, and Horney, who went her own way and formed a separate training institute) joined together in New York City as the founders of the William Alanson White Institute of Psychiatry, Psychoanalysis, and Psychology. The present volume, conceived by Carola Mann, Ph.D., is a memorial to that first generation of White Institute interpersonalists and to those psychoanalysts-to-be who enrolled at the White Institute in its very early days. Reprinted here are important, often classic, articles by the now-deceased pioneers of the interpersonal perspective. Our intention, in this era of theoretical tolerance and pluralism among psychoanalysts, is to draw attention back to the work of writers who worked in the interpersonal vein when it required genuine courage to do so. Since our purpose is to memorialize this vanished era and some of the people who made it what it was, we have reprinted the articles in the chronological order of their publication. Though we have not, of course, edited the articles for content or expression, we have recast their formats so they would appear here in a uniform style. Whenever it was possible, we also modernized and completed those references that were archaic and incomplete. In a few cases, we were unable to do this; those references appear in their original form. References cited in the introductions are listed at the back of the book, preceding the index.

This collection does not include writers who might well be considered pioneers of the interpersonal movement but who were not centered at the White Institute, such as Mabel Blake Cohen, Leslie Farber, Lewis Hill, Karen Horney, Edith Weigert, and Otto Will. Even limiting attention to past writers from the White Institute, though, did not allow us to reprint articles by all those we would have liked to include. Max Deutscher, Gloria Friedman, and Roberta Held-Weiss are the most notable of this group. Nor, given our intention to put together a memorial volume, could we include articles by living pioneers Gerard Chrzanowski, Marianne Horney Eckardt, Arthur H. Feiner, Edgar A. Levenson, Rollo May, Ruth Moulton, Rose Spiegel, Alberta Szalita, Earl Witenberg, Benjamin Wolstein, and Miltiades Zaphiropoulos, who are today the most influential senior contributors to the interpersonal psychoanalytic literature. Most of them have published throughout each of the last four decades. We are privileged that several of them have contributed introductions to the chapters in this volume.

Interpersonal psychoanalysts were among the first to think about the informative value of countertransference, and several of the classic articles in this book illustrate that fact. Janet Rioch Bard's paper appeared in 1943, Ralph Crowley's in 1952, and Edward Tauber's—unbelievably radical and open minded for his time—in 1954. Mabel Blake Cohen, Clara Thompson, and Benjamin Wolstein also published important work on the topic during the 1950s. The paper of Erwin Singer's chosen for this volume appeared some years later, in 1971, and its full embrace of the idea that psychoanalysis is inevitably a reciprocal interaction reflects the growth in interpersonal views of transference–countertransference during the 1960s.

Another area of early exploration among the interpersonal group was the intensive dynamic psychotherapy of psychotic patients, which Sullivan, Fromm-Reichmann, Otto Will, and a few others were the first to practice and conceptualize. Fromm-Reichmann's paper in this volume was part of that early thrust. Clara Thompson, along with Karen Horney and (within a few years) Ruth Moulton, recognizing the shortcomings of Freud's views of women, pioneered the neoFreudian psychology of women. One of Thompson's significant articles in this area appears here. Ernest Schachtel was an early and trenchant critic of libido theory, and his *Metamorphosis*, published in 1959, remains a masterwork of developmental psychoanalysis. Schachtel's article "On Memory and Childhood Amnesia" is undoubtedly his most widely known article, but because it has been republished frequently, we have chosen for this volume his equally important 1954 article on the development of focal attention and reality. Harry Bone, while not a prolific writer, did have a good deal of influence as a teacher. His article here illustrates the longstanding interest many interpersonalists have had in delineating the relationship between interpersonal and intrapsychic phenomena.

Several writers who obviously belonged in this book did not write an article that has attained the status of a classic; they are remembered instead for the body of their work. In the cases of these writers, articles that summarized their thinking or their orientation were selected. Silvano Arieti's whole career revolved around cognition, even when he was writing about depression and schizophrenia, so a summary article on "Cognition in Psychoanalysis" that he wrote late in life was a natural choice. Joseph Barnett, too, focused on cognition, though he used the concept in a way very much his own. His article here, also published late in his career, pulls together in one place much of his earlier thinking. David Schecter's paper summarizes his innovative and sensitive developmental thinking. John Schimel's article here is one of several clinical contributions that might have been chosen, all of which display his laconic wit and creative clinical interventions.

It was not easy to choose single articles by Sullivan and Fromm. After considering more specialized pieces, we settled on Sullivan's "Data of Psychiatry," probably the best single introduction to his thought. Most of the ideas Sullivan discusses here remain alive in interpersonal psychoanalysis today. In Fromm's case, we chose a brief and relatively obscure article that is remarkably contemporary. As far as we know, it has never been reprinted, though it certainly deserves to have been. Unlike most of Fromm's writing, its aim is entirely clinical. Reading it, one appreciates why so many analysts trained in the early days at the White Institute consider him to have been their most influential psychoanalytic supervisor. As a writer, Fromm was nearly always the social critic, seldom the clinician. He was best known to his students, though, as a brilliant and inspiring clinical psychoanalyst.

The writers in this volume all belonged to a single clinical and intellectual community, the William Alanson White Institute. Today that community is in the midst of a creative explosion, with more writers producing more new ideas than at any time since the years of Fromm and Sullivan. It seemed fitting for the work of these pioneers to be introduced by some of the productive contemporary members of their own group, and so each of the articles is prefaced by remarks written by a contemporary psychoanalyst/writer who has some sort of connection to the writer of the article.

That connection may be clinical, intellectual, or personal. The writer of the article may have been the introducer's analyst, supervisor, colleague, or friend—or may have occupied some combination of these roles. In three cases, the introducer did not actually know the writer of the article, though the connection between the two is no less salient for that: Marylou Lionells, who introduces Clara Thompson's article, is today the Director of the White Institute, as Thompson was in her own time; John Fiscalini, who introduces Sullivan's piece, is a highly regarded contemporary teacher and interpreter of Sullivan's thought; and Benjamin Wolstein, who introduces Harry Bone's article on the relation between the intrapsychic and the interpersonal, has made the theme Bone addresses a leitmotif across the several decades of his own work.

In the 11 other introducer/writer pairs, the relationship between the two people is sometimes described in the introductions, sometimes not. Some of the introductions are personal; others concern more the clinical and intellectual legacy of the writer in question. We are very grateful that the writers of the introductions were willing to contribute their time and talents, and we believe that their efforts make this book unique. It is more than a collection of classic articles—it contains informal history, too, and an interchange between the present and the past in interpersonal psychoanalysis.

1

THE DATA OF PSYCHIATRY

HARRY STACK SULLIVAN

[1938]

INTRODUCTION

John Fiscalini

As a contemporary perspective in psychoanalysis, the American school of interpersonal relations draws from the diverse contributions of several generations of interpersonal theorists. Constellatory, however, have been the seminal conceptions of Harry Stack Sullivan, who, more than any other theorist of his generation, laid the foundation for the development of an interpersonal school of thought. Though Sullivan did not invent interpersonal psychoanalysis single-handedly, he did provide a central theoretical armature upon which successive generations of interpersonal theorists could shape their own unique and diverse visions of interpersonal thought and practice. All contemporary interpersonal analysts, however they may differ from one another, have been profoundly influenced by Sullivan's seminal ideas.

Sullivan developed a psychological theory of human experience and behavior that in its comprehensiveness, elegance, and originality rivals Freud's. Sullivan's lifework—the development of an interpersonal theory of human nature and of human psychic disorder and its therapy—was a full metapsychological effort that has profoundly influenced not only all subsequent generations of interpersonalists but also the wider post-Freudian therapeutic community, often in ways that have remained invisible. Thus, such writers as

John Fiscalini, Ph.D. is a Fellow, Training and Supervising Analyst, William Alanson White Institute; coeditor, *Handbook of Interpersonal Psychoanalysis* (The Analytic Press, 1995), coeditor, *Narcissism and the Interpersonal Self;* and Director of Clinical Training, Faculty, Manhattan Institute of Psychoanalysis.

Leston Havens have proclaimed that Sullivan almost secretly dominates American psychiatry and, one might add, all of contemporary psychoanalytic praxis.

Sullivan was one of the seminal figures in the "interpersonal turn" in psychoanalysis, that profound paradigmatic shift, beginning in the 1920s and 1930s and continuing to this day, from drive theory to interpersonal, or object relations, theory and from an impersonal to an interpersonal or personal model of psychoanalytic inquiry. The American school of interpersonal relations, like British object relations and contemporary Freudian ego psychology, has focused on the study of the self, adaptation, character analysis, and the widening of analytic technique to accommodate therapeutic work with the severely disturbed. Unlike these cognate schools, however, interpersonal theory, guided by the democratic, pragmatic, pluralistic, and open-ended spirit of Sullivan and other American analysts, did not retain close ties, either in language or spirit, with orthodox metapsychology.

Though Sullivan did not identify himself as a psychoanalyst, his thinking and sensibility was clearly psychoanalytic, and he developed a psychoanalytic system of the first rank. Sullivan's theory of interpersonal relations deviated from Freud's libidinal metapsychology and proposed a radically new concept of the human as *communal being*—inextricably linked to others in a series of interpersonal fields from cradle to grave. For Sullivan, the communal human, first as infant and then as child and adult, can only be studied and known psychoanalytically through his or her nexus of interpersonal relations—this central idea is implicit in all of his interpersonal concepts of personality and praxis.

Two generations removed from the direct influence of Sullivan, I studied him largely through his posthumously published lectures and writings. From the beginnings of my study of psychoanalysis, I was drawn to Sullivan's ideas. Perhaps because I, like Sullivan, grew up on a relatively isolated farm, I understood intuitively his emphasis on the human need for social attachment—on the centrality of loneliness as a motivating force in human experience—and his concept of the self as socially formed. In the way that we always bring ourselves to our reading or understanding of others, I brought my own sense of personal loneliness and anxiety to my reading of Sullivan. Reading Sullivan was more than simply an intellectual adventure, for, in studying his ideas, I came to understand my own experience in new and deeper ways. Though I have evolved in my own way, and moved from traditional interpersonalism to what I think of as a radical empiricist perspective in interpersonal relations theory, I continue to find Sullivan's interpersonal concepts robust, evocative, and helpful. I continue to find, for example, new meanings in his simple, but profound, one-genus postulate that we are all more simply human than otherwise. I have always found Sullivan's writing filled with human insight and truth, a telling of human experience the way it is, in fact, lived. Sullivan's psychoanalytic concepts always seemed closer to what humans were about than Freudian ideas did. Thus such core concepts as dynamism, self-system, zones of interaction, tension, selective inattention, referential process, somnolent detachment, empathy, anxiety, personification, uncanny experience, and integrating tendency captured for me the dynamic, ever-moving quality and interpersonal complexity of human experience and motivation, and its functional, ever-emerging, developmental nature.

Similarly, Sullivan's interpersonal conceptions of clinical inquiry, his concepts of participant-observation and detailed inquiry caught, for me, the inherently dyadic and dynamically complex, always shifting nature of the psychoanalytic situation, in which the presumed certainty, anonymity, and absolute authority of the impersonal analyst, so characteristic of pre-Sullivanian psychiatry and psychoanalysis, proved mythic. Sullivan provided an alive alternative to what I felt to be the artificial and authoritarian constraints of orthodox technique.

Sullivan's interpersonal theory, in contrast to Freud's theory of personality, is more open ended and interactive in its concept of mind and more dynamic and process oriented in its understanding of human living. Freud's theory, with its hydraulic metaphor, libidinal focus, and psychosexual epigenetic scheme, is a more closed, narrowing concept of mind. In contrast, Sullivan's ideas always seemed to me to provide an expansive view of human personality and possibility. Sullivan's theory, in its operationalism and pragmatism is, in a way, a sparse one, one that stays close to the empirical and the clinical. The human, as Sullivan strove to understand him or her, was to be understood in the significant details of his or her relations with others and the experience of that relatedness, rather than in terms of a complex assemblage of reified mental structures. Though Sullivan outlined, and to some degree filled in, a comprehensive theory of psychological life, his successors, influenced more by his fruitful clinical ideas and guided by a clinical sensibility, have tended, with some major exceptions, to leave aside the development of a fuller, more complete, metapsychology in order to mine the clinical richness of Sullivan's thinking.

Sullivan's contributions to the human sciences are not limited solely to psychoanalytic science or praxis. An important figure in modern American intellectual history, Sullivan's influence has reached far beyond psychoanalysis or psychotherapy. His seminal ideas, particularly his revolutionary concept of empirical inquiry as participant observation, have had a profound impact on several disciplines of thought and continue to influence the nature of empirical methodology in the social sciences of anthropology, sociology, and political science. A complex, multi-faceted man with a broad range of interests in the society of his day, Sullivan was interested in applying his psychiatric and psychoanalytic understanding of human anxiety and disorder to the diagnosis and amelioration of various social evils, including such social and political problems as racial prejudice, international political tensions, and war. Even within the more narrow field of psychotherapy, Sullivan's influence has been extensive, if often unrecognized or unacknowledged. His interpersonal ideas have profoundly shaped contemporary conceptions of family therapy, milieu therapy, hospital psychiatry, social learning therapy, cognitive-behavior therapy, and group therapy, as well as modern psychoanalytic therapy.

Sullivan's mind was active and far-reaching; it was, at once, theoretical, clinical, political, intellectual, and organizational in its scope and interest. Sullivan was talented and multi-faceted in his interests and ambitions—he applied himself to editorial, organizational, and political, as well as to theoretical and therapeutic, developments in his field, and to its political and organizational implementation in related fields of inquiry and practice, for example, national and international politics. This urbane and complex man lived at the intellectual center of an America undergoing vast and complex social, economic, and political upheavals and changes. Sullivan's most enduring legacy, certainly for psychoanalysis, however, lies in the profound impact of his revolutionary interpersonal conceptions of the human psyche or "interpsyche" all, in one way or another, expressing his central view of humankind as irreducibly communal, *homo communis.*

"The Data of Psychiatry," published in 1938 in the first issue of the journal *Psychiatry,* is one of several papers published during the last decade of Sullivan's life that outline his central interpersonal conceptions. In these papers, Sullivan discusses his seminal theoretical and therapeutic concepts of dissociation, selective inattention, self-system, personification, anxiety, empathy, parataxis, "me–you" relations, participant-observation, and detailed inquiry.

Sullivan's concept of the *interpersonal situation* as the unit, the primary datum of psychoanalytic, or psychiatric study forms a central theme of the "Data of Psychiatry." As Sullivan states in this paper, psychiatry or psychoanalysis inevitably becomes "the study of interpersonal phenomena," for "personality is made manifest in interpersonal situations, and not otherwise." In this article, Sullivan clinically illustrates his concept of the interpersonal situation as the unit of psychoanalytic study by presenting a detailed study of the complex and shifting parataxic "me-you" relations of a married couple.

What does Sullivan mean by "interpersonal situation"? What, for example, does he mean when he states that personality is that "hypothetical entity" that is posited to account for "interpersonal fields"? Are individual personalities, thus, nonexistent, simply constructs? Is the interpersonal situation, or field, simply the concrete sum of the external, behavioral actions of two or more people? Does Sullivan, as many assume, deny the intrapsychic, or "inner life"?

A close look at Sullivan's definition of "situation" or "personality" indicates, however, the centrality of personal experience and its internal organization—the "intrapsychic"—in his theoretical system. As Sullivan makes clear in his clinical discussion in "The Data of Psychiatry," he had developed a theory of an internal representational world, an "inner life" of reflected appraisals, personifications, "conceptual me–you" relations, and dynamic "mental" operations—what he, in his latest theoretical statement, the posthumously published *Interpersonal Theory of Psychiatry,* referred to as "the functional interplay of persons and personifications, personal signs, personal abstractions, and personal attributions—which make up the distinctly human." The interpersonal field, in other words, always involves experience and imagination—the "inner workings" of the mind. As Sullivan notes in the "The Data of Psychiatry," interpersonal situations represent "configurations made of two or more people *all but one of whom may be more or less completely illusory."* For Sullivan, the distinction between the interpersonal and the intrapsychic, made by many theorists, is a mythic one. The intrapsychic is always interpersonal, an indivisible amalgam of event and self. Sullivan's internal world, however, in contrast to the closed intrapsychic world of Freudian and post-Freudian metapsychology, is an open one, interactively born and interpersonally dynamic.

Sullivan's theory of the intrapsychic, however, is incomplete, and along with other aspects of his theoretical system—most notably his theory of intimacy (the realm of the relational self) and his theory of sensuality (sexuality)—awaits further development by today's interpersonalists.

Sullivan's theory of experience is focused on the reactive, rather than proactive, aspects of the psyche. Consistent with his field orientation and positivist sensibility, Sullivan, in his interpersonal formulations of the mind, emphasized the communal, observable, and communicable, rather than the innate, private, and idiosyncratic. True to his interest in the communal and the consensual, Sullivan focused on the developmental vicissitudes of the adjusting person in adaptive response to his or her interpersonal surround. Sullivan emphasized how human experience and behavior are shaped (or misshaped) by one's acculturating social environment. He focused, in other words, on the representational self and how it is structured by the play of interpersonal factors, rather than on the organizing self (self as organizing and initiating process), or the creative self (self as spontaneous and a procreative agency). Although Sullivan himself notes in "The Data of Psychiatry" that a "selecting and organizing factor determines what part of . . . observed judgments of one's personal value . . . and which of the deductions and inferences that occur in one's own thinking, shall be incorporated into the self," he did not develop the implications of this and similar notions of a personal self. A theory of man as personifier, organizer, doer, or creator remained an unelaborated theme in Sullivan's system.

Sullivan, in his clinical and theoretical focus on the interpersonal self—the reactive, reflected "me," rather than on the personal self—the active or proactive "I," thus presented a truncated study of the self. Sullivan, like Kohut and many of the object-relations theorists years later, focused on the study of the selfobject aspects of human striving, to the relative neglect of its selfsubject aspects. Sullivan's focus was not on the uniquely individual self, but rather on its shaping interpersonal context. The interpersonal self, the reflected appraisals of significant others, the self shaped by anxious experience, is the dimension of human experience whose study Sullivan found most compelling. And in this area he made a signal contribution. Sullivan's unique view of anxiety is that it is wholly interpersonal in origin, that it springs from our communal humanness—originally "caught" empathically from one's significant caretakers. For Sullivan, anxiety, or social disapproval, plays a central role in human socialization, shaping much of anyone's living and awareness of that living. He, perhaps more than any other psychoanalytic theorist, understood the crippling power of social anxiety and its analytic significance. Sullivan, in his focus on the primary human need for social approval and affirmation, anticipated what has become the central clinical theme in contemporary, post-Freudian psychoanalysis—the inquiry into narcissism, the study of self esteem, and man's search for interpersonal security.

The dimension of anxiety, or the interpersonal self, as Sullivan profoundly understood, forms a central dimension of the human psyche. But this is only part of the story. In addition to the powerful shaping force of interpersonal anxiety, of the need for social affirmation, there are other powerful human yearnings equally formative in their influence on human living. There is, as interpersonalists of a more individualistic strain have pointed out, the equally crucial realm of the self-generative striving for personal fulfill-ment—a full and free living-out of one's uniquely individual psychic capaci-ties and interests.

Though Sullivan, given his strict operationalist philosophy, deemphasized these aspects of the psyche in his interpersonal studies, and eschewed what he called the delusion of unique individuality, other post-Sullivanian inter-personalists have studied this more personal aspect of the human psyche, thus contributing to an expanded interpersonal theory of the self. These contemporary interpersonalists, incorporating personalistic and humanis-tic concerns in their interpersonal orientation, have developed latent themes in Sullivan's work, and have thus contributed to the development of a more rounded interpersonal psychoanalytic psychology—one built upon Sul-livan's insights, but expanded to fulfill their creative potential—that has radical implications for the interpersonal theory of analytic participation and curative action.

Though Sullivan was a major contributor to the development of psycho-analytic theory, perhaps his most enduring and pervasive legacy lies in his contributions to psychoanalytic praxis. His revolutionary conception of the analytic situation as an "interpersonal field"—the notion that the ana-lyst's interpersonal participation forms an integral aspect of the data of psychoanalysis, formulated in terms of the clinical principle of participant observation—has influenced all modern post-Freudian conceptions of psy-choanalytic inquiry.

The radical implications of Sullivan's principle of participant observation, particularly for analysis of transference and countertransference, have occu-pied the clinical attention of several generations of post-Sullivanian analysts who, in various ways, have developed and extended this concept of interper-sonal psychoanalytic inquiry. Sullivan's clinical focus, like his theoretical emphasis, was on the study of the interpersonal self. For Sullivan, as for those contemporary interpersonalists who might be termed traditional preserva-tionists, the detailed psychoanalytic inquiry into the interpersonal self fo-cuses on how the interactive analytic dimension affects patients' narrative reports of historical or extratransference experiences. More radically, how-ever, many post-Sullivanian analysts, who could be called radical preserva-tionists, preserve Sullivan's clinical focus on the interpersonal self, but have extended his participant-observer model with a new emphasis on the inter-personal analysis of the here-and-now transference-countertransference ma-trix as the center of their work, often emphasizing radical diagnostic and expressive uses of countertransference experience. Building upon and ex-tending the implications of Sullivan's concept of participant-observation in a different way, other contemporary interpersonalists, the radical empiricists, focus, like the radical preservationists, on the analysis of transference and countertransference in the interpersonal field, but with a greater clinical emphasis on immediate experience and first-personal processes. This con-temporary view of Sullivan's participant-observer model of psychoanalytic inquiry as a coparticipant process emphasizes, in Ferenczian manner, the patient's role as a full copartner in the analytic inquiry. This extension of Sullivan's field principle, in its emphasis that both analyst and patient are participant observers and observed participants, calls for a radical individuation of psychoanalytic metapsychologies and methodologies.

All contemporary interpersonalists, though they apply Sullivan's field principle in many different and individual ways, are alike in that they emphasize the transactive, interactive, and intersubjective nature of the analytic process. Transference and countertransference are seen as mutually created by both analytic participants, rather than as exclusively endogenous expressions of either's closed intrapsychic world. The analytic expressions of transference and countertransference are, in this contemporary interpersonal view, variable amalgams of the unconscious of both patient and analyst. A central technical implication of this modern interpersonal approach is that understanding of the patient's personality inevitably involves an understanding of the analyst's personality. Countertransference analysis thus becomes an integral aspect of transference analysis. Interpersonal analysts focus variably on both their patients' and their own experiences of their analytic relatedness, often inviting the patient to do the same. Particularly for those post-Sullivanian analysts who embrace a more coparticipatory view of the analytic situation, this forms the interpersonal pathway to the understanding of patients' unconscious lives. From this point of view, a monadic and noninteractive approach to transference, even if relational in metapsychology, inevitably limits and often distorts the analyst's understanding of the patient and himself or herself. As Sullivan pointed out long ago, if analysts believe they can study their patients in some detached manner, their "data is incomprehensible."

The American school of interpersonal relations has evolved over the several decades since Harry Stack Sullivan's pioneering contributions. It has grown increasingly complex and now encompasses a rich and broadly diverse group of practitioners representing a variety of different viewpoints and clinical practices. Sullivan developed a new and radical set of psychoanalytic ideas—of interpersonal conceptions—that have been, and continue to be, developed by successive generations of interpersonal theorists in ever new, more radical, and fruitful ways.

P sychiatry as a science is concerned with the thinking and doings of persons, real and illusory. Everything personal is data for psychiatry, and relevant exactly to the extent that it is personal. Many of the phenomena of life that at first glance seem subpersonal or impersonal are found to have personal connections which make them of psychiatric interest. The whole subject of human biology is directly or indirectly psychiatric. All

Reprinted from *Psychiatry* (1938) 1:121–134. Reprinted in: *The Fusion of Psychiatry and Social Science*. Norton, 1971, pp. 32–55.

contemplations of human thinking and all study of social or group life are tributary to psychiatry. All that is man-made and used by man, all that the anthropologist calls culture, has personal and therefore psychiatric aspects and implications. The range of psychiatric relevance is vast indeed. The primary concern of psychiatry as a science, however, is relatively narrow. Psychiatry seeks to discover and formulate the laws of human personality. It is only indirectly concerned with the study of abstractions less or more inclusive than the person. Its peculiar field is the study of *interpersonal phenomena*. Personality is made manifest in interpersonal situations, and not otherwise. It is to the elucidation of interpersonal relations, therefore, that psychiatry applies itself.

1. The personality that can be studied by scientific method is neither something that can be observed directly nor something the unique individuality of any instance of which would be any concern of the psychiatrist. The individuality of a particular electron is of no concern to the physicist; the individuality of the biologist's dog is not apt to confuse his biology of the dog. It is quite otherwise, however, with the traditionally emphasized individuality of each of us, "myself." Here we have the very mother of illusions, the ever pregnant source of preconceptions that invalidate almost all our efforts to understand other people. The psychiatrist may, in his more objective moments, hold the correct view of personality, that it is the hypothetical entity that one postulates to account for the doings of people, one with another, and with more or less personified objects. In his less specialized operations this same psychiatrist joins the throng in exploiting his delusions of unique individuality. He conceives himself to be a self-limited unit that alternates between a state of insular detachment and varying degrees of contact with other people and with cultural entities. He arrogates to himself the principal role in such of his actions as he "happens" to notice.

2. Psychiatry is the study of the phenomena that occur in interpersonal situations, in configurations made up of two or more people, all but one of whom may be more or less completely illusory. This study has obvious relevance for the doings of everyone under most of the circumstances that characterize human life. Habitual operations on inanimate objects are an exception, in so far as they have come to include nothing personal. They are not the only exceptions, and some people manifest a somewhat less striking preponderance of interpersonal actions than do others. In general, however, anything that one *notices* is apt to be interpersonal and thus within the field of valid psychiatric data. Few interpersonal phenomena may appear in a mechanic's "listening" to a strange noise that has appeared in one's automobile. When he formulates his opinion, however, and particularly when he discovers that he is mistaken, this is no longer the case. Interpersonal factors in the latter situation may

overshadow his technical competence to the serious detriment of one's car, may ensue in alterations in one's personal organization such that interpersonal factors seriously complicate all of one's subsequent dealings with auto mechanics, with any mechanics, or even with engineers and experts in all fields pertaining to machinery.

3. Human behavior, including the verbal report of subjective appearances (phenomena), is the actual matter of observation of the psychiatrist; it is important, however, to note that the act of observing is in itself human behavior and involves the observer's experience. That which one cannot experience cannot be observed, but people seem all much more simply human than otherwise, and the data of psychiatry are for the most part events of frequent occurrence. At the same time, these data are often matters the *personal significance* of which is veiled from the person chiefly concerned, and more or less obscured in the process of being observed by another. This is always the case with processes that go on in sleep; it is often the case in the mental disorders called *parergasia;*[1] and it is not infrequently the case in the doings of everyday life. Thus, the experience of weariness is often a veiled expression of resentment; and unreasonable worry about someone, the disguised expression of a hostile wish.[2] Neither resentment nor hostility would appear in the person's verbal report of his mental state, because they exist outside of his awareness: it is from observation of his continued behavior towards the other person that one may demonstrate their presence "in him." We say that he is motivated to punish or to harm, but judge that these motives are denied his recognition, and are absent from his intentions. When he uses the pronoun "I," he includes in its reference only those motives of which he is aware, and refers to his *self,* a much less inclusive entity than the hypothetical

---

[1]"Mental disorder" as a term refers to interpersonal processes either inadequate to the situation in which the persons are integrated, or excessively complex because of illusory persons also integrated in the situation. It implies some—sometimes a great—ineffectiveness of the behavior by which the person is conceived to be pursuing the satisfactions that he requires. It is not, however, to be envisaged as an equivalent of *psychosis,* "insanity," or the like. The failure to remember the name of an acquaintance at the opportune moment is just as truly an instance of mental disorder as is a fixed delusion that one is Napoleon I.

The term *parergasia* is used throughout this text to refer to a group of serious mental disorders that make up the particular patterns of interpersonal maladjustment seen in more fully developed form in many patients diagnosed as suffering the *dementia praecox* of Kraepelin or the *schizophrenia* of Bleuler.

The term *parergasia* is a part of the psychiatric formulations of Professor Adolf Meyer, to whom the writer, like many another psychiatrist, is greatly indebted.

[2]So great are the difficulties in communicating the viewpoints of psychiatry—and so limited in particular are the capacities of the writer—that one may well distrust as a matter of principle the impressions gained on first reading of any part of this text. If the reader should seem to find something new and important, I must bespeak of him a rereading . . . of the whole. One of the sociologists who read the fourth version—this is the seventh— remarked that my ideas were contagious, but, like some other contagious things, they had a considerable incubation period.

personality with which the psychiatrist invests him. This self is an entity that is of little service as a general explanatory principle in the study of interpersonal relations. The weariness and the worry are fully real to the self, and provoke no feeling of incompleteness or obscurity. If the weariness should suddenly disappear when some new activity is suggested by a third person, or the worry be entirely assuaged by a game of bowling, no suggestion of inconsistency arises to disturb one's feeling of completeness, no awareness of the missing motive ensues. Even if an observer should suggest the probable motivation, no extension of awareness is to be expected, but instead a series of *rationalizations;* that is, plausible statements, in general appealing to prejudices (unwarranted beliefs), held by many persons known to the speaker, without particular regard to probability but only to interpersonal expediency, to the end that the observer shall defer to the "explanations" and thus withdraw the challenge to the other's self-esteem.

4. Psychiatry concerns itself with the way in which each of us comes to be possessed of a self which he esteems and cherishes, shelters from questioning and criticism, and expands by commendation, all without much regard to his objectively observable performances, which include contradictions and gross inconsistencies. We know that these self-dynamisms,[3] clearly the referent[4] of a great part of our conversation and other social behavior, are by no means inborn, relatively immutable, aspects of the person. Not only do they show significant differences between people from various parts of the world, and between the siblings of one family, but they change their characteristics in a more or less orderly fashion as one progresses from childhood to maturity. Sometimes they undergo rather abrupt and extensive modification in the course of a personal crisis; e.g., a grave mental disorder. These latter in particular (the vicissitudes of the self among the events that make up a severe psychosis) indicate that the content—the expressible convictions and uncertainties—of the self has been acquired in the life of the person, chiefly by communication with others. Much of the praise and some of the blame that has come from parents, teachers, friends, and others with

---

[3]The term *dynamism* is used throughout this text to connote a *relatively enduring configuration of energy which manifests itself in characterizable processes in interpersonal relations.* It is to be preferred to "mental mechanism," "psychic system," "conative tendency," and the like, because it implies only *relatively enduring capacity to bring about change,* and not some fanciful substantial engines, regional organizations, or peculiar more or less physiological apparatus about which our present knowledge is nil.

[4]A *referent* is that to which something refers. As should presently appear, all our information is closely related to the formulation of experience in terms that *might be* used in an attempt to communicate with some other person. The conception of referring pertains to the use in human mentation of abstractions from the events of life, the abstraction usually being closely related to verbal processes—secondary streams of events in which the characteristics of one's particular language are conspicuous factors.

whom one has been significantly related, have been organized into the content of the self. A selecting and organizing factor determines what part of these observed judgments of one's personal value, what of the information that one secures through secondary channels (e.g., reading), and which of the deductions and inferences that occur in one's own thinking, shall be incorporated into the self. The growth of the self is regulated in much the same way as is the growth of an organic system of the body; it is kept in vital balance with the rest of the personality in the functional activities of which it is peculiarly significant.

5. An outstanding activity involving the self is the having, organizing, and utilizing of *information*. Information is that part of our experience of which we are, or may easily become, aware. To be aware of something is to have information about it, and information varies from the merest hint within awareness to the most inclusive of abstract formulations. It is to be noted that information is never identical with any other aspect of reality and that, as in the case of the man's weariness in lieu of resentment, it is sometimes related in a most complicated fashion to the aspects of inter-personal reality of which it is a function within awareness. The man in question may be defined as "one motivated by resentment." This implies that he will behave in such a fashion as to punish the other person, at the same time ideally being more or less clearly aware of (a) an event that called out the motivation, (b) the state of being resentful, (c) the punitive activity, (d) the activity of the other person, and (e) the satisfactory resolution of the situation integrated by the resentment when the second person shall have been discomfited. Our particular man's resentment, however, is represented in awareness as weariness. He does not formulate the resentment in any such form as "you make me tired"; he has no information about his resentment, and little or no information about the other person's relation to his weariness. If now his behavior *unwittingly* thwarts or humiliates the other, the dynamic system which we call his "motivation by resentment" may be discharged. His weariness disappears. He would still have no information as to the punitive character of his behavior and would regard as unjust and unreasonable any imputation that he had been unkind. Under pressure, he might be led to regret the discomfiture of the other, whereupon weariness would probably return. That night, he might dream of some disaster befalling a more or less disguised representation of the object of his unrecognized resentment. He would thus be seen to have undergone (experienced)—quite dissociated from his personal awareness—resentment, its satisfaction in reality, and its reactivation and secondary satisfaction in fantasy, in the dream. Also, he "himself" has experienced two episodes of weariness, about which he may have an indefinite number of (erroneous) convictions, astonishment, or even uncomfortable uncertainty; these representations

within personal awareness amounting to definite misinformation about the interpersonal situation.

6. Suppose now that we review the events leading our hypothetical man to his "psychogenetic" weariness, and find that his wife made a derogatory remark to him a short time before he showed signs of his weariness. If it also appears that this weariness is interfering with some activity planned by his wife, we may be justified in surmising that the underlying resentment was aroused by her expressed disrespect for her husband. Let us now offer this interpretation of the situation to him. We find him anything but open-minded; he shows a definite resistance to our attempt to correct his faults of awareness. He seems determined to remain misinformed. Perhaps he says, "I *never* mind anything like that; my wife means *nothing* by it," or turns the situation against us by expressing chagrin at our imputing such motives to him and his wife. If he is integrated with us by strong motives of affection or respect, he may be led to entertain our interpretation—usually after a series of unsuccessful rationalizations of his weariness. Even though he thus becomes somewhat aware of, "admits," the fact that he is hurt by his wife's apparent lack of respect for him, he may still maintain that "It is her way; she doesn't know any better; that's the way they treated each other in her home," and so forth. In other words, he is claiming that he was made unpleasantly emotional by a fixed type of reaction of his wife's, which is alleged to have no reference to him personally and which, moreover, is habitual—a sad state of affairs, if true. Let us assume that it is *not* true, that his wife demonstrates a nice discrimination in her more or less contemptuous remarks, reserving them exclusively for her husband. It then appears that, though we have been able to improve the accuracy of his awareness of the character of his motivation, we have failed to correct his information as to the motivation of the other person in provoking his previously misrepresented resentment. He has been punishing the offending person, not for merely existing, but for the specific contumely, though he has been doing so unwittingly. It is really difficult for him to become clearly aware of his prehension[5] of his wife's hostile action; there is a specific limitation of his personal awareness of the manifestations of her negative attitude. Some supplementary process has been called out in the experiencing of

---

[5]The term *to prehend* is used throughout this text to mean an intelligible alteration of the personality by an impinging event. Barring familiarity (similarity) of the event, that which is prehended *tends* to be apprehended or clearly noticed within awareness. Unless under various circumstances to be discussed later, the effect of a particular prehension on self-consciousness may vary from focal awareness of the event and its personal meaning to a suppression of the self-consciousness, "complete abstraction" or "unconsciousness," or a massive falsification of the event and its personal implications.

To prehend is to have potential information (or misinformation) about an event; to perceive is to have information or misinformation in, or readily accessible to, awareness.

her offense to his self-esteem which has interfered with his having information about it. The substitution of weariness for resentment is a part of this self-deceptive pattern, a way of eliminating awareness of the motive called out by the event, and thus of diminishing the tendency to become informed as to "what is going on" in the situation. His wife, as she is represented in his personal awareness—as an objectification of certain of the relatively persistent processes that make up his self-dynamism—does not manifest hostility towards him. Yet destructive interpersonal processes are to be observed, and the observer may well wonder as to the future course of the marriage.

7. One may perhaps question the propriety of referring to hostility and to destructive processes in the matter of our hypothetical man and wife—whom we shall henceforth identify as Mr. and Mrs. A. A genial neighbor who was present at the scene we observed—Mr. A's weariness after a slight by Mrs. A—would perhaps brush the whole incident aside as trivial, would task us with making mountains out of molehills, might even, if he is superficially acquainted with "psychoanalysis," surmise that we wished the couple ill and therefore grossly misinterpreted their attitudes toward each other. He might ask, for instance, if it is not more constructive for one to substitute weariness for resentment, if Mr. A was not in fact doing the very best he could to keep the peace between himself and his wife, and to avoid exposing his friends to a disagreeable scene. The general statement that bears on all these considerations runs somewhat as follows: Whenever two people are collaborating towards the achievement of a common goal, they and their interpersonal relations make up, compose, and are integrated into a *personal situation*. Factors in this two-group which improve the collaboration, which increase the probability of achieving the goal, are constructive; factors that hinder the collaboration, diminish the probability, are destructive—with reference to the personal situation. If Mrs. A makes remarks which, were they directed to the observer, would be offensive, but which have no unpleasant effect whatever on A, we may be permitted some curiosity as to the phenomenon, but we would be in error in inferring the presence of destructive processes in the personal situation Mr.-and-Mrs.-A. If Mrs. A's remarks offend A and he is fully aware of his emotion (and retaliatory motivation towards her), the disintegrative effect on the personal situation might still be unimportant. He might resolve the subordinate and contradictory situation integrated by the hostility without particular damage to the major collaboration. In the given case, however, A is not aware of being offended; he is aware of being weary, without reference to Mrs. A or her provocative action. The situation of collaboration is attenuated or suspended by the weariness. He is more or less withdrawn from the A-and-Mrs.-A situation, which becomes subordinate to

his preoccupation with himself and his weariness. Under cover, so to speak, of this preoccupation, the action of retaliation goes on in a dominantly hostile, noncollaborative, A-and-Mrs.-A situation. A and Mrs. A are not collaborating in an exchange of hostility. She has acted against him, perhaps with full awareness of her motivation; but he "suffers weariness" while unwittingly acting against her, in his weariness ceasing to be aware of her relevance in his motivation, to this extent passing from a personal to a *parataxic* situation, a much more complicated entity in that two of the *four* or more persons now concerned, while illusory, are real antagonists to any collaboration of A and Mrs. A. Our Mr. A has become multiplex. There is the perduring A who is much the same day after day. There is a transient A who has no awareness of Mrs. A's expressed hostility and of resenting it, much less of hostile motives towards her; the transient A is dimly aware of an illusory Mrs. A, who has an unwaveringly friendly attitude, and is focally aware of his own weariness. Perduring A has to be recognized in any adequate explanation of the total behavior that is to be observed; transient A, however, has no awareness of incompleteness or inadequacy. This, however, does not imply that transient A is comfortable; on the contrary, he is suffering weariness. And, in final answer to our genial friend of the family, perduring A did not consciously make, show, or choose to manifest, transient A and his weariness, in preference to being angered by his wife; the shift from a more or less adequate pattern of interpersonal relations to the parataxically intricate one happened—and happened so swiftly and by steps so subtle that no trace of what is meant by volition can be discovered in the process.[6]

8. We have been content thus far in our discussion of hypothetical A and Mrs. A to refer to her showing some contempt for her husband, as a result of which he was in some obscure way hurt, slighted, humiliated, offended, angered, and moved to retaliation—although he was not aware of this, but instead felt weary. He *experienced*, lived, underwent, the hostile action; he manifested activity called out by it; but he was not clearly aware of either phase of this, rather avoided our efforts to correct his misinformation about it—and suffered an at first glance wholly irrelevant state, weariness. We have asserted that this course of events was not voluntary but parataxic, an automatic sequence resulting in a complex personal situation including an illusory Mr. A adjusted to an illusory Mrs. A. Let us

---

[6]The term *parataxis* to the writer's knowledge, was first used in a psychiatric sense by Dom Thomas V. Moore, M.D., in a paper entitled "The Parataxes" (*Psychoanalytic Rev.* [1921] 8:252–283). It is adopted for use in this text as a generic term with which to indicate sundry maladjustive or nonadjustive situations, some of which might be called in more conventional language "neurotic"—a misleading and much abused word which, with its substantive, "neurosis," might well be relegated to medical history along with "humors" and other monuments of discarded theories.

again review our fancied observations of the sequence, with some extraordinary aids to our senses.

Let us observe Mr. A in the focus of a "slow-motion" camera. When we study our record, we discover that there is ample evidence that Mr. A experienced something connected with Mrs. A's remarks. He glanced sharply at her and looked away very swiftly. The postural tensions in some parts of his face—if not, indeed, in other of his skeletal muscles—changed suddenly, and then changed again, more slowly. The first change may be hard to interpret; the second is apt to reflect the reductions in tone that are habitual in Mr. A when he is tired. Yet farther, let us suppose that, some time prior to the event, we have caused him to drink some "barium milk" and that we are observing the tone of the muscles in his alimentary canal by aid of the fluoroscope at the time that Mrs. A disturbs him. We have noticed that the shadows cast by the barium in the fluid that fills his stomach and small intestines are of a certain character. The insult comes. We observe, from change in the shape and position of the shadow, that the tone of his stomach walls is changing. His pylorus is becoming much more tense, may actually develop a spasm. The lumen or internal diameter of the small intestines is diminishing; their muscular walls are now more tense. Unlike the first changes in the skeletal muscles, these changes in the visceral muscles develop rather slowly but are persistent. We believe that they begin after the first fleeting shift of postural tension in the skeletal muscles, and that their persistence is connected with the continued feeling of weariness. One might surmise, from all these data, that the impulses which appeared in Mr. A, as he prehended the hostile action of Mrs. A, tended first to the ordinary expression of anger by changes of facial expression, and tensing of some of the other skeletal muscles—perhaps clenching a fist. It would seem that the impulses had very quickly been deflected from these objectively detectable expressive postures and movements, and that they had then discharged themselves by increasing the tension in the musculature of the alimentary tract.

Now if also in our apparatus for augmenting our observational abilities, we had included a device for phonographically recording the speech and adventitious vocal phenomena produced by Mr. A, we would have found interesting data in the field of this peculiarly expressive behavior. Here, too, there would appear a series of phenomena, beginning, perhaps, with an abrupt subvocal change in the flow of the breath. There might appear a rudimentary sort of a gasp. A rapid inhalation may be coincident with the shift in postural tension that we observed in the skeletal muscles. There may then have been a respiratory pause. When Mr. A speaks, we find that his voice has changed its characteristics considerably, and we may secure, in the record of his first sentence, phonographic evidence of a continuing shift of the vocal apparatus, first towards an "angry voice" and then to one somewhat expressive of a state of weary resignation. In brief, with refinements of observational technique applied to the performances of Mr. A as an organism, we find that we can no longer doubt that he experienced, even if he did not perceive, the personal significance of Mrs. A's hostile remark. We see rather impressive evidence of an *inhibition* of a direct, relatively simple, and presumably effective action on his part, and a series of phenomena that may represent the indirect, complicated, and only obscurely effective discharge of the situation. Along with this, we have already observed an inhibition of awareness of his wife's hostility, and the presence in his awareness of the parataxic, illusory, uniformly affectionate Mrs. A.

9. Some of the circumstances surrounding this illusory Mrs. A are peculiarly significant. She is not *all* that Mr. A perceives about his wife. He does not always deceive himself as to her amiability. He has learned, for example, that he cannot alter her dislike for one of his friends, Mr. B, nor can he persuade her to treat Mr. B civilly. Moreover, he has never inhibited his awareness of anger at his wife on occasions when she has been unpleasant to Mr. B. He has quarreled with her repeatedly about it; has condemned her insolence, her attitude of superiority, and her lack of consideration for his feelings for his friend; has finally informed her, with persisting unfriendly feeling, that he is continuing to see Mr. B at his club. In brief, we need assume that Mr. A has but the one illusion about his wife's disposition; namely, that she is uniformly amiable to him. "Of course, we have a spat now and then; but all married people do. We don't agree on everything, but we do agree on each other. We've been married ten years and she's never found a fault with me. And I—why, I'd do it over in a minute. She has made an ideal wife for me. In fact, I think she has been far too considerate of me, she never thinks of herself." As we hear these sentiments, we cannot doubt Mr. A's happiness, nor can we suspect his good faith. He believes; these are convictions that are a part of his self.

Let us explore farther into his views, and ask him, as tactfully as may be, to account for his wife's devotion to him. We learn that he married her because she was so keenly interested in his career. Even from the first, he had to remind himself that she came first, so self-effacing was she. She understands perfectly how exhausting his work can be; is perfectly content to stay at home when he is tired; of course, he sees to it that she has some good times; he has encouraged her to cultivate her natural gifts of musical appreciation and other artistic expression. He did not know this side of life, before marriage, but he has interested himself in it, for her sake, and is now able to enjoy the company of the artist friends that she has accumulated and, if he says it himself, to keep up his end in their conversations. It certainly has not been all on one side; he has gained quite as much as he has given, and his wife's influence has enriched his life very greatly. He did not know Bizet from Bach before he was married and could not tell a Corot from a Rembrandt. He goes with his wife to all the exhibitions now, is beginning a little collection. We recall, perhaps, at this point that the slighting remark that preceded his weariness showed his wife's contempt for his taste in painting. He almost never misses a symphony concert when he is in town, and has season tickets for the Opera. Here we recall to ourselves a friend's comment that Mr. A sleeps through everything but the "Habanera." In a word, while we know that Mr. A does not deceive himself as to his business abilities, does not make many errors of judgment in appraising himself as an executive, and errs rather on the side of underestimating the regard in which he is held by his men friends and acquaintances, it is quite otherwise when he thinks of himself as a husband. His conception of himself as his wife's husband is sadly awry, quite as much in error as is his conception of Mrs. A as his wife. With illusory Mrs. A there goes an illusory Mr. A—the gentleman who is never slighted by this embodiment of amiability and devotion, regardless of the data that our scrutiny of the A-and-Mrs.-A situation reveals. I seek by this fanciful tale to illustrate one of the specific *me-and-you conceptions* that we encounter in any exploration of a person's account of his relations with a (to him) significant person.

We shall now suppose that, instead of participating in the scene of domestic harmony, we are invisibly present at one of the family quarrels—perhaps about Mr. B. Mrs. A has just remarked on the number of evenings that she has had to shift for herself recently, owing, she remarks sarcastically, to her husband's devotion to his cronies. Up to this time, Mr. A has maintained equanimity in the face of her slightly veiled hostility. Now abruptly, he takes a deep breath, glares at her, flings down the newspaper, and in a frankly angry voice says that at least he does not have to listen to crackpots discussing art when he is with his friends. This acts as a cue to his wife, who now sheds all pretense of patience with him. "Don't judge my friends by the fools you spend your evenings with, telling each other what big shots you are and how you'd run the government." There follow sundry extravagant abuses about each other's apparently all-encompassing defects, about the imbecility of each other's friends and preoccupations, and, finally, as the heat mounts steadily, Mrs. A shouts, "And if I ever see that swine B around here again, I'll tell him to his face what he is; and what you are to go around with him." Mr. A undergoes an abrupt change. His color changes, his loud-voiced anger gives place to low-voiced rage. He speaks slowly, perhaps "thickly," as if he had difficulty in articulating his words. He is focally aware of a desire to strike, tear, kill, the illusory Mrs. A who is now before him. She is the epitome of malicious persecutions, a human viper whom the law protects while she taunts him with her ability to destroy his every chance of happiness. He says things about her that would shock him if he were to recall them when he is calm again. She laughs at him as he leaves the room. He is trembling as he goes to the hall closet for his coat and hat. He leaves the house, looks unseeingly at a taxi that pulls in towards the curb, and walks on towards the corner—to find a taxicab. A strange woman who passes him is startled by the hateful look he gives her. At the corner he enters the cab he had previously ignored, gives crisp instructions to take him to the club, and becomes lost in revery. Divorce, mayhem, finding his wife in the arms of a lover—whereupon he, in the presence of witnesses, kills both of them; these are some of the courses of action that flow through his mind. He begins to feel better, overtips the chauffeur at his destination, and orders himself a stiff drink. After sipping it in silence, lost in a revery so deep that he would scarcely be able to recall it, he bethinks himself of companionship, and joins in a game of bridge. In the course of his second rubber, Mr. B comes in and waves a greeting to him. Mr. A nods somewhat jerkily in return. In retrospect, he would have no information about having seen Mr. B. When the game is interrupted, he asks Mr. C to join him in a drink. As the evening wears on, they become immersed in a discussion of women. The views that A now expresses leave no place for the vaguely amiable, self-effacing woman that we encountered in the first of the illusory Mrs. A's. One gathers that women are the factual source of the belief in personal devils. As the refinements of his self-restraint become progressively beclouded, A proceeds to unfold his personal experiences with marriage. He has been deceived, exploited, cheated, humiliated, ignored, ridiculed. The self-confidence that is so necessary in his business has been undermined systematically. He has listened to so much "wishful thinking" that he is getting unrealistic himself. In short, Mr. A, as he now expresses himself, is quite as different from the happy benedict of his previous self-revelation, as is the second illusory Mrs. A from the first. A different "me" corresponds to the different illusory Mrs. A.

10. Each "me" and its appropriate "you" are part aspects of different configurations that recur in the A-and-Mrs.-A situation as it is extended in time, as the two go on living together. We might speak of an A'-and-Mrs.-A' pattern which is characterized in his consciousness by mutual respect and affection, and an A"-and-Mrs.-A" pattern which is characterized by mutual contempt and hostility. Scrutiny might reveal a third, a fourth, a fifth of these me–you patterns in the interaction of A and his wife. Had we chosen to attend to the wife instead of the husband, we would have found a series of recurrent me-you patterns in her

consciousness of herself and her husband. Her several me-conceptions would have been rather simply related to her several conceptions of A as "you." Each, too, would be a part-aspect of a configuration that recurs in their relations.

Let us now consider the circumstances that call out these various me–you patterns in the interactions of A and Mrs. A. We have seen A'-and-Mrs.-A' and A"-and-Mrs.-A". Let us assume a Mrs. A'-and-A' that is an illusion-pair of the tolerant wife-mother to a rather incompetent, absurdly conceited, but devoted husband; and a Mrs. A"-and-A", the disillusioned victim of an utterly selfish man who regards women as inferior creatures for whose services almost anything is extravagant overpayment. It will be apparent that these two sets of patterns can be fairly congruous aspects of two configurations in the A-and-Mrs.-A situation. Mrs. A has a me–you pattern that permits an approximate agreement of mutual illusion when A's motivation is friendly. She has a pattern that "suits" their integration in a frankly hostile relationship. This is usually the case, and the reader, considering his own relations with some intimate, may wonder why I have depicted the pairs of illusions as only imperfectly congruous. The series of me–you patterns and their more or less congruous me–you patterns in the awareness of one's intimate are seldom, severally or collectively, of much value as objectively verifiable descriptions of the two personalities concerned. All that A conceives of Mrs. A, or Mrs. A of A, may be beside the point, excepting in rationalizing their actions with each other. Moreover, the approach towards congruence that we have depicted need not be present; A'-and-Mrs.-A' may coincide with Mrs. A"-and-A". Mr. A will then feel that he is misunderstood, for this or that reason not to his wife's discredit; and Mrs. A, that she is penetrating one of his crafty attempts to mislead her. If situations of this kind recur fairly frequently, new sets of me–you patterns are apt to develop which are less incongruous aspects of the unitary interpersonal situation with which they are associated. This, however, need not be the case. The incongruity in the coincident me-you patterns may grow to such a point that A comes to think "something is wrong" with Mrs. A, and consults a psychiatrist about her. He reports that "she seems to have undergone a complete change. She misunderstands everything I do, thinks I deceive her about everything. The more I try to reassure her, the more suspicious she gets, the more firmly she believes I am doing underhanded things to her. It doesn't make any sense at all, and you can't reason with her." He speaks of a change having occurred in his relation with his wife. While she has always shown some suspiciousness about people, has attributed bad motives to them more frequently than he himself felt was justifiable, this tendency at first did not involve him. As he looks back, he sees that the tendency to think ill of others had been growing on Mrs. A for some considerable time before she centered her hostility on him.

11. The psychiatrist knows that the present state of the A-and-Mrs.-A situation cannot possibly be formulated in meaningful terms until there are extensive data as to its history. He will wish to secure an outline of the whole history of the situation, will take pains to elucidate the events which culminated in the marriage, will inquire as to the circumstances in which the two became acquainted, the events leading up to their engagement, and the course of their relationship up to the marriage. He will ask as to the history of Mr. A's interest in women; was this his first love; if not, what of the earlier attachments. He will ask as to A's impressions regarding the wife's earlier attachments. He will want to know about the course of the courtship; did either of them have periods of uncertainty. He will ask particularly about their setting the date for marriage; was it precipitate, were there difficulties in deciding on it, did either of them have a change of mind once the date had been set—was the marriage perhaps actually postponed. He will inquire about instances of bad feeling between them that had preceded marriage. He will encourage Mr. A to talk about how these incidents affected him, as to how he disposed of his doubts as to her ideal suitability. He will be interested in almost anything that can be recalled from the very beginning of their relationship and will gradually clarify to himself the chronology (the order in time) of A's me-you patterns. Knowing that in most instances of durable relations there is a rather high degree of congruence in the me–you patterns that develop in the two or three people concerned, he will attend to any indications as to Mrs. A's series of me–you patterns about her husband. It will be evident that from early in their acquaintance, there have been me–you patterns that included some measure of hostility or unfriendliness. It will become clear that this type of me–you pattern has tended to increase in significance as they have gone on living together. Disagreeable scenes between them were originally quite infrequent. "Until my friend B began to visit us, we got on quite well together. My wife took a violent dislike to him. I could never understand it. We got so we never discussed him because it always led to a fight." Careful inquiry will cast some doubt on this peculiar significance given to Mrs. A's dislike of B. The psychiatrist may come to feel that the importance of this particular one of her negative attitudes resides chiefly in its disturbing effect on A. The increasing friction between them could be overlooked by the husband until it involved one of his close personal friends. Had their relations been as harmonious as A thinks, Mrs. A would have offered extensive rationalizations to "account for" her antipathy for Mr. B. Mr. A states that she never explained it, that she was entirely unreasonable about it. The psychiatrist then assumes that A's relationship up to the

appearance of Mr. B included complex processes of the general type that we have seen in the substitution of weariness for felt resentment.

The probability that any A has imperfect information about his married life is in every case very considerable. A high degree of objectivity about someone who is important to one is as rare as the conviction is common that one is objective. The psychiatrist presumes that all the informant's accounts will be markedly one-sided, will show strong personal warp. He knows also that he cannot hope to separate truth and illusion unless his own integration with the informant is studied carefully. In securing this part of the history of the A-and-Mrs.-A relationship, the psychiatrist is integrated with Mr. A. Me–you patterns develop in this as in all significant relationships. Somewhere in their conversation, Mr. A may remark, "I do not have very much faith in doctors; and I have even less faith in psychiatrists." He then refers to the case of a relative who developed mental disorder which, he was told, was incurable. She had subsequently recovered, thereby demonstrating the unreliability of psychiatric prognosis. The story goes on to reveal that the patient was seen by several psychiatrists, all but the first of whom—an intern in a psychopathic hospital—having expressed opinions to the effect that she would probably recover. The one incorrect unfavorable opinion seems to have been especially significant in crystallizing A's lack of faith in psychiatry as presented in the current interview. As it is unfriendly to the psychiatrist, it must be recognized to be the presenting feature of a me–you pattern that will have something to do with the information which Mr. A imparts. This does not mean that Mr. A will wittingly omit significant data, will deliberately deceive the psychiatrist as to the facts. It suggests that certain data will not occur to him during the interview; if they occur to him afterwards, they will be dismissed as of no interest to a psychiatrist. Mr. A will have no sense of inadequacy to judge what is important and of interest to a psychiatrist, and the particular data, once recalled and dismissed between interviews, are not apt to appear subsequently.

Let us suppose now that the psychiatrist seeks to expand his acquaintance with the history of the A-and-Mrs.-A situation by consulting other informants. He will desire to confer with some personal friend of Mrs. A and of the husband. For purposes of exposition, we shall presume that these friends are unacquainted one with another. We shall have him confer with Mr. C, Mr. D, Mrs. E, and Miss F. It may become apparent that the impressions of Mrs. A which C has gained from years of acquaintance with the husband are strikingly different from the impressions gained by D during an equally extended acquaintance. Similarly, Mrs. E's impression of A gained over the years from the wife will be rather strikingly different from the impression that Miss F has formed. D's information about Mrs. A differs from C's. Mrs. E's information about A differs from Miss F's. A has never "happened to" tell D about events that he has related to C; and vice versa. Mrs. A has never "happened to" tell Mrs. E some of the things about A that she had told to Miss F; and vice versa.

Factors in the A-and-C situation have influenced the communication of information about the third person, Mrs. A. While there have been some two, three, or four illusory Cs in A's objectification of C; and several more or less congruous illusory As in C's objectification of A; the underlying configurations of the A-and-C situation have precluded the reporting of certain of his illusory Mrs. As in A's conversation with C. If we were able to call this to A's attention, he might say that C was not the sort of person to be interested in such and such attributes of Mrs. A. He might tell us that he had on certain occasions mentioned to C some matters concerning Mrs. A in these unrepresented aspects. Mr. C had paid no attention to this information, had forgotten it, or left it out of consideration in subsequent discussions of Mrs. A. C's opinion of A did not include the possibility of his feeling toward his wife in these unrepresented ways. C's objectification of the personality of Mrs. A, his illusory Mrs. A, is thus seen to be a fairly simple function of the A-and-C situation, but it is also a function of a C-imaginary-Mrs.-A situation; that is, it includes complex processes that are suggested when C says, "Well, if she were my wife. . . ." It might well seem that anything which C can offer as his impression of the, to him, actually unknown Mrs. A will be of little use in formulating an outline of her personality. The psychiatrist could perhaps make little headway if all of his information about A and Mrs. A came through these highly mediate interpersonal channels.

The mental disorder of Mrs. A, the psychiatrist's focal problem, has eventuated in the course of her life with A. While she has been living with A, A has been an important factor in her life. She knows something about his significance, and he knows something about his significance. Her accessible information is bound up in a series of me–you patterns, the variety of which has become restricted to a very hostile Mrs. A" '-and-A" ' pattern. While the psychiatrist by appropriate steps could probably recover data on the whole series of A's illusory Mrs. As, as they are recorded in his memory, a parallel recall could not be obtained in Mrs. A as she now is. In other words, among the changes that she has undergone, there is one that makes it difficult to remind her of the me–you patterns about her husband which are at striking variance with the now dominant pattern. Even though the psychiatrist, in the course of a long conversation, reminds her of an earlier me–you pattern in which Mr. A was represented as anything but a hostile and dangerous person—an achievement that may be quite difficult—he will be no nearer to convincing Mrs.

A that she has undergone a striking change in the freedom with which she objectifies her husband. She will probably account for the earlier friendly illusions about her husband as mistakes which she has subsequently corrected. As an alternative, she may hold that Mr. A himself has undergone a marked change. In the first case, when next she sees the psychiatrist, Mrs. A will have elaborated some data with which to prove that her former favorable impressions were the result of the fraud and dishonesty in Mr. A which she has finally come to understand. While the psychiatrist may have made her somewhat uncomfortable when first she recalled the earlier personification, this is no longer possible in that connection. She believes entirely the correctness of her present me-you pattern and the belief is not to be shaken.

In the face of so potent a factor, the psychiatrist in pursuit of information as to the history of Mrs. A's me–you patterns must have recourse to her friends. Again, in his conferences with Mrs. E and Miss F, he has to formulate the relation of each with him as best he can, [that is,] he must make some inquiries purposed to illuminate the characteristics of the illusory psychiatrist to whom each is addressing her remarks. He will seek mediate data on the Mrs. A-and-A situation. He will know that Mrs. E, for example, has developed an illusory A as a particular manifestation of some of the recurrent configurations that have characterized the enduring Mrs. E-and-Mrs.-A situation. His inquiry will bear significantly on the history of the latter. Without considerable information on this, Mrs. E's impressions about Mr. A would be practically beyond interpretation. As Mrs. E herself has a husband, the psychiatrist may encourage her to present contrasts between her married life and that of her friend, and between Mr. E and Mr. A as she knows him. Similarly, in his conferences with Miss F, having obtained some clues from time to time as to the illusory psychiatrist with whom she is communicating, he will develop the history of the Miss F-and-Mrs. A relationship. In all these conferences, he will attend to many phenomena besides the actual verbal contexts. He will note, for example, that whenever Miss F is discussing men, her voice, intonation, attitude, and set facial expression indicate something of a rigid attitude. Her replies to not-too-direct questions confirm his surmise that Miss F has an unfriendly view of men in general. This has value as collateral information concerning the configurations that have characterized the Miss F-and-Mrs. A situation. He comes ultimately to inquire as to Miss F's views of marriage, her preference for the single state, and how Mrs. A may have influenced her in this particular. He may ask finally if Mrs. A in bygone years urged Miss F to marry. She is surprised to recall that such was indeed the case. These contexts shed light on the factors which have resulted in the exclusion of some favorable illusions concerning A from the wife's discussion of him with her unmarried friend.

For parallel reasons, Miss F in her account recalls certain facts that may have "escaped" not only Mrs. A herself, but also Mrs. E. In particular, the time-ordering of events—which preceded which—in the recollections respectively of Mrs. E and Miss F, may vary widely. Some of these discrepancies may be especially useful bases for exploration in subsequent conferences with any one of the informants.

12. Everyone with whom one has been in any significant relationship, from birth onward, is a potential informant about one. Informants are able to express a body of illusions that they have developed in the interpersonal situations in which they have been integrated. In the body of illusions that they can communicate, there are data capable of elaboration into more valid information than they themselves have formulated. This is chiefly because everyone prehends much more than he perceives; at the same time, one's behavior is affected by all that one has experienced, whether it was prehended or consciously perceived. The psychiatrist, in developing his skill in interrogating informants, learns to integrate situations the configurations of which provoke the elaboration of information that was previously potential. He thus obtains more data from the informant than the latter has clearly perceived. The informant, so to speak, tells more than he knows. The data are more significant to the psychiatrist because he has more experience and more freedom in formulating interpersonal processes. He is alert to implications; his alertness is oriented to understanding interpersonal processes; and he has many fewer specific inhibitions of alertness in the interpersonal configurations in which he participates. From the relative accessibility of his own past, and from intimate contact with the developmental history of a number of people, he has a considerable grasp on the actual dynamics of interpersonal relations. He knows more about the processes that can occur in these configurations; in particular, he knows that certain alleged processes are highly improbable. Report of these alleged events are, therefore, most probably rationalizations, and he is able, from experience or by inquiry, to secure clues to the unwitting motivations that underlie these conventional statements.

Certainty about interpersonal processes is an ideal that should seldom concern one. Information about any situation should be considered as a formulation of probability. Information about a person may vary from very high probability—my companion is in the same room; to extremely low—my companion understands me perfectly. The physical factors in situations are often quite accurately measurable; they can be described in specialized language in a manner that contributes to an approximate *consensus* in the people who are considering the situation. This requires similarity of experience with the specialized language. Two people looking at this page may express different opinions as to the color of the paper. One may say it is yellow;[7] the other, that it is yellow-green. It is quite possible that a third observer may call it a deep orange; it is equally possible that a fourth may call it a vivid green. In the first pair of observers, the probability is that they had much the same initial prehensions, that the difference is primarily a difference in language. In the third and fourth observer, we must suspect differences in the initial prehensions. The spectral reflection of light by this paper includes green, yellow, orange, and red—the last three in approximately equal degree. The visual efficiency of light of different wave-lengths is rather widely variable in different people, the average maximum being in the yellow-green, falling off rather steeply in the green and orange. The long and the short waves producing relatively little effect when they impinge on the retina, the paper *looks* yellow (or yellow-green). In color-blind persons the experience caused by encountering colored light is markedly different from the average, and, while the meaning of their terms for these experiences are also necessarily different from the average, the more striking difference is in the initial prehension. A person in whom the prehension of green is lacking may, none the less, state that a green object is green. When we investigate this anomalous situation, we find that he has learned to call a particular gray appearance by the name of green—people have always been talking to him about how beautiful the green fields are, how bright this or that green is, how the traffic light is now green. Despite a fundamental defect in color-perception, he has come to talk about colors much as others do. While he can be led to mention his color-blindness, he has found that it is a difference that does not enhance the regard in which he is held by others. It may make people "nervous" to ride with him when he is driving his car. Some people amuse themselves by testing his color-perception. His language behavior has been developed to shield him from these and many other unpleasant consequences of difference. A discussion with him of the merits of a Monet is obviously a much more complex process than an unsuspecting companion might believe.

When one has regard for the multiple me–you patterns that complicate interpersonal relations, for the possible differences in individual prehension of events, and for the peculiarities of language behavior which characterize each of us . . . the practical impossibility of one-to-one correspondence of mental states of the observer and the observed person should be evident. We never know all about another, we are fortunate when we achieve an approximate consensus and can carry on meaningful communication about relatively simple contexts of experience. Most of us spend the greater part of our social life in much less adequate

---

[7]This was originally printed on the yellow paper of the journal *Psychiatry*.

contact with our interlocutors, with whom we manifest considerable skill at avoiding frank misunderstanding, with whom in fact we agree and disagree quite often with very little consensus as to subject of discussion. The psychiatrist of all people knows the relative character of his formulation of the other person, even if he has gained such skill that he is often quite correct.

2

TRANSFERENCE PROBLEMS IN SCHIZOPHRENICS

FRIEDA FROMM-REICHMANN

[1939]

INTRODUCTION

Gerard Chrzanowski

From the time that she settled at Chestnut Lodge, Frieda Fromm-Reichmann belonged to a small number of psychoanalysts who devoted themselves to working mainly with schizophrenic or otherwise severely disturbed patients. Psychoanalysts in general tend to see her as a representative of the interpersonal approach to psychoanalysis. Nevertheless, having been trained in the classical tradition, she considered not only Harry Stack Sullivan, but also Sigmund Freud (as well as Kurt Goldstein and Georg Groddeck) to have been a major influence on her thinking and practice. She payed homage to all these teachers in her classic book *Principles of Intensive Psychotherapy* (Fromm-Reichmann, 1950). Given the divergence of thinking among Fromm-Reichmann's teachers, together with her independence of spirit, it is not surprising that her views of psychoanalysis, particularly in reference to the treatment of schizophrenics, have her own individual stamp. In the paper under discussion Fromm-Reichmann (1939) acknowledges that "other analysts may feel that treatment as we have outlined it is not psychoanalysis" (p. 126). She goes on to say, however, that according to Freud's definition of psychoanalysis, her own approach, which accepts Freud's concepts of the unconscious, of transference and of resistance, as well as of infantile sexuality, is indeed psychoanalytic although technical rules of psychoanalysis, that is, use of the couch, free association, and interpretation, are not followed.

Gerard Chrzanowski, M.D. is a Training and Supervising Analyst, William Alanson White Institute; and Training and Supervising Analyst, Clinical Professor of Psychiatry, New York Medical College.

It may be of interest to the reader that the paper under discussion was delivered at the 41st annual meeting of the American Psychoanalytic Association in Chicago in May 1939. More than half a century later Frieda Fromm-Reichmann's views regarding the use of psychoanalysis in the treatment of schizophrenic patients are still relevant. Her early attention to transference phenomena in the treatment of schizophrenia was courageous. She confronted her classical colleagues by challenging their view that adherence to technical rules was the essence of psychoanalysis. For her, psychoanalysis provided a platform for therapeutic collaboration between a therapist attuned to the highly specific resonance between the patient and herself. Frieda Fromm-Reichmann's descriptions of her work are poignant proof that schizophrenic patients can develop strong relationships of love and hate to the analyst, and do not remain narcissistically detached as suggested by Freud in his later writings.

The paper under discussion, "Transference Problems in Schizophrenics" (Fromm-Reichmann, 1939), had not heretofore been familiar to me. Reading it at this time proved to be evocative of my many personal contacts with Frieda. While still a candidate in training at the William Alanson White Institute I had the privilege of being the discussant of one of her many papers on schizophrenia. She was most gracious in her response to my comments. My own training at the Burghoelzli,[1] Zurich, focused exclusively on work with schizophrenics and I was supervised by Dr. Meta Lutz, an analysand of Frieda Fromm-Reichmann, when both were still in Frankfurt, Germany. When I left for the United States, Dr. Lutz gave me a personal introduction to Frieda Fromm-Reichmann, and I became her supervisee once I began analytic training at the White Institute. Being her discussant before a large audience, however, filled me with anxiety and I appreciated her sensitivity to my discomfort.

Psychoanalysis and schizophrenia have had a stormy relationship over the years. Early on, Freud (1907) had praised the Zurich group of psychoanalysts, and particularly Eugen Bleuler and Carl Jung, for promoting psychoanalysis in the scientific community. Bleuler had devoted his entire professional life to the vicissitudes of schizophrenia, and Jung's interest in the study of the dreams of schizophrenic patients had caught Freud's attention. Jung had found that the dreams of schizophrenics were useful tools for working with these patients. Freud (1907) was elated that Jung applied the analytic method of interpretation to the dreams of patients suffering from the until-then obscure phenomenon of dementia praecox. In Jung's interpretations the histories and experiences of these patients came clearly to light. Psychiatry could no longer claim that psychoanalysis was irrelevant to the treatment of the more seriously disturbed individual. Fromm-Reichmann (1939) shared this early psychoanalytic interest in schizophrenic patients. She intended her work to be a contribution to the problem she recognized in the first lines of her article reprinted here: "Freud, Fenichel, and other authors have recognized that a new technique of approaching patients psychoanalytically must be found if analysts are to work with psychotics" (p. 117).

---

[1]Burghoelzli was then and is still the Psychiatric Clinic of the University of Zurich, Switzerland.

Fromm-Reichmann was a European-born psychiatrist who, early on in her professional career in Germany, became involved in Freud's psychoanalytic movement. Having been forced to flee Hitler's Germany, she eventually settled in the United States. Her career was exclusively and intimately tied to Chestnut Lodge, then considered a haven for schizophrenics, if their families could afford it.

It was at Chestnut Lodge that Fromm-Reichmann became acquainted with Sullivan. While Sullivan had in part rejected Freudian metapsychology, he did, according to Clara Thompson (1964), "stand on Freud's shoulders" (p. 94). In a similar vein Fromm-Reichmann called herself an interpersonalist with a Freudian matrix.

Frieda Fromm-Reichmann, as clinician, was primarily interested in alleviating the emotional suffering of her patients and enabling them to relinquish their symptoms. She felt that it was important to gain insight into the meaning of symptoms and to understand their unconscious roots. However, her dialogue with patients was not based on theory and she relied as much on nonverbal communication as on the spoken word.

I recall from my own supervision with Fromm-Reichmann that she often spoke of "scientific language" in contrast to subjective feelings about a patient. Her emphasis was invariably on the subjective, demonstrating her firm belief that neurotics and psychotics are similar in their dealings with the complexities of everyday life and, most importantly, that analysts themselves must realize their own similarity to the patients they treat. Fromm-Reichmann had deep feelings for her fellow humans and she objected to the notion that the analyst is sane while the patient is sick. In this she followed Sullivan (1940) who felt that the therapist's attitude toward the patient determines the therapist's value. In a similar vein Winnicott (1945) considered therapists to be doing poor work if they depended exclusively on their own sanity.

While Fromm-Reichmann's work has much to offer today's analysts, parts of it are no longer current. I will now turn to two of these issues. While the second arises in the paper reprinted here, the first is based on material appearing widely in her published work (Fromm-Reichmann, 1950, 1959), but not specifically here.

1. *Diagnosis and Etiology* The diagnosis of schizophrenia has varied over the years. At different times it has included psychosis, borderline, bipolar, and panic states as well as endogenous disorders. If definitions of a syndrome are unclear or vary with the times, notions of etiology remain equally confusing. In retrospect, Fromm-Reichmann, akin to Freud, believed simplistically that schizophrenia could be traced to a specific cause. For her the so-called "schizophrenogenic mother" was the root cause of a schizophrenic adaptation in later life. Such a mother is one who constantly double-binds her offspring. Today's psychoanalysts, even those of an interpersonalist persuasion, no longer accept a simple cause-and-effect relationship between mother and child. It is my opinion that Fromm-Reichmann's adherence to the concept of the schizophrenogenic mother and its underlying notion of direct causality may have had to do with her European psychoanalytic heritage with its affinity for Freudian determinism. Fromm-Reichmann's clinical stance and empathetic attitude towards her schizophrenic patients were clearly

more in tune with the pragmatic notions of American Interpersonalism than with the more rigidly Freudian notions of causality.

2. *Transference and Countertransference* Racker (1968) has pointed out that transference evokes countertransference. Fromm-Reichmann, talking about the transference of the schizophrenic patient, asks: "why is it inevitable that the psychoanalyst disappoints his schizophrenic patients again and again?" (p. 119). Today we would counter this with the question: How does the analyst deal with his own inevitable disappointments with the schizophrenic's rage, and with his destructiveness, which is directed both toward himself and toward the analyst?

From the classical point of view countertransference is a neurotic block in the analyst that interferes with treatment and must be avoided. Contemporary psychoanalysis, however, views countertransference as an essential component of treatment, offering important clues to the analyst in terms of his resonance with and understanding of the patient. When contemporary analysts stress the need for authenticity on the part of the analyst in his work with patients, their clinical approach underscores the need for an element of subjectivity.

Frieda Fromm-Reichmann certainly did not adhere to the classical definition of countertransference, but after reading her paper on transference I am left to question whether, at least at this point in her career, she paid much attention to the notion of countertransference. I myself consider subjective resonance with patients a sine qua non of effective treatment. Considering Frieda Fromm-Reichmann's work with her schizophrenic patients, and particularly her emphasis on both verbal and nonverbal communication, I can only aver that her work was indeed characterized by subjective resonance, even though specific, theoretical attention to countertransference is absent in the paper at hand.

In summary, Frieda Fromm-Reichmann was a firm believer that schizophrenia can always be traced to early childhood traumas, particularly in connection with a schizophrenogenic mother, and that it can be cured by helping the schizophrenic recall the traumatic events. Today the concept of cure, particularly in working with schizophrenic patients, is no longer used. this does not, however, diminish Frieda Fromm-Reichmann's pioneering contribution to the treatment of schizophrenics. She was clearly a pioneer, particularly in terms of the genuine respect she felt for her patients, and her ability to empathize with their fears and horrors. Frieda Fromm-Reichmann worked at a time when psychopharmacology was still in its infancy. Those of us who, like myself, worked with hospitalized schizophrenic patients and their psychotic "cousins" prior to the advent of tranquilizers and antipsychotic medication, can only marvel at Fromm-Reichmann's pioneering spirit. Of diminutive build herself, she had the courage, empathy, and patience to reach out to even the most agitated and threatening individual. Revisiting her writings brings to mind what Santayana (1894) said about Columbus:

> Columbus found a world, and had no chart,
> Save one that faith deciphered in the skies
> To trust the soul's invincible surmise
> Was all his science and his only art.

$\mathbf{M}$ ost psychoanalytic authors maintain that schizophrenic patients cannot be treated psychoanalytically because they are too narcissistic to develop with the psychotherapist an interpersonal relationship that is sufficiently reliable and consistent for psychoanalytic work (Abraham, 1927; Freud, 1935, 1946). Freud, Fenichel, and other authors have recognized that a new technique of approaching patients psychoanalytically must be found if analysts are to work with psychotics (Brill, 1929; Fenichel, 1934; Freud, 1905a; Jelliffe, 1907; Muller, n.d.; Waelder, 1926; Weininger, 1938, n.d.; White, 1917, 1935; White and Jelliffe, n.d.). Among those who have worked successfully in recent years with schizophrenics, Sullivan, Hill, and Karl Menninger and his staff have made various modifications of their analytic approach (Hill, 1936; Kamm, 1937; Sullivan, 1925, 1927, 1929, 1931a,b; Tidd, 1937, 1938).

In our work at the Chestnut Lodge Sanitarium we have found similar changes valuable. The technique we use with psychotics is different from our approach to psychoneurotics (Bullard, n.d., a,b; Weininger, 1938, n.d.). This is not a result of the schizophrenic's inability to build up a consistent personal relationship with the therapist but is due to his extremely intense and sensitive transference reactions.

Let us see, first, what the essence of the schizophrenic's transference reactions is and, second, how we try to meet these reactions.

In order to understand them, we must state those parts of our hypothesis about the genesis of these illnesses that are significant for the development of the patient's personal relationships and thus for our therapeutic approach.

We think of a schizophrenic as a person who has had serious traumatic experiences in early infancy at a time when his ego and its ability to examine reality were not yet developed. These early traumatic experiences seem to furnish the psychological basis for the pathogenic influence of the frustrations of later years. At this early time the infant lives grandiosely in a narcissistic world of his own. His needs and desires seem to be taken care of by something vague and indefinite which he does not yet differentiate. As Ferenczi (1916) noted, they are expressed by gestures and movements, since speech is not yet developed. Frequently, the child's desires are fulfilled without any expression of them, a result that seems to him a product of his magical thinking.

Psychoanalytic Quarterly, Vol. 8, Oct. 4. Also published in *Psychoanalysis and Psychotherapy: Selected Papers,* ed. D. M. Bullard and E. V. Weigert. Chicago: University of Chicago Press, 1959, pp. 117–128.

Traumatic experiences in this early period of life will damage a personality more seriously than those occurring in later childhood, such as
are found in the history of psychoneurotics. The infant's mind is more
vulnerable, the younger and less used it has been; further, the trauma is a
blow to the infant's egocentricity. In addition, early traumatic experience
shortens the only period in life in which the individual ordinarily enjoys
complete security, thus endangering the ability to store up, as it were, a
reasonable supply of assurance and self-reliance for the individual's later
struggle through life. Thus such a child is sensitized considerably more
toward the frustrations of later life than by later traumatic experience.
Hence many experiences in later life which would mean little to a
"healthy" person and not much to a psychoneurotic mean a great deal of
pain and suffering to the schizophrenic. His resistance against frustration is easily exhausted.

Once he reaches his limit of endurance, he escapes the unbearable
reality of his present life by attempting to re-establish the autistic, delusional world of the infant; but this is impossible because the content of his
delusions and hallucinations is naturally colored by the experiences of
his whole lifetime (Freud, 1905b,c,d, 1946; Sullivan, 1925, 1927, 1929,
1931a,b).

How do these developments influence the patient's attitude toward the
analyst and the analyst's approach to him?

Because of the very early damage and the succeeding chain of frustrations which the schizophrenic undergoes before finally giving in to illness,
he feels extremely suspicious and distrustful of everyone, particularly of
the psychotherapist, who approaches him with the intention of intruding
into his isolated world and personal life. To him the physician's approach
means the threat of being compelled to return to the frustrations of real
life and to reveal his inadequacy to meet them or—still worse—a repetition of the aggressive interference with his initial symptoms and peculiarities which he has encountered in his previous environment.

In spite of his narcissistic retreat, every schizophrenic has some dim
notion of the unreality and loneliness of his substitute delusionary world.
He longs for human contact and understanding, yet is afraid to admit it
to himself or to his therapist for fear of further frustration. That is why
the patient may take weeks and months to test the therapist before being
willing to accept him.[1]

However, once he has accepted him, his dependence on the therapist is
greater, and he is more sensitive about it than is the psychoneurotic
because of the schizophrenic's deeply rooted insecurity; the narcissistic,
seemingly self-righteous attitude is but a defense.

---

[1]Years in the case reported by Clara Thompson (1938).

Whenever the analyst fails the patient from reasons to be discussed later—one cannot at times avoid failing one's schizophrenic patients—it will be a severe disappointment and a repetition of the chain of frustrations that the schizophrenic has previously endured.

To the primitive part of the schizophrenic's mind that does not discriminate between himself and the environment, it may mean the withdrawal of the impersonal supporting forces of his infancy. Severe anxiety will follow this vital deprivation.

In the light of his personal relationship with the analyst, it means that the therapist seduced the patient by giving him a bridge over which he might possibly be led from the utter loneliness of his own world to reality and human warmth, only to have him discover that this bridge is not reliable. If so, he will respond helplessly with an outburst of hostility or with renewed withdrawal, as may be seen most impressively in catatonic stupor.

One patient responded twice with a catatonic stupor when I had to change the hour of my appointment with her; both times it was immediately dispelled when I went to see her and explained the reasons for the change. This withdrawal during treatment is a way the schizophrenic has of showing resistance and is dynamically comparable to the various devices which the psychoneurotic utilizes to show resistance.[2]

The schizophrenic responds to alternations in the analyst's defections and understanding by corresponding stormy and dramatic changes from love to hatred, from willingness to leave his delusional world to resistance and renewed withdrawal.

As understandable as these changes are, they nevertheless may come as quite a surprise to the analyst, who frequently has not observed their source. This is in great contrast to his experience with psychoneurotics, whose emotional reactions during an interview he can usually predict. These unpredictable changes seem to be the reason for the conception of the unreliability of the schizophrenic's transference reactions; yet they follow the same dynamic rules as the psychoneurotics' oscillations between positive and negative transference and resistance. *If the schizophrenic's reactions are more stormy and seemingly more unpredictable than those of the psychoneurotic, I believe it to be due to the inevitable errors in the analyst's approach to the schizophrenic, of which he himself may be unaware, rather than to the unreliability of the patient's emotional response.*

Why is it inevitable that the psychoanalyst disappoint his schizophrenic patients time and again?

The schizophrenic withdraws from painful reality and retires to what resembles the early speechless phase of development in which consciousness

---

[2]Edith Weigert-Vowinckel (1938) observed somewhat similar dynamics in what she calls the "automatic attitudes" of schizoid neurotics.

is not yet crystallized. As the expression of his feelings is not hindered by the conventions he has eliminated, so his thinking, feeling, behavior, and speech—when present—obey the working rules of the archaic unconscious (Storch, 1931). His thinking is magical and does not follow logical rules. It does not admit a *no*, and likewise no *yes*; there is no recognition of space and time. I, you, and they are interchangeable. Expression is by symbols; often by movements and gestures rather than by words.

As the schizophrenic is suspicious, he will distrust the words of his analyst. He will interpret them and the analyst's incidental gestures and attitudes according to his own delusional experience. The analyst may not even be aware of these involuntary manifestations of his attitudes; yet they mean much to the hypersensitive schizophrenic, who uses them as a means of orienting himself to the therapist's personality and intentions toward him.

In other words, the schizophrenic patient and the therapist are people living in different worlds and on different levels of personal development with different means of expressing and of orienting themselves. We know little about the language of the unconscious of the schizophrenic, and our access to it is blocked by the very process of our own adjustment to a world that the schizophrenic has relinquished. So we should not be surprised that errors and misunderstandings occur when we undertake to communicate and strive for rapport with him.

Another source of the schizophrenic's disappointment arises from the following: since the analyst accepts and does not interfere with the behavior of the schizophrenic, his attitude may lead the patient to expect that the analyst will assist in carrying out all the patient's wishes, even though they may not seem to be to his interest or to the analyst's and the hospital's in their relationship to society. This attitude of acceptance, so different from the patient's previous experiences, readily fosters the anticipation that the analyst will try to carry out the patient's suggestions and take his part, even against conventional society, should occasion arise. Frequently, it will be wise for the analyst to agree with the patient's wish to remain unbathed and untidy until he is ready to talk about the reasons for his behavior or to change spontaneously. At other times he will, unfortunately, be unable to take the patient's part, without being able to make the patient understand and accept the reasons for the analyst's position.

For example, one day I took a catatonic patient who asked for a change of scene to a country inn for lunch, another time to a concert, and a third time to an art gallery. After that he asked me to permit him with a nurse to visit his parents in another city. I told him I would have to talk this over with the superindependent and, in addition, suggested notifying his people. Immediately he became furious and combative because this meant that I was betraying him by consulting with others about what he regarded as a purely personal matter. From his own detached and child-like viewpoint he was right. He had given up his isolation in exchange for my personal interest in him, but he was not yet ready to have other persons admitted to his intimate relationship.

If the analyst is not able to accept the possibility of misunderstanding the reactions of his schizophrenic patient and, in turn, of being misunderstood by him, it may shake his security with his patient.

The schizophrenic, once he accepts the analyst and wants to rely upon him, will sense the analyst's insecurity. Being helpless and insecure himself—in spite of his pretended grandiose isolation—he will feel utterly defeated by the insecurity of his would-be helper. Such disappointment may furnish reasons for outbursts of hatred and rage that are comparable to the negative transference reactions of psychoneurotics, yet more intense than these because they are not limited by the restrictions of the actual world.

These outbursts are accompanied by anxiety, feelings of guilt, and fear of retaliation, which, in turn, lead to increased hostility. Thus is established a vicious circle: we disappoint the patient; he hates us, is afraid we hate him for his hatred, and therefore continues to hate us. If, in addition, he senses that the analyst is afraid of his aggressiveness, it confirms his fear that he is actually considered to be dangerous and unacceptable, and this augments his hatred.

This establishes that *the schizophrenic is capable of developing strong relationships of love and hatred toward his analyst.*

"After all, one could not be so hostile if it were not for the background of a very close relationship," said one catatonic patient after emerging from an acutely disturbed and combative episode.

In addition, I believe that the *schizophrenic develops transference reactions in the narrower sense*, which he can differentiate from the actual interpersonal relationship.

A catatonic artist stated the difference between the two kinds of relations while he was still delusional and confused when he said, pointing to himself, "There is the artist, the designer, and the drawer," then, looking around my office at the desk and finally at me, "the scientist, the research worker, the psychiatrist. . . . As to these two my fears of changes between treatment and injury do not hold true. Yet there is also something else between us—and there is fear of injury and treatment—treatment and injury." Then he implored me: "Understand! Try to be psychic—that will constitute real communism between us" (here using a political symbol to indicate a personal bond).

Another instructive example was given by an unwanted and neglected middle child of a frigid mother. He fought all his life for the recognition denied him by his family. Ambitious, he had a successful career as a researcher. During the war he was called to a prominent research center some distance from his home. Ten years later, after several frustrating repetitions of his childhood conflicts, he became sick.

The first 18 months of his analysis were spent in a continuous barrage of hatred and resentment. He would shout: "You dirty little stinking bitch" or "You damned German Jew; go back to your Kaiser!" or "I wish you had crashed in that plane you took!" He threatened to throw all manner of things at me. These stormy outbursts could be heard all over the hospital.

After a year and a half he became less disturbed and began to be on friendly terms with me, accepting willingly some interpretations and suggestions. Asked about his hatred of me, he said, "Oh, I think I did not actually hate you; underneath I always liked you. But when I had that call to the Institute—do you remember?—I saw what the Germans had done to our men, and I hated you as a German for that. Besides, mother, far from being proud of me as you would have expected, hated me for going instead of staying home and supporting her pet, my younger brother. You were mother, and I hated you for that. My sister, although living near the Institute, did not even once come to see me, although she had promised to. So you became sister, and I hated you for that. Can you blame me?"

From these examples can one doubt that the schizophrenic demonstrates workable transference reactions?

As the usual psychoanalytic approach is effective only with psychoneurotics, what modifications are necessary in our current technique in order to meet the particular needs of schizophrenics?

Contact with the schizophrenic must begin with a long preparatory period of daily interviews (as in psychoanalysis with children), during which the patient is given the opportunity of becoming acquainted with the analyst, of finding out whether the analyst can be of value to him, and of overcoming his suspicion and his anxiety about the friendship and consideration offered to him by the analyst. After that the patient may gain confidence in his physician and at last accept him.

One patient shouted at me every morning for six weeks, "I am not sick; I don't need any doctor; it's none of your damned business." At the beginning of the seventh week the patient offered me a dirty, crumpled cigarette. I took it and smoked it. The next day he had prepared a seat for me by covering a bench in the yard, where I met him, with a clean sheet of paper. "I don't want you to soil your dress," he commented. This marked the beginning of his acceptance of me as a friend and therapist.

Another very suspicious patient, after two days of fear and confusion ushering in a real panic, became stuporous for a month—mute, resistive to food, and retaining excretions. In spite of this rather unpromising picture, I sat with him for an hour every day. The only sign of contact he gave to me or anyone was to indicate by gestures that he wanted me to stay; all that he said on two different days during this period was: "Don't leave!"

One morning after this I found him sitting naked and masturbating on the floor of his room, which was spotted with urine and sputum, talking for the first time, yet so softly that I could not understand him. I stepped closer to him but still could not hear him, so I sat down on the floor close to him, upon which he turned to me with genuine concern: "You can't do that for me, you too will get involved." After that he pulled a blanket around himself saying, "Even though I have sunk as low as an animal, I still know how to behave in the presence of a lady." Then he talked for several hours about his history and his problems.

Finally I offered him a glass of milk. He accepted the offer, and I went to get it. When I came back after a few moments his friendliness had changed to hostility, and he threw the milk on me. Immediately he became distressed: "How could I do that to you?" he asked in despair. It seemed as though the few minutes I was out of the room were sufficient time for him to feel that I had abandoned him.

His confidence was regained by my showing that I did not mind the incident. And for eight months of daily interviews he continued to talk. Unfortunately, he was then removed from the sanitarium by his relatives.

This also serves to illustrate the difference between the schizophrenic's attitude toward time and ours. One patient, after I told him I had to leave for a week, expressed it thus: "Do you know what you are telling me? It may mean a minute and it may mean a month. It may mean nothing; but it may also mean eternity to me."

Such statements reveal that there is no way to estimate what time means to the patient; hence the inadvisability of trying to judge progress by our standards. These patients simply cannot be hurried, and it is worse than futile to try. This holds true in all stages of treatment (Hinsie, n.d.).

This was brought home to me by a catatonic patient who said at the end of five months of what seemed to me an extremely slow movement in the direction of health: "I ought to tell you that things are going better now; but [with anxiety in his voice] everything is moving too rapidly. That ought to make us somewhat skeptical."

As the treatment continues, the patient is asked neither to lie down nor to give free associations; both requests make no sense to him. He should feel free to sit, lie on the floor, walk around, use any available chair, lie or sit on the couch. Nothing matters except that the analyst permit the patient to feel comfortable and secure enough to give up his defensive narcissistic isolation and to use the physician for resuming contact with the world.

If the patient feels that an hour of mutual friendly silence serves his purpose, he is welcome to remain silent: "The happiness to dare to breathe and vegetate and just to be, in the presence of another person who does not interfere," as one of them described it.

The only danger of these friendly silent hours is that the patient may develop more tension in his relationship with the analyst than the patient can stand, thereby arousing great anxiety. It belongs among the analyst's "artistic" functions, as Hill (1936) has called them, to sense the time when he should break his patient's friendly silence.

What are the analyst's further functions in therapeutic interviews with the schizophrenic? As Sullivan (1931) has stated, he should observe and evaluate all the patient's words, gestures, changes of attitudes and countenance, as he does the associations of psychoneurotics. Every single production—whether understood by the analyst or not—is important and makes sense to the patient. Hence the analyst should try to understand and let the patient feel that he tries.[3] He should, as a rule, not attempt to prove his understanding by giving interpretations because the schizophrenic himself understands the unconscious meaning of his productions better than anyone else.[4] Nor should the analyst ask questions when he does not understand, for he cannot know what trend of thought, far-off dream, or hallucination he may be interrupting. He gives evidence of understanding, *whenever he does*, by responding cautiously with gestures or actions appropriate to the patient's communication; for example, by lighting his cigarette from the patient's cigarette instead of using a match when the patient seems to indicate a wish for closeness and friendship.

"Sometimes little things like a small black ring can do the job," a young catatonic commented after I had substituted a black onyx ring for a silver bracelet I had been wearing. The latter had represented to him part of a dangerous armor of which he was afraid.

What has been said against intruding into the schizophrenic's inner world with superfluous interpretations also holds true for untimely suggestions. Most of them do not mean the same thing to the schizophrenic that they do to the analyst. The schizophrenic who feels comfortable with his analyst will ask for suggestions when he is ready to receive them. So long as he does not, the analyst does better to listen. The following incident will serve as an illustration:

A catatonic patient refused to see me. I had disappointed him by responding to his request that someone should spend the whole day with

---

[3]Diethelm (1936) also stresses this viewpoint.

[4]LaForgue (1936) attributes the cure of a case of schizophrenia to his interpretive work with the patient. According to my experience, I believe it was due to his sensitive emotional approach and not the result of his interpretations.

him by promising to make arrangements for a nurse to do so instead of understanding that it was I whom he wanted. For the following three months he threatened me with physical attack when I came to see him daily, and I could talk with him only through the closed door of his room.

Finally he reaccepted me and at the end of a two-and-a-half-hour interview stated very seriously: "If only you can handle this quite casually and be friendly and leave the young people [the nurses] out of it, I may be able to work things out with you." The next day in the middle of another hour of confused hallucinatory talking, he went on: "This is a great surprise to us. There were lots of errors and misunderstandings between us, and we both learned quite a bit. If you could arrange for me to see my friends and to spend more time on an open ward, and if you remain casual, we might be able to co-operate." It is scarcely necessary to say that we acted in accordance with his suggestions.

In contrast to fortunate experiences like these, there will remain long stretches on every schizophrenic's lonely road over which the analyst cannot accompany him. Let me repeat that this alone is no reason for being discouraged. *It is certainly not an intellectual comprehension of the schizophrenic but the sympathetic understanding and skilful handling of the patient's and physician's mutual relationship that are the decisive therapeutic factors.*

The schizophrenic's emotional reactions toward the analyst have to be met with extreme care and caution. The love which the sensitive schizophrenic feels as he first emerges and his cautious acceptance of the analyst's warmth of interest are really most delicate and tender things. If the analyst deals unadroitly with the transference reactions of a psychoneurotic, it is bad enough, though as a rule not irreparable; but if he fails with a schizophrenic in meeting positive feeling by pointing it out, for instance, before the patient indicates that he is ready to discuss it, he may easily freeze to death what has just begun to grow and so destroy any further possibility of therapy.

Here one has to steer between Scylla and Charybdis. If the analyst allows the patient's feelings to grow too strong without providing the relief of talking about them, the patient may become frightened at this new experience and then dangerously hostile toward the analyst.

The patient's hostility should ideally be met without fear and without counterhostility. The form it sometimes takes may make this difficult to do. Let it be remembered, however, that the less fear patients sense in the therapist the less dangerous they are.

One patient explained this to me during the interviews we had in her postpsychotic stage of recovery. "You remember," she said, "when you once came to see me and I was in a wet pack and asked you to take me out? You went for a nurse and I felt very resentful because that meant to me that you were afraid to do it yourself and that you actually believed that I was a dangerous person. Somehow you felt that, came back, and did it yourself. That did away with my resentment and hostility toward you at once, and from then on I felt I could get well with you because if you were not afraid of me, that meant that I was not too dangerous and bad to come back into the real world you represented."

Sometimes the therapist's frank statement that he wants to be the patient's friend but that he is going to protect himself, should he be assaulted, may help in coping with the patient's combativeness and relieve the patient's fear of his own aggression.

Some analysts may feel that the atmosphere of complete acceptance and of strict avoidance of any arbitrary denials which we recommend as a basic rule for the treatment of schizophrenics may not accord with our wish to guide them toward reacceptance of reality. We do not believe this is so.

Certain groups of psychoneurotics have to learn by the immediate experience of analytic treatment how to accept the denials that life has in store for each of us. *The schizophrenic has, above all, to be cured of the wounds and frustrations of his life before we can expect him to recover.*

Other analysts may feel that treatment as we have outlined it is not psychoanalysis. The patient is not instructed to lie on a couch, he is not asked to give free associations (although frequently he does), and his productions are seldom interpreted other than by understanding acceptance.

Freud says that every science and therapy that accepts his teachings about the unconscious, about transference and resistance, and about infantile sexuality may be called psychoanalysis. According to this definition, we believe that we are practicing psychoanalysis with our schizophrenic patients.

Whether we call it analysis or not, it is clear that successful treatment does not depend on technical rules of any special psychiatric school but rather on the basic attitude of the individual therapist toward psychotic persons. If he meets them as strange creatures of another world whose productions are not understandable to "normal" beings, he cannot treat them. If he realizes, however, that the difference between himself and the psychotic is only one of degree and not of kind, he will know better how to meet him. He will be able to identify himself sufficiently with the patient to understand and accept his emotional reactions without becoming involved in them.

To summarize: *Schizophrenics are capable of developing workable relationships and transference reactions, but successful psychotherapy with schizophrenics depends upon whether the analyst understands the significance of these transference phenomena and meets them appropriately.*

REFERENCES

Abraham, K. (1927), The psychosexual difference between hysteria and dementia praecox. *Selected Papers*. London: Hogarth Press.

Brill, A. A. (1929), Schizophrenia and psychotherapy. *Amer. J. Psychiat.*, 9.

Bullard, D. M. (n.d. a), Organization of psychoanalytic procedure in the hospital. *J. Nerv. & Ment. Dis.*

———(n.d. b), The application of psychoanalytic psychiatry to the psychoses. *Psychoanal. Rev.*

Diethelm, O. (1936), *Treatment in Psychiatry*. New York: Macmillan.

Fenichel, O. (1934), *Outline of Clinical Psychoanalysis*. New York: Norton.

Ferenczi, S. (1916), Stages in the development of the sense of reality. *Contributions to Psychoanalysis*. Boston: Richard G. Badger.

Freud, S. (1905a), On psychotherapy. *Collected Papers, Vol. I*. London: Hogarth Press.

———(1905b), The loss of reality in neurosis and psychosis. *Collected Papers*, Vol. II. London: Hogarth Press.

———(1905c), Neurosis and psychosis. *Collected Papers, Vol. II*. London: Hogarth Press.

———(1905d), Psycho-analytic notes upon an autobiographical account of a case of paranoia (dementia paranoides). *Collected Papers, Vol. III*. London: Hogarth Press.

———(1946), On narcissism: An introduction. *Collected Papers, Vol. IV*. 4th ed. London: Hogarth Press.

———(1935), *A general introduction to psychoanalysis*, Lecture XVI. New York: Liveright.

Hill, L. B. (1936), Treatment of the psychotic ego. Presented to annual meeting of the American Psychiatric Association, St. Louis, MO, May.

Hinsie, L. E. (n.d.), *Treatment of Schizophrenia*. Baltimore, MD: Williams & Wilkins.

Jelliffe, S. E. (1907), Predementia praecox. *Amer. J. Med. Sci.*, p. 157.

Kamm, B. (1937), A technical problem in the psychoanalysis of a schizoid character. *Bull. Menn. Clin.*, 1 (8).

LaForgue, R. (1936), A contribution to the study of schizophrenia. *Internat. J. Psycho-Anal.*, 18 (pt. 2).

Lewis, N. D. C. (1936), *Research in Dementia Praecox*. Scottish Rite of Freemasonry for the Northern Masonic Jurisdiction of the United States of America.

Muller, M. (n.d.), *Über Heilungsmechanismen in der Schizophrenie*. Berlin: S. Karger.

Schilder, P. (n.d.), *Entwurf zu einer Psychiatrie auf psychoanalytischer Grundlage*. (Internationaler Psychoanalytische Bibliothek, No. XVII.) Vienna: Internationaler Psychoanalytische.

Storch, A. (1931), *The Primitive Archaic Forms of Inner Experiences and Thought in Schizophrenia*. (Nervous and Mental Disease Monograph Series, No. 36.) New York: Nervous & Mental Disease.

Sullivan, H. S. (1925), The oral complex. *Psychoanal. Rev.*, 12 (1).

———(1927), Affective experience in early schizophrenia. *Amer. J. Psychiat.*, 6 (3).

———(1929), Research in schizophrenia. *Amer. J. Psychiat.*, 9 (3).

———(1931a), The modified psychoanalytic treatment of schizophrenia. *Amer. J. Psychiat.*, 11 (3).

———(1931b), Sociopsychiatric research: Its implications for the schizophrenia problem and for mental hygiene. *Amer. J. Psychiat.*, 10 (6).

Thompson, C. (1938), Development and awareness of transference in a markedly detached personality. *Internat. J. Psycho-Anal.*, 19 (3).

Tidd, C. W. (1937), Increasing reality acceptance by a schizoid personality during analysis. *Bull. Menninger Clin.*, 1 (5).

———(1938), A note on the treatment of schizophrenia. *Bull. Menninger Clin.*, 2 (3).

Waelder, R. (1926), Schizophrenic and creative thinking. *Internat. J. Psycho-Anal.*, 7.

Weigert-Vowinckel, E. (1938), A contribution to the study of schizophrenia. *Internat. J. Psycho-Anal.*, 19 (3).

Weininger, B. (1938), Psychotherapy during convalescence from psychosis. *Psychiatry*, 1 (2).

——(n.d.), The importance of reeducational therapy in recovered psychotic patients.

White, W. A. (1917), Study on the diagnosis and treatment of dementia praecox. *Psychoanal. Rev.*, 8.

——(1935), *Outlines of Psychiatry*. Washington, DC: Nervous & Mental Disease.

——& Jelliffe, S. E. (n.d.), *The Modern Treatment of Nervous and Mental Diseases*. Philadelphia: Lea & Febiger.

3

THE TRANSFERENCE PHENOMENON IN PSYCHOANALYTIC THERAPY

JANET MACKENZIE RIOCH

[1943]

INTRODUCTION

Earl G. Witenberg

I first met Janet Rioch when I applied to become a candidate for analytic training at the William Alanson White Institute. I was somewhat apprehensive about my interview with her and was most pleasantly surprised by how easy and seemingly casual it turned out to be. Early on in the interview, Janet found out that she and I had graduated from the same medical school, and our talk took on a relaxed, chatty character, as if we were old acquaintances comparing reminiscences about former teachers and experiences. Only several years later did I become aware of the skill with which Janet had conducted the interview, simultaneously putting me at ease and yet getting to know me by way of information I found easy to share. In short, her interview bore the genuinely Sullivanian, interpersonal stamp: she drew on her own knowledge of experiences and people we had in common and helped me be at ease.

The easy manner with which Janet approached the interview masked the clear mind, theoretical rigor, and innovative thinking that she brought to her work; it also masked her thorough familiarity with Sullivan's approach to clinical work and with interpersonal thinking. It is regrettable that the paper reprinted in this volume is her only written contribution to psychoanalysis. The paper stands as a model of clarity, of freedom from jargon, of respectful disagreement with Freud; and in its own way it embodies a pioneering spirit

Earl G. Witenberg, M.D. is Training and Supervising Analyst and Faculty, William Alanson White Institute.

that was able to encompass some core interpersonal concepts and concerns that have become central to contemporary interpersonal psychoanalysis.

It is noteworthy that Janet Rioch (Bard) was only 38 years old when her paper was published in 1943. She had been working as psychiatrist and psychoanalyst for 10 years. She had obtained her medical degree in 1930. Following a year's internship in medicine and surgery, she became house physician at Shepard and Enoch Pratt Hospital in Baltimore and met Harry Stack Sullivan, Clara Thompson, William Silverberg, Karen Horney, Frieda Fromm-Reichmann, and Erich Fromm. At her age she was the junior member among this dynamic and innovative group of psychoanalysts.

Later on she worked in psychosomatic medicine at Columbia and became a founder of the division of Child Psychiatry at Roosevelt Hospital. During these years, Janet began her psychoanalytic training at the New York Psychoanalytic Institute and by 1941 had become an advanced candidate in the program. That was also the year that Karen Horney was deprived of her academic appointment at the Institute following her challenge of the concept of penis envy and her (then daring) notions about female psychology. Janet Rioch, together with Karen Horney, Clara Thompson, Herman Ephron, Bernard Robbins, Sarah Kelman, Harold Kelman, Judd Marmor, and others left the New York Psychoanalytic Institute in protest against the censoring of Horney and formed the Association for the Advancement of Psychoanalysis. In 1943, Rioch joined the New York Division of the Washington School of Psychiatry, which later became the White Institute. She was appointed Training and Supervising analyst at both the White Institute and the Washington School.

Janet's interest in psychoanalysis was broad, as can be gleaned from the sources she cites. They include the most noted interpersonalists of her time, many of whom are still considered prominent today and some of whose papers are included in this volume; but she also quotes kindred spirits such as Maslow, Sherif, and others who were not psychoanalysts.

Janet's discussion of transference is remarkable for its day. Remember that this was the early 1940s. She not only took the concept of transference out of the realm of biology and drive theory—a radical move for the time—but she did it without diminishing Freud's contribution. Instead of biology, Janet grounded transference in interpersonal experience, and she dated the relevant patterns of interpersonal experience all the way back to infancy. In doing so, she placed transference squarely in two-person psychology, just as present-day psychoanalysts seem to be rediscovering. Rioch and her colleagues were there first. In addition, she was one of the first psychoanalysts to appreciate that transference is not merely a repetition, but an event determined by the patient's character. Character, of course, is heavily influenced by the interactive patterns of the past, but that fact does not diminish the reality of transference as an event in the present tense. It may be difficult for recently trained analysts to appreciate how novel and radical these ways of thinking were 50 years ago.

But perhaps the greatest contribution of this paper lies in Janet's understanding of the effect of the analyst as a real person. Clara Thompson and other early interpersonalists were arguing similar points, but it may be Janet who saw the issues earliest and most clearly. She saw that no patient can work out a transference problem with an analyst who has the same kind of problem as does the parent with whom the patient first developed that very problem. The personality of the analyst was, for Janet the limit beyond which any patient's analysis could not go, and she managed to understand this point without succumbing to something like Alexander's less subtle "corrective emotional experience." Janet did not recommend, as Alexander had, that the analyst should try to create an interactive situation that purposely avoided the problematic aspects of the relationship with the patient's parents. She understood that the issue was more profound than a solution of that kind could solve. The analyst had to *be* different, not just *act* differently. In this, Janet was absorbing and creatively expanding a lesson that had been taught both by Ferenczi and by Sullivan. This point also makes her paper one of the earliest statements about the power and unavoidable significance of the countertransference.

Janet expected from her colleagues and students the sense of ethical commitment and analytic rigor that she herself adhered to. This expectation was brought home to me by two personal experiences with Janet, who, after having been my analyst, also became my supervisor. While I was in supervision with her, she referred to me the spouse of one of her patients. After seeing this person for a while, I sensed that something was going on in the marriage that was not spelled out by my patient but that intrigued and puzzled me. I asked Janet if she knew from her patient whether something was amiss in the marriage. She did not say a word. A few months later, the marriage of these two people indeed broke up. But true to her commitment to confidentiality, Janet had not shared with me her knowledge of the upcoming break-up. For her, respect for the patient, his trust in her, and her belief in the sanctity of analytic confidentiality took precedence over a colleague's concern about what was going on.

On a more personal note: I had finished my analysis with Janet many years before, when I lost a close member of my family during summer vacation. When Janet heard about the death after she returned from her own vacation, she simply and without being asked took the train to New York and saw me for a session. She went back to Washington the same day, and nothing further was said about it. Just as her analytic work was straightforward and direct, so was her expression of concern and compassion.

"The Transference Phenomenon in Psychoanalytic Theory" was a ground-breaking paper for its time. Much of what is contained in it is being increasingly discussed today. A brief summary of its ideas scarcely can do it justice, but the ideas will be familiar to all who are acquainted with contemporary interpersonal thought, including its echo in the wider psychoanalytic community. Among these ideas is the notion that development depends on the interpersonal context in which it occurs; that the interpersonal context is similarly important in the analytic setting; that the analytic goal, the true independence or selfhood of the patient, can come about only if the interpersonal analytic experience is a novel one for the patient; that there is no transference without countertransference; and that ultimately it is the relationship between patient and analyst, not the recovery of repressed memory, that facilitates addressing difficulties in living. In writing her paper, Janet Rioch developed many of Harry Stack Sullivan's ideas with great clarity. We can only wish that she had written more.

T he significance of the transference phenomenon impressed Freud so profoundly that he continued through the years to develop his ideas about it. His classical observations on the patient Dora formed the basis for his first formulations of this concept. He says,

> What are transferences? They are the new editions or facsimiles of the tendencies and phantasies which are aroused and made conscious during the progress of the analysis; but they have this peculiarity, which is characteristic for their species, that they replace some earlier person by the person of the physician. To put it another way: a whole series of psychological experiences are revived, not as belonging to the past, but as applying to the person of the physician at the present moment [Freud, 1933, p. 139].

According to Freud's view, the process of psychoanalytic cure depends mainly upon the patient's ability to remember that which is forgotten and repressed, and thus to gain conviction that the analytical conclusions arrived at are correct. However, "the unconscious feelings strive to avoid the recognition which the cure demands" (p. 321); they seek instead, emotional discharge, regardless of the reality of the situation.

Freud believed that these unconscious feelings which the patient strives to hide are made up of that part of the libidinal impulse that has turned away from consciousness and reality, due to the frustration of a desired gratification. Because the attraction of reality has weakened, the libidinal energy is still maintained in a state of regression attached to the original infantile sexual objects, although the reasons for the recoil from reality have disappeared (p. 316).

Freud states that in the analytic treatment, the analyst pursues this part of the libido to its hiding place, "aiming always at unearthing it, making it accessible to consciousness and at last serviceable to reality" (p. 316). The patient tries to achieve an emotional discharge of this libidinal energy under the pressure of the compulsion to repeat experiences over and over again rather than to become conscious of their origin. He uses the method of transferring to the person of the physician past psychological experiences and reacting to this, at times, with all the power of hallucination (p. 321). The patient vehemently insists that his impression of the analyst is true for the immediate present, in this way avoiding the recognition of his own unconscious impulses.

The transference phenomenon in psychoanalytic therapy. *Psychiatry,* 6:147–156.

Thus, Freud regards the transference-manifestations as a major problem of the resistance. However, Freud said, "It must not be forgotten that they (the transference-manifestations) and they only, render the invaluable service of making the patient's buried and forgotten love-emotions actual and manifest" (p. 322).

Freud regards the transference-manifestations as having two general aspects—positive and negative. The negative, he at first regarded as having no value in psychoanalytic cure and only something to be "raised" (p. 319) into consciousness to avoid interference with the progress of the analysis. He later (Freud, 1940) accorded it a place of importance in the therapeutic experience. The positive transference he considered to be ultimately sexual in origin, since, Freud (1933) said, "To begin with, we knew none but sexual objects" (p. 319). However, he divides the positive transference into two components—one, the repressed erotic component, which is used in the service of resistance; the other, the friendly and affectionate component, which, although originally sexual, is the "unobjectionable" aspect of the positive transference, and is that which "brings about the successful result in psychoanalysis, as in all other remedial methods" (Freud, 1933, p. 319). Freud refers here to the element of suggestion in psychoanalytic therapy, about which I wish to speak in detail a little later on.

At the moment, I should like to state that, although not agreeing with the view of Freud that human behavior depends ultimately on the biological sexual drives, I believe that it would be a mistake to deny the value and importance of his formulations regarding transference phenomena. As I shall indicate shortly, I differ on certain points with Freud, but I do not differ with the formulation that early impressions acquired during childhood are revived in the analytical situation, and are felt as immediate and real—that they form potentially the greatest obstacles to analysis if unnoticed—and, as Freud put it, the greatest ally of the analysis when understood. I agree that the main work of the analysis consists in analyzing the transference phenomena, although I differ somewhat as to how this results in cure. It is my conviction that the transference is a strictly interpersonal experience. Freud gives the impression that under the stress of the repetition-compulsion the patient is bound to repeat the identical pattern, regardless of the other person. I believe that the personality of the analyst tends to determine the character of the transference illusions, and especially to determine whether the attempt at analysis will result in cure. Horney (1939) has shown that there is no valid reason for assuming that the tendency to repeat past experiences again and again has an instinctual basis. The particular character structure of the person requires that he integrate with any given situation according to the necessities of his character structure.

In discussing my own views regarding the transference and its use in therapy, it is necessary to begin at the beginning and to point out in a very schematic way how a person acquires his particular orientation to him-self and the world—which one might call his character structure, and the implications of this in psychoanalytic therapy.

The infant is born without a frame of reference, as far as interpersonal experience goes. He is already acquainted with the feeling of bodily movement—with sucking and swallowing—but, among other things, he has had no knowledge of the existence of another *person* in relationship to himself. Although I do not wish to draw any particular conclusions from this analogy, I want to mention a simple phenomenon, described by Sherif (1936), connected with the problem of the frame of reference. If you have a completely dark room, with no possibility of any light being seen, and you then turn on a small pin-point of light, which is kept stationary, this light will soon appear to be moving about. I am sure a good many of you have noticed this phenomenon when gazing at a single star. The light seems to move and it does so, apparently, because there is no reference point in relation to which one can establish it at a fixed place in space. It just wanders around. If, however, one can at the same time see some other fixed object in the room, the light immediately becomes stationary. A reference point has been established, and there is no longer any uncertainty, any vague wandering of the spot of light. It is fixed. The pin-point of light wandering in the dark room is symbolic of the original attitude of the person to himself, undetermined, unstruc-tured, with no reference points.

The newborn infant probably perceives everything in a vague and uncertain way, including himself. Gradually, reference points are estab-lished; a connection begins to occur between hunger and breast, between a relief of bladder tension and a wet diaper, between playing with his genitals and a smack on the hand. The physical boundaries and poten-tialities of the self are explored. One can observe the baby investigating the extent, shape, and potentialities of his own body. He finds that he can scream and mother will come, or will not come, that he can hold his breath and everyone will get excited, that he can smile and coo and people will be enchanted, or just the opposite. The nature of the emotional reference points that he determines depends upon the en-vironment. By that still unknown quality called "empathy," he dis-covers the reference points which help to determine his emotional atti-tude toward himself. If his mother does not want him, is disgusted with him, treats him with utter disregard, he comes to look upon himself as a thing-to-be-disregarded. With the profound human drive to make this rational, he gradually builds up a system of "reasons why." Underneath all these "reasons" is a basic sense of worthlessness, undetermined and undefined, related directly to the original reference frame. Another child discovers that the state of being regarded is dependent upon specific factors—all is well as long as one does not act spontaneously, as long as one is not a separate person, as long as one is good, as the state of being good is continuously defined by the parents. Under these conditions, and these only, this child can feel a sense of self-regard.

Other people are encountered with the original reference frame in mind. The child tends to carry over into later situations the patterns he first learned to know. The rigidity with which these original patterns are retained depends upon the nature of the child's experience. If this has been of a traumatic character so that spontaneity has been blocked and further emotional development has been inhibited, the original orientation will tend to persist. Discrepancies may be rationalized or repressed. Thus, the original impression of the hostile mother may be retained, while the contact with the new person is rationalized to fit the original reference frame. The new person encountered acts differently, but probably that is just a pose. She is just being nice because she does not know me. If she really knew me, she would act differently. Or, the original impressions are so out of line with the present actuality, that they remain unconscious, but make themselves apparent in inappropriate behavior or attitudes which remain outside the awareness of the person concerned.

The incongruity of the behavior pattern, or of the attitude, may be a source of astonishment to the other person involved. Sullivan (1940) provides insight into the process by the elucidation of what he calls the "parataxic distortions." He points out that in the development of the personality, certain integrative patterns are organized in response to the important persons in the child's past. There is a "self-in-relation-to-A" pattern, or "self-in-relation-to-B" pattern. These patterns of response become familiar and useful. The person learns to get along as a "self-in-relation-to-A" or B, C, and D, depending on the number of important people to whom he had to adjust in the course of his early development. For example, a young girl, who had a severely dominating mother and a weak, kindly father, learned a pattern of adjustment to her mother which could be briefly described as submissive, mildly rebellious in a secret way, but mostly lacking in spontaneity. Toward the father she developed a loving, but contemptuous attitude. When she encountered other people, regardless of sex, she oriented herself to them partly as the real people they were, and partly as she had learned to respond to her mother and father in her past. She thus was feeling toward the real person involved as if she were dealing with two people at once. However, since it is very necessary for people to behave as rational persons she suppressed the knowledge that some of her reactions were inappropriate to the immediate situation, and wove an intricate mesh of rationalizations, which permitted her to believe that the person with whom she was dealing really was someone either to be feared and submitted to, as her mother, or to be contemptuous of, as her father. The more nearly the real person fitted the original picture of the mother and father, the easier it was for her to maintain that original "self-in-relation-to-A" or B was the real and valid expressions of herself.

It happened, however, that this girl had had a kindly nurse who was not a weak person, although occupying an inferior position in the household. During the many hours when she was with this nurse, she was able to experience a great deal of unreserved warmth, and of freedom for self-realization. No demands for emotional conformity were made on her in this relationship. Her own capacities for love and spontaneous activity were able to flourish. Unfortunately, the contact with this nurse was all too brief. But there remained, despite the necessity for the rigid development of the patterns towards the mother and father, a deeply repressed, but still vital experience of self, which most closely approximated the fullest realization of her potentialities. This, which one might call her *real self*, although "snowed under" and handicapped by all the distortions incurred by her relationship to the parents, was finally able to emerge and become again active in analysis. In the course of this treatment, she learned how much her reactions to people were "transference" reactions, or as Sullivan would say, "parataxic distortions."

I have deliberately tried to schematize this illustration. For instance, when I speak of the early frame of reference and then just mention the parents, I do not overlook all the other possible reference frames. Also, one has to realize that one pattern connects with another—the whole making a tangled mass that only years of analysis can unscramble. I also have not taken the time to outline the compensatory drives that the neurotic person has to develop in order to handle his life situation. Each compensatory maneuver causes some change in his frame of reference, since the development of a defensive trait in his personality sets off a new set of relationships to those around him. The little child who grows more and more negativistic, because of injuries and frustrations, evokes more and more hostility in his environment. However, and this is important, the basic reactions of hostility on the part of the parents, which originally induced his negativism, are still there. Thus, the pattern does not change much in character—it just gets worse in the same direction. Those persons whose later life experience perpetuate the original frames of reference are more severely injured. A young child, who has a hostile mother, may then have a hostile teacher. If, by good luck, he got a kind teacher and if his own attitude were not already badly warped, so that he did not induce hostility in this kind teacher, he would be introduced into a startlingly new and pleasant frame of reference, and his personality might not suffer too greatly, especially if a kindly aunt or uncle happened to be around. I am sure that if the details of the life histories of healthy people were studied, it would be found that they had had some very satisfactory experiences early enough to establish in them a feeling of validity as persons. The profoundly sick people have been so early injured, in such a rigid and limited frame of reference, that they are not able to make use of kindliness, decency, or regard when it does come their way. They meet the world as if it were potentially menacing. They have already developed defensive traits entirely appropriate to their original experience, and then carry them out in completely inappropriate situations rationalizing the discrepancies, but never daring to believe that people are different from the ones they early learned to distrust and hate. By reason of bitter early experience, they learn never to let their guards down, never to permit intimacy, lest at that moment the death blow would be dealt to their already partly destroyed sense of self-regard. Despairing of real joy in living, they develop secondary neurotic goals which give a pseudo-satisfaction. The secondary gains at first glance might seem to be what the person was really striving for—revenge, power and exclusive possession. Actually, these are but the expressions of the deep injuries sustained by the person. They can not be fundamentally cured until those interpersonal relationships that caused the original injury are brought back to consciousness in the analytic situation. Step by step, each phase of the long period of emotional development is exposed, by no means chronologically; the interconnecting, overlapping reference frames are made conscious; those points at which a distortion of reality, or a repression of part of the self *had* to occur, are uncovered. The reality gradually becomes "undistorted," the self, re-found, in the personal relationship between the analyst and the patient. This personal relationship with the analyst is the situation in which the transference distortions can be analyzed.

In Freud's view, the transference was either positive or negative, and was related in a rather isolated way to a particular person in the past. In my view, the transference is the experiencing in the analytic situation of the entire pattern of the original reference frames, which included at every moment the relationship of the patient to himself, to the important persons, and to others, as he experienced them at that time, in the light of his interrelationships with the important people.

The therapeutic aim in this process is not to uncover childhood memories that will then lend themselves to analytic interpretation. Here, I think, is an important difference to Freud's view, which Fromm (1943) has also pointed out. Psychoanalytic cure is not the amassing of data, either from childhood, or from the study of the present situation. Nor does cure result from a repetition of the original injurious experience in the analytic relationship. What is curative in the process is that in tending to reconstruct with the analyst that atmosphere which obtained in child-hood, the patient actually achieves something new. He discovers that part of himself which had to be repressed at the time of the original experi-ence. He can only do this in an interpersonal relationship with the analyst, which is suitable to such a re-discovery. To illustrate this point: if a patient had a hostile parent towards whom he was required to show deference, he has to repress certain of his own spontaneous feelings. In the analytic situation, he tends to carry over his original frame of refer-ence and again tends to feel himself to be in a similar situation. If the analyst's personality also contains elements of a need for deference, that need will unconsciously be imparted to the patient, who will, therefore, still repress his spontaneity as he did before. True enough, he may act or try to act as if analyzed, since by definition, that is what the analyst is attempting to accomplish. But he will *never* have found his repressed self, because the analytical relationship contains for him elements actu-ally identical with his original situation. Only if the analyst provides a genuinely *new* frame of reference—that is, if he is truly non-hostile, and truly not in need of deference—can this patient discover, and it is a real *discovery*, the repressed elements of his own personality. Thus, the transference phenomenon is used so that the patient will completely reexperience the original frames of reference, and himself within those frames, in a truly different relationship with the analyst, to the end that he can discover the invalidity of his conclusions about himself and others.

I do not mean by this to deny the correctness of Freud's view of trans-ference also acting as a resistance. As a matter of fact, the tendency of the patient to reestablish the original reference frame is precisely because he is afraid to experience the other person in a direct and unreserved way. He has organized his whole system of getting along in the world, bad as that system might be, on the basis of the original distortions of his personality and his subsequent vicissitudes. His capacity for spontaneous feeling and acting has gone into hiding. Now it has to be sought. If some such phrase as the "capacity for self-realization" is substituted in place of Freud's concept of the repressed libidinal impulse, much the same conclusions can be reached about the way in which the transference-manifestations appear in the analysis as resistance. It is just in the safest situation, where the spontaneous feeling might come out of hiding, that the patient develops intense feelings, sometimes of a hallucinatory character, that relate to the most dreaded experiences of the past. It is at this point that the nature and the use by the patient of the transference distortions have to be understood and correctly interpreted, by the analyst. It is also here that the personality of the analyst modifies the transference reaction. A patient cannot feel close to a detached or hostile analyst and will therefore never display the full intensity of his transference illusions. The complexity of this process, whereby the transference can be used as the therapeutic instrument and, at the same time, as a resistance may be illustrated by the following example: a patient had developed intense feelings of attachment to a father surrogate in his every day life. The transference feelings towards this man were of great value in elucidating his original problems with his real father. As the patient became more and more aware of his own personal validity, he found this masochistic attachment to be weakening. This occasioned acute feelings of anxiety, since his sense of independence was not yet fully established. At that point, he developed very disturbing feelings regarding the analyst, believing that she was untrustworthy and hostile, although prior to this, he had succeeded in establishing a realistically positive relationship to her. The feelings of untrustworthiness precisely reproduced an ancient pattern with his mother. He experienced them at this particular point in the analysis in order to retain and to justify his attachment to the father figure, the weakening of which attachment had threatened him so profoundly. The entire pattern was elucidated when it was seen that he was reexperiencing an ancient triangle, in which he was continuously driven to a submissive attachment to a dominating father, due to the utter untrustworthiness of his weak mother. If the transference character of this sudden feeling of untrustworthiness of the analyst had not been clarified, he would have turned again submissively to his father surrogate, which would have further postponed his development of independence. Nevertheless, the development of this transference to the analyst brought to light a new insight.

I wish to make one remark about Freud's view of the so-called narcissistic neuroses. Freud felt that personality disorders called schizophrenia or paranoia cannot be analyzed because the patient is unable to develop a transference to the analyst. It is my view that the real difficulty in treating such disorders is that the relationship is essentially nothing but transference illusions. Such persons hallucinate the original frame of reference to the exclusion of reality. Nowhere in the realm of psychoanalysis can one find more complete proof of the effect of early experience on the person than in attempting to treat these patients. Frieda Fromm-Reichmann (1939) has shown in her work with schizophrenics the necessity to realize the intensity of the transference reactions, which have become almost completely real to the patient. And yet, if one knows the correct interpretations, by actually feeling the patient's needs, one can over years of time do the identical thing that is accomplished more quickly and less dramatically with patients suffering a less severe disturbance of their interpersonal relationships.

Another point I wish to discuss for a moment is the following:

Freud (1933) takes the position that all subsequent experience in normal life is merely a repetition of the original one. Thus love is experienced for someone today *in terms of* the love felt for someone in the past. I do not believe this to be exactly true. The child who has not had to repress certain aspects of his personality enters into a new situation dynamically, not just as a repetition of what he felt, say, with his mother, but as an active continuation of it. I believe that there are constitutional differences with respect to the total capacity for emotional experience, just as there are with respect to the total capacity for intellectual experiences. Given this constitutional substrate, the child engages in personal relationships not passively as a lump of clay waiting to be molded, but most dynamically, bringing into play all his emotional potentialities. He may possibly find someone later whose capacity for response is deeper than his mother's. If *he* is capable of that greater depth, he experiences an expansion of himself. Many later in life have met a "great person" and have felt a sense of newness in the relationship which is described to others as "wonderful" and which is regarded with a certain amount of awe. This is not a "transference" experience, but represents a dynamic extension of the self to a new horizon.

In considering the process of psychoanalytic cure, Freud (1933) very seriously discussed the relationship of analysis to suggestion therapy and hypnosis. He believed as I previously mentioned that part of the positive transference could be made use of in the analysis to bring about the successful result. He says:

> In so far we readily admit that the results of psychoanalysis rest upon a basis of suggestion; only by suggestion we must be understood to mean that which we, with Ferenczi, find that it consists of—influence on a person through and by means of the transference-manifestations of which he is capable. The eventual independence of the patient is our ultimate object when we use suggestion to bring him to carry out a mental operation that will necessarily result in a lasting improvement in his mental condition [p. 319].

Freud elsewhere indicates very clearly that in hypnosis the relationship of the patient to the hypnotist is not worked through, whereas in analysis the transference to the analyst is resolved by bringing it entirely into consciousness. He also says that the patient is protected from the unwitting suggestive influence of the analyst by the awakening of his own unconscious resistances (p. 226).

I should like to discuss hypnosis a little more in detail and to make a few remarks about its correlation with the transference phenomenon in psychoanalytic therapy.

According to White (1941), the subject under hypnosis is a person striving to act like a hypnotized person as that state is continuously defined by the hypnotist. He also says that the state of being hypnotized is an "altered state of consciousness." However, as Maslow (Maslow and Mittelman, 1941) points out, it is not an abnormal state. In everyday life transient manifestations of all the phenomena that occur in hypnosis can be seen. Such examples are cited as the trance-like state a person experiences when completely occupied with an absorbing book. Among the phenomena of the hypnotic state are the amnesia for the trance; the development of certain anesthesias, such as insensitivity to pain; deafness to sounds other than the hypnotist's voice; greater ability to recall forgotten events; loss of capacity to spontaneously initiate activities; and a much greater suggestibility. This heightened suggestibility in the trance state is the most important phenomenon of hypnosis. Changes in behavior and feeling can be induced, such as painful or pleasant experiences, headaches, nausea, or feelings of well-being. Post-hypnotic behavior can be influenced by suggestion, this being one of the most important aspects of experimental hypnosis for the clarifying of psychopathological problems.

The hypnotic state is induced by a combination of methods which may include relaxation, visual concentration, and verbal suggestion. The methods vary with the personality of the experimenter and the subject.

Maslow has pointed out the interpersonal character of hypnosis, which accounts for some of the different conclusions by different experimenters. Roughly, the types of experimenters may be divided into three groups—the dominant type, the friendly or brotherly type, and the cold, detached, scientific type. According to the inner needs of the subject, he will be able to be hypnotized more readily by one type or the other. The brotherly hypnotist cannot, for instance, hypnotize a subject whose inner need is to be dominated.

Freud (1922) believed that the relationship of the subject to the hypnotist was that of an emotional, erotic attachment. He comments on the "uncanny" character of hypnosis and says that "the hypnotist awakens in the subject a portion of his archaic inheritance which had also made him compliant to his parents." What is thus awakened is the concept of "the dreaded primal father," "towards whom only a passive-masochistic attitude is possible, towards whom one's will has to be surrendered."

Ferenczi (1916) considered the hypnotic state to be one in which the patient transferred onto the hypnotist his early infantile erotic attachment to the parents with the same tendency to blind belief and to uncritical obedience as obtained then. He calls attention to the paternal or frightening type of hypnosis and the maternal or gentle, stroking type. In both instances the situation tends to favor the "conscious and unconscious imaginary return to childhood."

The only point of disagreement with these views that I have is that one does not need to postulate an *erotic* attachment to the hypnotist or a "transference" of infantile sexual wishes. The sole necessity is a willingness to surrender oneself. The child whose parent wished to control it, by one way or another, is forced to do this, in order to be loved, or at least to be taken care of. The patient transfers this willingness to surrender to the hypnotist.[1] He will also transfer it to the analyst or to the leader of a group. In any one of these situations the authoritative person, be he hypnotist, analyst or leader, promises by reason of great power or knowledge the assurance of safety, cure or happiness, as the case may be. The patient, or the isolated person, regresses emotionally to a state of helplessness and lack of initiative similar to the child who has been dominated.

If it is asked how in the first place the child is brought into a state of submissiveness, it may be discovered that the original situation of the child had certain aspects that already resemble a hypnotic situation. This depends upon the parents. If they are destructive or authoritarian they can achieve long lasting results. The child is continuously subjected to being told *how* and *what* he is. Day in and day out, in the limited frame of reference of his home, he is subjected to the repetition, over and over again: "You are a naughty boy." "You are a bad girl." "You are just a nuisance." "You are always giving me trouble." "You are dumb," "you are stupid," "you are a little fool." "You always make mistakes." "You can never do anything right"; or, "That's right; I love you when you are a good boy." "That's the kind of boy I like." "Now you are a nice boy." "Smile sweetly." "Pay attention to mother." "Mother loves a good boy who does what she tells him." "Mother knows best, mother always knows best." "If you would listen to mother, you would get along all right. Just listen to her." "Don't pay attention to those naughty children. Just listen to your mother."

Over and over again, with exhortations to pay attention, to listen, to be good, the child is brought under the spell. "When you get older, never forget what I told you. Always remember what mother says, then you will never get into trouble." These are like post-hypnotic suggestions. "You will never come to a good end. You will always be in trouble." "If you are not good, you will always be unhappy." "If you don't do what I say, you will regret it." "If you do not live up to the right things—again, "right" as continuously defined by the mother—you will be sorry."

It was called to my attention that the Papago Indians deliberately make use of a certain method of suggestion to influence the child favorably. When the child is falling asleep at night the grandfather sits by him and

---

[1]I am indebted to Erich Fromm for suggestions in the following discussion.

repeats over and over—"You will be a fast runner. You will be a good hunter" (Underhill, 1939).

Hypnotic experiments, according to Hull (1933), indicate that children, on the whole, are more susceptible than adults. Certainly, for many reasons, including that of learning the uses and misuses of language, there is a marked rise of verbal suggestibility up to five years, with a sharp dropping off at around the eighth year. Ferenczi refers to the subsequent effects of threats or orders given in childhood as "having much in common with the post-hypnotic command-automatisms." He points out how the neurotic patient follows out, without being able to explain the motive, a command repressed long ago, just as in hypnosis a post-hypnotic suggestion is carried out for which amnesia has been produced.

It is not my intention in this paper to try to explain the altered state of consciousness that is seen in the hypnotized subject. I have had no personal experience with hypnosis. The reason I refer to hypnosis in discussing the transference is in order to further an understanding of the analytic relationship. The child may be regarded as being in a state of "chronic hypnosis," as I have described, with all sorts of post-hypnotic suggestions thrown in during this period. This entire pattern—this entire early frame of reference—may be "transferred" to the analyst. When this has happened the patient is in a highly suggestible state. Due to a number of intrinsic and extrinsic factors, the analyst is now in the position of a sort of "chronic hypnotist." First, by reason of his position of a doctor he has a certain prestige. Second, the patient *comes* to him, even if expressedly unwillingly; still if there were not something in the patient which was cooperative he would not come at all, or at least he would not stay. The office is relatively quiet, external stimuli relatively reduced. The frame of reference is limited. Many analysts maintain an anonymity about themselves. The attention is focussed on the interpersonal relationship. In this relatively undefined and unstructured field the patient is able to discover his "transference" feelings, since he has few reference points in the analytic situation to go by. This is greatly enhanced by having the patient assume a physical position in the room whereby he does not see the analyst. Thus the ordinary reference points of facial expression and gesture are lacking. True enough, he can look around or get up and walk about. But for considerable periods of time he lies down—itself a symbolically submissive position. He does what is called "free association." This is again giving up—willingly, to be sure—the conscious control of his thoughts. I want to stress the willingness and cooperativeness of all these acts. That is precisely the necessary condition for hypnosis. The lack of immediate reference points permits the eruption into consciousness of the old patterns of feeling. The original frame of reference becomes more and more clearly outlined and felt. The power which the parent originally had to cast the spell is transferred to the analytical situation. Now it is the analyst who is in the position to do the same thing—placed there partly by the nature of the external situation, partly by the patient who comes to be freed from his suffering.

There is no such thing as an impersonal analyst, nor is the idea of the analyst's acting as a mirror anything more than the "neatest trick of the week." Whether intentionally or not, whether conscious of it or not, the analyst does express, day in and day out, subtle or overt evidences of his own personality in relationship to the patient.

The analyst may express explicitly his wish not to be coercive, but if he has an unconscious wish to control the patient, it is impossible for him correctly to analyze and to resolve the transference distortions. The patient is thus not able to become free from his original difficulties and for lack of something better, adopts the analyst as a new and less dangerous authority. Then the situation occurs in which it is not "my mother says" or "my father says," but now "my analyst says." The so-called chronic patients who need lifelong support may benefit by such a relationship. I am of the opinion, however, that frequently the long-continued unconscious attachment—by which I do *not* mean genuine affection or regard—is maintained because of a failure on the analyst's part to recognize and resolve the [patient's] sense of being under a sort of hypnotic spell that originated in childhood.

To develop an adequate therapeutic interpersonal relationship, the analyst must be devoid of those personal traits that tend unconsciously to perpetuate the originally destructive or authoritative situation. In addition to this, he must be able, by reason of his training, to be aware of every evidence of the transference phenomena; and lastly, he must understand the significance of the hypnotic-like situation which analysis helps to reproduce. If, with the best of intentions, he unwittingly makes use of the enormous power with which he is endowed by the patient, he may certainly achieve something that looks like change. His suggestions, exhortations and pronouncements, based on the patient's reevaluation of himself, may certainly make an impression. The analyst may say, "You must not do this just because I say so." That is in itself a sort of posthypnotic command. The patient then strives to be "an analyzed person acting on his own account"—because he was told to do so. He is still not really acting on his own.

It is my firm conviction that analysis is terminable. A person can continue to grow and expand all his life. The process of analysis, however, as an interpersonal experience, has a definite end. That end is achieved when the patient has rediscovered his own self as an actively and independently functioning entity.

REFERENCES

Ferenczi, S. (1916), *Sex in Psycho-Analysis*. Boston: Badger.

Freud, S. (1922), *Group Psychology and the Analysis of the Ego*. London: International Psycho-Analytic Press.

——(1933), *Collected Papers, Vol. 3*. London: Hogarth Press.

——(1940), *Gesammelte Werke, Vol. 12*. London: Imago.

Fromm, E. (1943), Lectures on ideas and ideologies. Presented at New School for Social Research, New York.

Fromm-Reichmann, F. (1939), Transference problems in schizophrenics. *Psychoanal. Quart.*, 8:412–426.

Horney, K. (1939), *New Ways in Psychoanalysis*. New York: Norton.

Hull, C. L. (1933), *Hypnosis and Suggestibility*. New York: Appleton-Century.

Maslow, A. H. & Mittelman, B. (1941), *Principles of Abnormal Psychology*. New York: Harper.

Sherif, M. A. F. (1936), *The Psychology of Social Norms*. New York: Harper.

Sullivan, H. S. (1940), Conceptions of modern psychiatry. *Psychiatry*, 3:1–117.

Underhill, R. (1939), *Social Organization of the Papago Indians*. New York: Columbia University Press.

White, R. W. (1941), A preface to the theory of hynotism. *J. Abn. & Soc. Psychol.*, 36:477–505.

4

SOME EFFECTS OF THE DEROGATORY ATTITUDE TOWARD FEMALE SEXUALITY

CLARA M. THOMPSON

[1950]

INTRODUCTION

Marylou Lionells

Psychoanalysts are fond of tracing their professional genealogies, illustrating through linkage to the psychoanalytic pioneers how they are legitimate heirs of a rich intellectual legacy. Clara Thompson met Sándor Ferenczi, one of Freud's early disciples, in 1927. She traveled to Budapest in the summers of 1928 and 1929 to start analytic treatment with him and then lived in that city to complete her analysis from 1931 until Ferenczi died in 1933. In the early 1940s, my own analyst, Ruth Moulton, began her training analysis with Thompson who was then on the faculty of the New York Psychoanalytic Institute. Moulton joined the group that defected from the New York Institute in 1942. She completed analytic training through an affiliation with Sullivan's Washington-Baltimore psychoanalytic center, and worked with Thompson and others to found the William Alanson White Institute as a free-standing enterprise in New York City. Among the ideals that distinguished the White Institute from other psychoanalytic training programs was its commitment to heterodoxy, a refusal to assert any psychoanalytic theory as dogma, and its willingness to train psychologists on an equal basis with medical practitioners. Thompson served as the first Director of the White Institute, a position she maintained until her death in 1958. She was a revered and beloved leader, universally referred to simply as "Clara." Moulton filled many central administrative posts at the growing Institute,

Marylou Lionells, Ph.D. is Director, Training and Supervising Analyst, and Fellow, William Alanson White Institute; and coeditor, *Handbook of Interpersonal Psychoanalysis* (The Analytic Press, 1995).

notably heading the Training Committee from 1960 to 1970. She also followed Clara's lead in becoming a major figure of her generation who championed the study of women's issues. In 1992 I was appointed Director of the White Institute, the second woman and the first psychologist, heir to a tradition that includes Clara's standards of personal fairness, pragmatism, intellectual rigor, humanitarian concerns, philosophical openness, and determination to avoid factionalism and ideological dogma. Clara provided an inspirational role model, but indeed, a very hard act to follow.

At times this sort of exercise in detailing one's psychoanalytic roots is criticized as a constricting form of ancestor worship, a litmus test of orthodoxy. But such historical analysis serves a legitimate purpose in scholarly research. Theory, whether about nuclear physics or literary criticism, is to some extent influenced by the personality of its author, and it is particularly true that psychoanalytic thought is inevitably shaped by personal experiences. Both the interpretations in the consulting room and the ideas presented in the journals are subject to the broad impact of culture and historical epoch, and are subtly affected by personal life history, developmental patterns, family life, professional training, and the patients chosen for study. To offer a context for the following paper by Clara Thompson, I will focus on three aspects of her personal situation: her psychoanalytic experience with Ferenczi; her involvement with two powerful and competing psychoanalytic theorists, Sullivan and Fromm; and her gender.

Freud's relationships with his colleagues were notably stormy, and his friendship with Ferenczi was no exception. While other early psychoanalysts rejected Freud's thesis concerning the centrality of intrapsychic sexual motivations and went on to found competing schools, Ferenczi worked independently in Budapest, elaborating theory and technique along lines that he understood to be continuous with the libido theory, at least as originally conceived. While Freud moved ever further away from the so-called "seduction hypothesis," seeking the causes of psychic distress in the realm of internally generated fantasy instead of in the area of the patient's experiences in the real world, Ferenczi remained focused on the interaction between the internal and the external, between impulse, need, and wish on the one hand, and interpersonal encounters and traumatic events on the other.

It is unclear how the political and personal storms between Freud and Ferenczi affected Thompson's personal experience in psychoanalysis. Probably of more importance was the effect of Ferenczi's own personality and his professional quest that, at the time, was to expand the scope of psychoanalytic inquiry. Ferenczi carried on the spirit of psychoanalytic innovation. He was patient oriented, willing to experiment in order to find a technique that would be helpful in alleviating symptoms and exploring the unconscious. His was a more emotional temperament than Freud's, perhaps characteristically Hungarian. Thompson herself asserts that "he preferred his sentimental tendencies and struggled against his conventional trends" (Green, 1964, p. 73). He was less suited to anonymity, more willing to use his reactions and to reveal his personal feelings. He was convinced that an important ingredient in helping the patient involved the analyst's willingness and ability to communicate personal feelings of care and concern. As was the custom of the day, he comfortably maintained social as well as professional relationships with patients, a tradition carried on by Thompson throughout her lifetime, and later perpetuated by Moulton as well.

Clara has written that when she told Harry Stack Sullivan of her interest in obtaining experience in psychoanalysis he advised her to seek out Sándor Ferenczi (Green, 1964, p. 355). While emerging from totally different intellectual traditions, there is a basic compatibility and remarkable similarity between Sullivan's interpersonal psychoanalytic viewpoint and Ferenczi's modifications of Freud's ideas. In her personal analysis, Thompson experienced the classical view of transference, and the interpretation of oedipal conflict within the matrix of an exploration of the real encounter between patient and analyst. Thompson's bibliography is heavily weighted in favor of questions concerning female sexuality and feminine psychology. We may speculate that this trend in her work is at least in part due to the influence of her analytic experience that emphasized the centrality of sexual issues and the necessity that any theory of the human psyche grapple with problems of drive, impulse, and biological and evolutionary requirements.

Sullivan and his followers, who rejected Freudian definitions of psychoanalysis, held that the effects of interpersonal experience as formative of personality and psychic life are more important than sexual drive. Among the early interpersonalists, Thompson stands out for having studied the origins, meanings, representations, and implications of the sexual aspects of human experience. She alone within the interpersonal school, in concert with her contemporary iconoclastic innovator, Karen Horney, explored the dimensions of sexuality as both a fundamental motivation in human life and as a product of the complex interweaving of biological, social, cultural, and personal factors. I would suggest that her recognition that the sexual dimension must be incorporated as a major component of any psychoanalytic understanding of human experience was in some measure a result of her personal analytic experience.

In 1993–94 the White Institute celebrated its fiftieth anniversary. Each of the founders of the Institute was memorialized with biographical sketches, personal anecdotes, and reminiscences. In the discussion, some spoke of the personal qualities that enabled Clara to create and lead a psychoanalytic institute that has been remarkably free of the factionalism and schisms which are so typical of the field. One participant wondered how this independent yet shy woman could manage to maintain an atmosphere where two such powerful and contentious spirits as Harry Stack Sullivan and Erich Fromm could feel equally appreciated and comfortable.

Although Fromm was reputed to be a consummate clinician, his published legacy emphasizes understanding human nature as a function of conflicting biological, social, and cultural pressures. And while Sullivan's humanitarian efforts and social concerns are well documented, his most influential writings pertain to the psychological ramifications of interpersonal interactions. In studying her writings it is abundantly clear that Clara was deeply indebted to both men. Without explicitly acknowledging it, she seems to have built a series of bridges between the sociopolitical concerns of Fromm and the innovations of Sullivan in the realm of deep pathology and clinical technique. In the article reprinted here, a brief but representative gem, Thompson accepts Fromm's analysis of the relationship between anatomy, physiology, and sensory experience. She then considers how the differing phenomenology of each sex contributes to a differing psychological state, and to particular patterns of interaction which have implications for self-image and self-esteem. She also locates these experiences within a conception of the sociocultural milieu, understanding how time and place define social conditions, and these, in turn, shape individual feelings.

Psychoanalysis is unusual among the professions in that throughout its history there have been a number of women among its major figures. Unlike her most notable contemporaries, Horney and Klein, Thompson did not found a new psychoanalytic school based on her own theory. While seen as a formidable intellect and seriously interested in the expansion of psychoanalytic ideas, she seems to have been more dedicated to interpreting, extending, clarifying, and synthesizing the ideas of others, than in being innovative herself. For example, her most enduring work is her major opus, *Psychoanalysis: Evolution and Development* (Thompson, 1950), the first systematic synthesis of the various schools of psychoanalytic thought. She brought a strong personal ethic to her administrative work as well as to her scholarship, and was seen as maternal, sensitive, and demonstrating a deep, perhaps stereotypically feminine concern for minorities, the underprivileged, and the underserved.

Her comfort with using her personal feelings to guide her intellectual concerns is nowhere more apparent than in her writing about the psychology of women. She assailed the Freudian establishment for reliance upon a phallocentric view of human psychology. She was appalled that ideas about the development of females should be derived from the fantasies of males, and especially from the neurotic distortions of men who suffered from severe pathologies in their own personalities. She even argued that it is impossible for one gender to truly appreciate, much less to empathize with any degree of accuracy, with the sensory awareness and psychological reactivity of the other sex. Thompson championed the inductive development of theory, starting from the data of actual experience. Long before the contemporary feminist critique, she observed how prejudice, stereotype, sociocultural standards, and even psychological defenses such as insecurity, envy, and the quest for power, all contributed to an erroneous understanding of women. She was aware of how theory can be used as a mechanism of social control, and how it can serve purposes of narcissistic protection.

Despite the quality of her intellect and the passion of her arguments, Thompson's writings do not seem to have received the attention they might warrant. There are of course many reasons for it, not the least of which was her untimely death that occurred before she was able to complete her manuscript concerning the psychology of women. It is also true that she was not particularly interested in theory per se. Like her mentor Harry Stack Sullivan, she denounced abstract conceptualizations and fancy hypothetical constructions. In addition, and unlike Sullivan, she had the rare gift of being plainspoken. She was known for her clearheadedness and common sense. Her prose is clear and simple, a virtue that often has the contradictory effect of not being considered profound. But, as her article will illustrate, she had much to say, and she said it very well. There is great value in returning to her writings, not simply as artifacts in the history of psychoanalysis but as useful

documents of clinical insight, technical skill, and genuine dedication to
psychoanalytic healing.

In an earlier paper (Thompson, 1943) I stressed the fact that the actual
envy of the penis as such is not as important in the psychology of women
as their envy of the position of the male in our society. This position of
privilege and alleged superiority is symbolized by the possession of a
penis. The owner of this badge of power has special opportunities while
those without it have more limited possibilities. I questioned in that
paper whether the penis in its own right as a sexual organ was necessarily
an object of envy at all.[1]

That there are innate biological differences between the sexual life of
man and woman is so obvious that one must apologize for mentioning it.
Yet those who stress this aspect most are too often among the first to
claim knowledge of the psychic experiences and feelings of the opposite
sex. Thus for many centuries male writers have been busy trying to
explain the female. In recent years a few women have attempted to
present the inner life of their own sex, but they themselves seem to have
had difficulty in freeing their thinking from the male orientation. Psychoanalysts, female as well as male, seem for the most part still to be
dominated by Freud's thinking about women.

Freud was a very perceptive thinker but he was a male, and a male quite
ready to subscribe to the theory of male superiority prevalent in the
culture. This must have definitely hampered his understanding of experiences in a woman's life, especially those specifically associated with her
feminine role.

Of course this thinking can be carried to extreme lengths and one can
say that no human being can really know what another human being
actually experiences about anything. However, the presence of similar
organs justifies us in thinking that we can at least approximate an
understanding of another person's experiences in many cases. A head-
ache, a cough, a pain in the heart, intestinal cramps, weeping, laughter,
joy, a sense of well-being—we assume that all of these feel to other people
very similar to what we ourselves experience under those titles.

In the case of sexual experiences, however, one sex has no adequate
means of identifying with the experience of the other sex. A woman, for
instance, cannot possibly be sure that she knows what the subjective

---

Interpersonal Psychoanalysis: The Selected Papers of Clara M. Thompson, ed. M. R. Green. New
York: Basic Books, 1964, pp. 229–242.
[1]I do not wish to leave the impression that there is never a woman who thinks she desires
to possess the male genital as such, but I believe such women are found relatively rarely.

experience of an erection and male orgasm is. Nor can a man identify with the tension and sensations of menstruation, or female genital excitation, or childbirth. Since for many years most of the psychoanalysts were men this may account for the prevalence of some misconceptions about female sexuality. Horney (1926) pointed out that Freud's theory that little girls believed that they had been castrated and that they envied boys their penises is definitely a male orientation to the subject. In this paper she listed several ideas which little boys have about girls' genitals. These ideas, she shows, are practically identical with the classic psychoanalytic conception of the female. The little boys' ideas are based on the assumption that girls also have penises, which results in a shock at the discovery of their absence. A boy, reasoning from his own life experience, assumes this is a mutilation, as a punishment for sexual misdemeanor. This makes more vivid to him any castration threats which have been made to him. He concludes that the girl must feel inferior and envy him because she must have come to the same conclusions about her state. In short, the little boy, incapable of imagining that one could feel complete without a penis, assumes that the little girl must feel deprived. It is doubtless true that her lack of a penis can activate any latent anxiety the boy may have about the security of his own organ, but it does not necessarily follow that the girl feels more insecure because of it.

Freud (1959) assumes that masochism is a part of female sexuality, but he gives as his evidence the fantasies of passive male homosexuals. What a passive male homosexual imagines about the experience of being a woman is not necessarily similar to actual female sexual experience. In fact, a healthy woman's sexual life is probably not remotely similar to the fantasies and longings of a highly disturbed passive male personality.

Recently I heard to my amazement that a well-known psychiatrist had told a group of students that in the female sexual life there is no orgasm. I can only explain such a statement by assuming that this man could not conceive of an orgasm in the absence of ejaculation. If he had speculated that the female orgasm must be a qualitatively different experience from that of the male because of the absence of ejaculation, one could agree that this may well be the case. I think these examples suffice to show that many current ideas about female psychosexual life may be distorted by being seen through male eyes.

In "Sex and Character" Fromm (1943) has pointed out that the biological differences in the sexual experience may contribute to greater emphasis on one or the other character trends in the two sexes. Thus he notes that for the male it is necessary to be able to perform, while no achievement is required of the female. This, he believes, can have a definite effect on the general character trends. This gives the man a greater need to demonstrate, to produce, to have power, while the woman's need is more in the direction of being accepted, being desirable. Since her satisfaction is dependent on the man's ability to produce, her fear is in being abandoned, being frustrated, while his is fear of failure. Fromm points out that the woman can make herself available at any time and give satisfaction to the man, but the man's possibility of satisfying her is not entirely within his control. He cannot always produce an erection at will.

The effect of basic sexual differences on the character structure is not pertinent to this paper. Fromm's thesis that the ability to perform is important to male sexual life, that it is especially a matter of concern to the male because it is not entirely within his control, and that the female may perform at all times if she so wishes, are points of importance in my thesis. But I should like to develop somewhat different aspects of the situation. Fromm shows that the woman can at any time satisfy the male, and he mentions the male's concern over successfully performing for the female, but he does not at any point discuss how important obtaining satisfaction for themselves is in the total reaction.

In general the male gets at least some physiological satisfaction out of his sexual performance. Some experiences are more pleasurable than others, to be sure, and there are cases of orgasm without pleasure. However, for the very reason that he cannot force himself to perform, he is less likely to find himself in the midst of a totally uncongenial situation.

The female, however, who permits herself to be used when she is not sexually interested or is at most only mildly aroused, frequently finds herself in the midst of an unsatisfactory experience. At most she can have only a vicarious satisfaction in the male's pleasure. I might mention parenthetically here that some male analysts, for example, Ferenczi, are inclined to think that identification with the male in his orgasm constitutes a woman's true sexual fulfillment. This I would question.

One frequently finds resentment in women who have for some reason consented to being used for the male's pleasure. This is in many cases covered by an attitude of resignation. A frequent answer from women when they are asked about marital sexual relations is: "It is all right. He doesn't bother me much." This attitude may hold even when in other respects the husband and wife like each other; that is, such an attitude may exist even when the woman has not been intimidated by threats or violence. She simply assumes that her interests are not an important consideration.

Obviously the sexual act is satisfactory to the woman only when she actively and from choice participates in her own characteristic way. If she considered herself free to choose, she would refuse the male except when she actually did desire to participate.

This being the case, it might be fruitful to examine the situations in which the woman submits with little or no interest. There are, of course, occasions when she genuinely wishes to do this for the man's sake; this does not create a problem. More frequently the cause is a feeling of insecurity in the relationship; this insecurity may arise from external factors—that is, the male concerned may insist on his satisfaction or else! The insecurity may also arise from within because of the woman's own feelings of inadequacy. These feelings may arise simply from the fact that the woman subscribes to the cultural attitude that her needs are not as insistent as the man's; but, in addition she may have personal neurotic difficulties.

The question arises: How has it become socially acceptable for a man to insist on his sexual rights whenever he desires? Is this because rape is a possibility, and the woman is physically relatively defenseless? This must have had some influence in the course of society's development. However, it has often been proved that even rape is not easy without some cooperation from the woman. The neurotic condition of vaginismus illustrates that in some conditions even unconscious unwillingness on the part of the woman may effectively block male performance. So while the superior physical power of the male may be an important factor in the frequency of passive compliance, there must be other factors. These other factors are not of a biologic nature, for the participation in sexual relations without accompanying excitement is most obviously possible in human females, although not definitely impossible in other animals.

One must look to cultural attitudes for the answer. There are two general concepts which are significant here, and to which both men and women subscribe in our culture. One is that the female sexual drive is not as pressing or important as the male. Therefore there is less need to be concerned in satisfying it or considering it. The other is the analytically much-discussed thesis that the female sex organs are considered inferior to those of the male.

In recent years there has been a definite tendency to move away from the first ideas as far as actual sexual performance is concerned. With the increasing tendency to be more open in observing facts about sex, women in many groups have become able not only to admit to themselves but also to men that their sexual needs are important. However, this is still not true of all groups. Moreover, at almost the same time another important aspect of woman's sexual life has diminished in importance; that is, the bearing of children. Woman's specific type of creativeness is no longer highly desired in many situations. This is an important subject in itself and will not be discussed here.

As we know, during the Victorian era a woman's sexual needs were supposed to be practically nonexistent. A woman was expected to be able to control her sexual desires at all times. Thus an extramarital pregnancy was allegedly entirely due to the woman's weakness or depravity. The man's participation in such an extramarital relationship was looked upon with more tolerance, and there was little or no social disgrace attached to him. The double standard of sexual morality also implied an assumption that woman's sexual drive was not as insistent as the male's.

The fact that evidence of erotic excitement could be concealed much better by a woman than by a man made the development of such thinking possible. Since she was not supposed to be erotic and since the man must have his satisfaction, a pattern was developed in which the dutiful wife offered herself to her husband without actively participating in the act herself. I am sure many women were sufficiently normal to find nonparticipation difficult, and doubtless many men did not subscribe to the feeling that they should be horrified at any evidence of passion in their wives. Nevertheless, as recently as twenty years ago a woman, who consulted me about her marital difficulties, reported that her husband felt disgust, it seemed, whenever she responded sexually to him. She tried to conceal her sexual responses, including orgasm, from him, then would lie awake the rest of the night in misery and rage. Since I saw this woman only twice, I am not in a position to say how much this situation contributed to her suicide about a year later. Undoubtedly there were many other difficulties in her relation to her husband, of which the sexual may have been only one expression. Certainly this extreme denial of sexual interest is seldom required of women today, but an attenuated form still remains, especially in marriage. Here it is found not only in frigid women who, realizing their inadequacy as mates, make amends as best they can by a nonparticipating offering of themselves. But one also finds the attitude even in women with adequate sexual responsiveness in many situations. They have accepted the idea that the male's needs are greater than their own and that therefore his wishes and needs are paramount.

So the feeling that woman's sexual life is not as important or insistent as the male's may produce two unfortunate situations. It may inhibit the woman's natural expression of desire for fear of appearing unwomanly, or it may lead her to feel she must be ready to accommodate on all occasions—that is, she has no rights of her own. Both extremes mean an interference with her natural self-expression and spontaneity with resulting resentment and discontent.

Moreover, since the male has often been indoctrinated with the idea that woman's sexual life is not important, he may not exert himself much to make her interested. He fails to see the importance of the art of love.

When an important aspect of a person's life becomes undervalued, this has a negative effect on the self-esteem. What a woman actually has to offer in sexual responsiveness becomes undervalued and this in turn affects her own evaluation of herself as a person.

The second way in which our culture has minimized woman's sexual assets is in the derogation of her genitals. This in classic terminology is connected with the idea of penis envy. I wish to approach the problem differently. As I said earlier, the idea of penis envy is a male concept. It is the male who experiences the penis as a valuable organ and he assumes that women also must feel that way about it. But a woman cannot really imagine the sexual pleasure of the penis—she can only appreciate the social advantages its possessor has. What a woman needs rather is a feeling of the importance of her own organs. I believe that much more important than penis envy in the psychology of woman is her reaction to the undervaluation of her own organs. I think we can concede that the acceptance of one's body and all its functions is a basic need in the establishment of self-respect and self-esteem.

The short, plump, brunette may feel that she would be more acceptable if she were a tall, thin blond—in other words, if she were somebody else. The solution of her problem lies not in becoming a blond but in finding out why she is not accepting what she is. The history will show either that some significant person in her early life preferred a tall blond or that being a brunette has become associated with other unacceptable characteristics. Thus in one case in which the envy of the blond type was present, being brunette meant being sexy, and being sexy was frowned upon.

Sex in general has come under the disapproval of two kinds of thinking in our culture. The puritan ideal is denial of body pleasure, and this makes sexual needs something of which to be ashamed. Traces of this attitude still remain today in the feelings of both sexes.

We also have another attitude which derogates sexuality, especially female sexuality. We are people with great emphasis on cleanliness. In many people's minds the genital organs are classed with the organs of excretion and thus become associated with the idea of being unclean. With the male some of the curse is removed because he gets rid of the objectional product. The female, however, receives it, and when her attitude is strongly influenced by the dirty excretion concept, this increases her feeling of unacceptability. Moreover, the men who feel the sexual product is unclean reinforce the woman's feeling that her genitals are unclean.

The child's unrestrained pleasure in his body and its products begins to be curbed at an early age. This is such a fundamental part of our basic training that most of us would have difficulty imagining the effect on our psychic and emotional life of a more permissive attitude. What has happened is that this training has created a kind of moral attitude toward our body products. Sphincter morality, as Ferenczi has called it, extends to more than the control of urine and feces. To some extent genital products come also under the idea of sphincter morality. Obviously this especially has an influence on attitudes toward the female genitals where no sphincter control is possible. My attention was first called to this by a paper written in German by Bertram Lewin (1930) twenty years ago. In this paper he presented, among other things, clinical data in which the menses were compared to an unwanted loss of feces and urine due to lack of sphincter control. In one case which he reported, the woman had become very proficient at contracting the vaginal muscles so that she attained some semblance of control of the quantity of menstrual flow. Although in my own practice I have never encountered a patient who actually tried to produce a sphincter, I have frequent evidence that the inability not only to control menstruation but all secretions of the female genitals has contributed to a feeling of unacceptability and dirtiness. One patient on being presented by her mother with a perineal napkin on the occasion of her first menses refused to use it. To her it meant a baby's diaper, and she felt completely humiliated. Obviously she presently felt even more humiliated because of the inevitable consequences of her refusal.

Also because of the culture's overvaluation of cleanliness another attribute of the female genital can be a source of distress, that is, the fact that it has an odor. Thus one of the chief means by which the female attracts the male among animals has been labeled unpleasant, to many even disgusting. For example, a female patient whose profession requires her appearing before audiences has been greatly handicapped for many years by a feeling of being "stinking" which is greatly augmented whenever she is in a position to have her body observed. Thus she can talk over the radio but not before an audience. Another patient felt for years that she could never marry because she would not be able to keep her body clean at every moment in the presence of her husband. Whenever she had a date with a man she prepared for it by a very vigorous cleansing of the genitals, especially trying to make them dry. When she finally had sexual relations she was surprised and greatly helped in her estimation of her body by discovering that this highly prized dryness was just the opposite of what was pleasing to the man.

In two cases the feeling of genital unacceptability had been a factor in promiscuity. In each case an experience with a man who kissed her genitals in an obviously accepting way was the final step in bringing about a complete transformation of feeling. In both cases all need to be promiscuous disappeared, and each of the women felt loved for the first time.

I am obviously oversimplifying these cases in order to make my point clear. I do not wish to leave the impression that the feeling of dirtiness connected with the genitals was the sole cause of a feeling of unacceptability in these patients. There was in each case a feeling from early childhood of not being acceptable, produced by specific attitudes in the parents. The feeling of unacceptability became focused on the genitals eventually for different reasons in each case. For example, in three cases the woman had risen above the lowly social position of her parents and with each of these three women the feeling of having dirty genitals became symbolic of her lowly origin of which she was ashamed. The parents had not placed such an emphasis on baths as they found to be the case in the new social milieu. Therefore any evidence of body secretion or odor betrayed them, and this made sex itself evidence of lower-class origin. On the other hand, two other patients suffered from their own mother's overemphasis on body cleanliness. In each of these two cases the mother was cold and puritanical as well as over clean, and the patient felt humiliated because she had a more healthy sexual drive which she felt was proclaimed to the world by her body's odors and secretions.

From these observations I hope I have emphasized the fact that the problem of a woman's sexual life is not in becoming reconciled to having no penis but in accepting her own sexuality in its own right. In this she is hampered by certain attitudes in the culture such as that her sexual drive is not important and her genitals are not clean. With these two deprecatory cultural attitudes in the background of women's lives, it is to be expected that both are important points at which difficulties in interpersonal relations may be expressed.

REFERENCES

Freud, S. (1959), The economic problem of masochism. *Collected Papers, Vol. 2.* New York: Basic Books.

Fromm, E. (1943), Sex and character. *Psychiatry,* 6:21–31.

Horney, K. (1926), Flight from womanhood. *Internat. J. Psycho-Anal.,* 7:324–339.

Lewin, B. (1930), Kotschmieren, Menses and weibliches Uber-Ich. *Internat. Z. Psychoanal.,* 16:43–56.

Thompson, C. (1943), Penis envy in women. *Psychiatry,* 6:123–125.

5

HUMAN REACTIONS OF ANALYSTS
TO PATIENTS

RALPH M. CROWLEY

[1952]

INTRODUCTION

Miltiades L. Zaphiropoulos

Ralph Manning Crowley was my first analyst, so-called training or otherwise. Analysis with him was experiencing the man whose article "Human Reactions of Analysts to Patients" is presented here. Starting analysis on the first of April seems to have boded well for finding out, among other things, what a fool I had been for not trusting myself enough to really trust others when I did feel that way. Crowley's natural manner made it relatively easy to enter this new venture without undue or lasting anxiety, be it about influence or other issues.

I soon rewarded him with a dream that struck my fancy and my funny bone more than it did his. This was not for lack of humor on his part since he proved to have plenty of it and was capable of using it judiciously and effectively. Rather, analysis being a serious though not grim enterprise for him, calling for involvement and curiosity while acknowledging one's feelings, he raised some questions with me and in me—a revelation in the midst of my revelry.

There was something uncanny about his timing, the unselfconscious tentativeness of his sparse interpretations, actually more a kind of responsive intervention, and his willingness to be a participant in an eventually collaborative interchange. He did not begrudge or belabor the early absence of true collaboration, caused by an unreadiness on my part, nor prematurely force

Miltiades Zaphiropoulos, M.D. is Training and Supervising Analyst, William Alanson White Institute; and Special Lecturer in Psychiatry, College of Physicians and Surgeons, Columbia University.

on me its effect on him. This being a so-called training analysis, and in the light of a brief earlier experience at a classical institute where training analysts participated in the evaluation and progress of their analysand candidates, and although the William Alanson White Institute forbade such participation, I asked him if he considered me ready to start courses and to enter supervision. I believe this was the first time that he addressed me by my first name, no doubt aware that my early cultural background made it difficult for me to brook egalitarianism between hierarchical superiors and inferiors. His response conveyed to me the probable presence of conflicting concerns of my own, concerns that were partly being transferred and projected on him, and yet acknowledged some wish for consensual validation.

Years later, after graduation, I returned to him for supervision thinking that this might prove edifying and productive. It did. His stance was one of respect and responsibility, using what each of us had known about the other, essentially eliciting what got in the way of using my capabilities or what resulted in lapses. Once, in supervision with Harry Stack Sullivan, he had been told about some lapse of his own: "Either you were asleep or careless or both." Crowley may not have been as trenchant with me but he could and did challenge my petty complaints or any of my unwarranted attributions to others of failings that I could do something about.

The paper presented here was first delivered in 1950, and is part of a series of efforts by analysts of the interpersonal school to redefine and refine the concept of countertransference, establish the validity of its components and consider its uses. It also aims to differentiate between countertransferential developments and possible transferential intrusions by analysts into the analytic situation and, most important, to reach a better understanding of the multiple nature and sources of the analyst's reactions so as to obviate "a paranoid reaction to one's own countertransference."

From our present vantage point, the Crowley paper may suggest an obsolescent candor. But in 1950, its premises and purpose were pioneering and pathfinding. They highlighted the ubiquitousness and inevitability of the analyst's human emotional reactions to the patient and the waste implicit in denying or ignoring them instead of using them. They also pointed out the desirability of studying countertransferential reactions in terms of their potential to shed light on the psychoanalytic process. To some extent, both concerns have led to subsequent developments in interpersonal psychoanalysis as well as in mainstream analysis, thus reflecting the essence and endurance of Crowley's contribution. Without resorting to precious or tendentious parsing, it is interesting to note the use of the terms rational and irrational in differentiating appropriate human reactions, that is, those likely to occur on the part of most people to actual attitudes or behaviors displayed by an individual in dealing with one or many others, and inappropriate ones likely to reflect unresolved difficulties on the part of a particular analyst with a particular patient. Were one to use the word natural, there would still be a question as to whether that would also refer to either rational or irrational.

I want to stress that Crowley was particularly concerned with the role of ambiguity in analytic work as well as in life. In discussing the analyst's wish to help and referring to needs the analyst shares with his patients and all of humanity, Crowley (1964) writes:

They are neither exclusively infantile nor exclusively mature; they are neither exclusively rational nor exclusively irrational; they are neither exclusively appropriate nor exclusively inappropriate; and they are neither totally conscious nor totally unconscious. They are a mixture of all of these [p. 34].

He mused on the statement that life is irrational, meaning that it is both rational and irrational and, as such, paradoxical. He did not believe in complete and exclusive rationality as an achievable state of human affairs no matter what the effort or the wish for it, and he wrote: "Every therapist to be helpful must accept in part, he and his patient will remain to the end irrational as well as rational" (1964, p. 34). In another vein, Crowley stated:

Rationality belongs only to the mind itself; its epitome is in mathematical systems, which tell us nothing about the nature of external reality. As soon as the rational is expressed in action, something of the nonrational is present . . . the assumption of the original innocence of man is even more destructive than that of original sin . . . a farewell to innocence requires the admission of evil in ourselves" [1975, pp. 385–387].

A faithful interpreter of Harry Stack Sullivan and discerning critic of his critics, Crowley (1975) compiled Sullivan's definitive bibliography. He lived and breathed participant observation in the analytic situation, saw consensual validation as process and content, viewed the intrapersonal as lasting or changing configurations within a person operating in an interpersonal field, and told no one how to live but helped free them to make personal and responsible choices. Having venerated his well-chosen teachers and honored them through his own creative use of what they taught, he communicated what he could, eventually paraphrasing Marcel Proust with a poignant cri de coeur: "But how does one teach seeing with new eyes? One can only encourage" (Crowley, 1983, p. 132).

Analysts have all been patients. When they finish their analyses and stop being patients, they cannot stop being human. If they could, they would not do their patients any good. Yet analysts' emotional reactions to patients are often termed counter-transference with connotations of something disparaging and to be avoided. I believe that the human emotional reactions of analysts to their patients not only cannot be avoided, but can be used to facilitate analytic understanding and progress. They also deserve attention as phenomena worthy of study. Such study and research can cast further light on the nature of the psychoanalytic process.[1]

Samiksa, 6:212–219.
Based on a paper read as part of a symposium on counter-transference held by the William Alanson White Association, New York, December 6, 1950.

I use counter-transference to mean those reactions of an analyst to a patient that are inappropriate and irrational. I agree with Mabel Cohen (1952) that for counter-transference to be present, anxiety must be aroused in the analyst. As she points out, this definition of counter-transference has the advantage of including all situations where an analyst is unable to be useful to a patient because of difficulties with his own responses (p. 231).

This way of distinguishing counter-transference from the totality of an analyst's reactions has its precedent in distinguishing a patient's transference reactions from the totality of his reactions to his analyst. Clara Thompson (1945) has pointed out in her paper on transference that not all the reactions a patient has to his analyst are abnormal, inappropriate, irrational, or transferred from somewhere in his past. Some of these reactions are quite germane to the actual analytic situation and to the actual behaviour or character of the analyst. In other words, the reactions are products of rational judgment and rational attitudes and emotions and correspond to the reality of the person of the analyst. Thompson distinguishes these attitudes and reactions from transference. The latter term she reserves for irrational attitudes.

Similarly, an analyst may have rational and reality-based feelings and attitudes toward his patient, which I do not include in my use of the term counter-transference.[2] Some authors use that term to include these appropriate, unexaggerated non-defensive, and non-anxious reactions of an analyst to patients (Heimann, 1950).[3] These responses, however, are neither counter, that is, provoked only by the patient, nor are they transference reactions in the sense of being unanalyzed and irrational. They are much neglected. Their significance is belittled and their usefulness to therapy is not realized.[4] Although in practice it is difficult to separate them from counter-transference reactions, I think there is a scientific advantage in so doing. There is also a practical advantage in that such a distinction emphasizes the existence of rational reactions especially when irrational reactions are mixed with them. Since the literature is liberal with illustrations of the irrational counter-transference responses of analysts, I shall not add more here (see Reich,

---

[1]See Cohen, 1952, p. 231. This paper is a beginning toward such research in that it advances the theory that counter-transference reactions are characterized by anxiety on the part of the analyst.

[2]There is wide variation among psycho-analysts in their definition and use of the term counter-transference (see Cohen, 1952; Berman, 1949; Gitelson, 1952; Weigert, 1952.

[3]Here the term counter-transference is used "to cover all the feelings that the analyst experiences toward his patient."

[4]The following papers are exceptions to this statement and stress the unavoidability and usefulness of the analysts' emotional reactions: DeForest (1951); Heimann (1950); Little (1951); Gitelson (1952); Weigert (1952).

1951; Gitelson, 1952; Little, 1951). I shall, however, illustrate the other types, namely, mixed counter-transference–appropriate reactions and the more or less totally appropriate reactions.

Analysts, like others, do have emotional reactions that are almost entirely rational and appropriate. For example, during a session in which a patient is telling a story about himself and his wife, the analyst notices he, himself, is irritated and impatient. He next asks himself why, and he discovers he would like to know the significance the story has for the patient. This leads the analyst to observe the patient's story was wordy, circumstantial, and unduly prolonged. This is something that is normally productive of annoyance in most people, and is an example of a reaction appropriate to the stimulus. As we shall see later, it can be easily utilized to advance therapy.

The following example illustrates a partially appropriate and partially counter-transference reaction. An analyst finds that he has not been listening to the patient and, in fact, feels quite angry, and is thinking, "what a stupid story" or "how can anyone be so boring?" Being an analyst, he realizes that he is not understanding something, and remembers that he often listened to long-winded talks from his father with mounting rage and inability to extricate himself. He sees this is something he has frequently done with this patient, feeling angry, withdrawing, and saying nothing, and that his reaction to him has become in many respects like that he had toward his father and that he has to anyone who tells circumstantial tales. Irrational elements are plain here—the transference from the father to the patient, the character defenses of submitting and becoming enraged and blaming and belittling the other person. It is these elements that make for the analyst's exaggerated anger. Nevertheless, there was also a real provocation. The patient was being long-winded and pointless, and this fact should not be overlooked to the detriment of therapy and to unwarranted loss of self-esteem on the part of the analyst.

To return to the rational reactions of analysts, I wish briefly to illustrate a number of these. An analyst feels sorry for a patient, and discovers from examining his feeling that the way the patient operates with many people is to make them sorry for her as a helpless victim of circumstances. An analyst feels afraid of a certain patient, and a Rorschach shows active homicidal tendencies. An analyst notices sexual phantasies about a patient, who, it turns out, was behaving in coyly seductive ways and having sexual phantasies herself, without mentioning them. Another analyst wonders why he especially liked a certain patient and discovers this patient is the only one in his practice who is really moving in his analysis while all the others are sitting passively waiting for him to get them out of it. Is the analyst's liking for this patient irrational?

An analyst becomes amazed at continued dramatic demands, and discovers that the patient is expressing his impatience at not being able to get over a lifelong problem in a few weeks. It is not counter-transference when an analyst feels astonished at a tale of unrealistic self-damaging aggressive behaviour toward a superior, nor when he is surprised at hearing from a sociologist, who is studying racial relations, of feeling rage against a Negro who held on to the same subway strap with him on a crowded subway. The patient who feels at home with anger will certainly find ways of provoking his analyst to anger.

Several remarks can be made about these rational emotional reactions. First they not only include simple likes and dislikes, and feeling well disposed or angry, but also a great many reactions such as amusement, astonishment, disgust, dismay, pity, fear, tenderness—in fact, all the wonderful possibilities in the varied gamut of human feelings. While I have mentioned mainly emotions and attitudes, appropriate reactions include as well, ideas, opinions, judgments, and phantasies about patients.

Second, many of these reactions have to do with a patient's motives. Theodor Reik (1949) states that "the nature of an individual's unconscious motives is revealed by the effect of his actions and behaviour on others" (p. 487). I think it is also true that what a person is like generally, not only his unconscious motivations, is revealed by his effect on others. This would then be especially true of his effect on an analyst who is a person trained to observe himself and others. It follows, then that from noticing at any given moment our own reactions with patients, we, as analysts, can learn much about what our patients are really like and what they are doing with us in the analysis.

This brings me to the question of the utilization of rational emotional reactions in psycho-analytic therapy. Since studying this topic I have begun to notice how seldom we and our supervisees seem to use our own emotional reactions in therapy. We are perhaps not aware of them sufficiently, or we may belittle them, or we may not be admitting their existence due to what has been called a paranoid reaction toward one's own counter transference.

Let me return to one of the examples of appropriate emotional reactions, namely, the irritation in response to the circumstantially told tale. This irritation is valuable in therapy in helping make the analyst aware of what the patient is doing at the moment, namely, being circumstantial. Not only this, the therapist may become aware that this is something the patient does often, that it is a manifestation of his character structure. It can inspire him to go further and wonder "why" this pointless storytelling—perhaps even ask the patient about it. In this way his attention, and that of the patient, is called to the fact that the patient does not know why he tells pointless stories and, further, attempts to evade knowing. He does not wish to take responsibility for the meaning of what he says, but leaves all this up to the analyst. With the help of other material, still further exploration of the various facets of the patient's character structure is made possible. In fact, I believe analysis cannot be done successfully in any other way than by use of the analyst's own personal reactions to the material—otherwise his comments and inter-pretations are bound to be mediocre.

Similarly, any counter-transference feeling can be so used, including those exaggeratedly irrational and defensive reactions. In these, it is tre-mendously important for the analyst to burrow through the exaggerated parts of his reactions to the healthy rational substratum, and not to be distracted from doing this by the conventional evaluation of his personal reactions as valueless, useless, harmful, or as a reflection on the complete-ness of his analysis. For example, the irrational anger at aimlessness must not be dismissed as foolish and inappropriate. The anger may be inap-propriate in great part. This must be recognized, and then the anger must be used to detect what the patient did to provoke it and exactly why, as one would in a reaction that was entirely rational and appropriate.

So far I have discussed utilizing emotional reactions to one's patient only in terms of revealing something about the patient or his part in the emotional climate of the analysis. Another possibility is that of revealing to the patient something about the analyst and his part in the analysis at the moment. Heimann (1950) states that the analyst's feelings should not be communicated to the patient on the basis that they would constitute a burden to him. This, however, is not always the case. Often the patient is aware, at least dimly, of his analyst's feelings, whether communicated or not, and it is helpful for the patient to know that the analyst knows these feelings, too. Such revelation may be a help in reassuring the patient as to his power of testing reality, leading to the reassuring feeling, "I am not entirely crazy." It can help make real the fact that complete rationality is a phantastic goal and that an analyst is human, not superhuman.[5]

Another type of appropriate feeling for patients that is not directly provoked by what patients are or what they do or by how they are currently motivated toward the analyst (although it is not unrelated to these) is the interest in people which analysts bring to their work, if it has not been too trained out of them. Healthy analysts are naturally inter-ested in people. Discussion arose in a small group as to what makes for a person's choosing the discipline of analysis rather than, for example, dentistry. There was much learned discussion and then one of the group

---

[5]For a more detailed discussion of indications for such revelations and the dangers involved, see Cohen, 1952; DeForest, 1951; Gitelson, 1952; Little, 1951; Weigert, 1952.

asked, "Is my conception too naive? I always thought people went into dentistry because they were interested in teeth, and that they went into analysis because they were interested in people." And "people" include analysts' patients.

This interest in patients is not unrelated to what the analyst can perceive of the actual character of his patient. For example, an analyst who sees his patient as basically aggressive and destructive, at times, with good reason, cannot be interested in helping that patient. If he sees in this aggression a fearful, trapped child who, when he has a chance to be uninvolved, is really a warm person, the analyst's interest is aroused. Now that we have established that analysts do have an interest in helping their patients, would it not be natural that, in some instances, analysts will not only discuss helpfully patients' problems, but also take appropriate action when necessary? Yet taking action is often belittled as an evidence of counter-transference just as a patient's action in giving his analyst a gift is belittled as transference when it often expresses, at least in part, an appropriate sentiment of regard for the analyst's helpfulness.

This helpfulness may be simply that of the analysis itself or may also include extra-analytic help. There are indications for an analyst's helping a patient extra-analytically. It is not irrational counter-transference that makes an analyst call his patient's attention to behaviour destructive to himself, and even forbid it. An extremely anxiety-ridden patient who had been involved in a homo-sexual incident, could not, himself, deal with a blackmailer to whom the patient, between two analytic hours, had given $800. Although the analyst ascertained it was personally safe for the patient to go to the district attorney's office, the patient was too afraid to go. The analyst refused to continue analysis unless either the patient or he went to the district attorney. The patient finally allowed the analyst to go, the blackmailing was nipped in the bud, and the analysis began, for the first time, to take shape. The patient's tremendous anxieties lessened to the extent that he became able to take some charge of his own life.

There are other less dramatic ways in which one may wish to help patients; for example, to have an hour in the home during illness, to carry a patient through an unemployed period without fee, to demand that the patient consult a doctor about his health, to bring a doctor to a physically ill patient or to suggest that he stay home from an analytic hour when he has a cold. There are countless other examples that any analyst may recall from his own experience.

I wish now to mention another situation—that of the analysis of a patient who has been a friend prior to analysis. While for good reason one may not have any social relations with certain patients, it is not irrational counter-transference if, in appropriate situations, one has a social relationship with a patient and gives concrete evidence of one's attitudes toward him such as what one likes or does not like about him, what interests one shares with him, and which ones are not shared. This real relationship some patients cannot stand, but in many instances it can serve as an immense help both in reducing the analyst to his proper proportions in the eyes of the patient and in increasing his stature when the patient harbours irrational belittling and negative attitudes toward his analyst.

It has been pointed out that transference is the chief means available for making the patient conscious of his unconscious trends. I should like to point out that study of the analyst's feelings and attitudes toward his patient is a much-neglected means of achieving the same purpose. I find it valuable to ask a patient to become aware of my attitudes and feelings about him. I ask him this: "Now what do you think I really think of you?" or: "How do you think I regard you?" This calls the patient's attention to hitherto-unnoticed aspects of his personality that are affecting other people, including his analyst. It may also call attention to unnoticed tendencies in the analyst that are affecting the patient.

Emotional reactions of analyst to patients are shown to be ever present and as little to be avoided as are transference reactions of patients to analysts. Their study promises to shed much light on such questions as the nature of analytic cure, and how an analysis ends, if it does. Their precise utilization in practice leaves much room for clinical and technical exploration. Both types of study should lead to a more rational and scientific attitude on the part of analysts and their students to their counter-transference phenomena, and eventually, to the disappearance of a paranoid attitude of avoidance and condemnation.

REFERENCES

Berman, L. (1949), Countertransference and attitudes of the analyst in the therapeutic process. *Psychiatry*, 12:159.

Cohen, M. B. (1952), Countertranference and anxiety. *Psychiatry*, 15:231.

DeForest, I. (1951), The significance of the countertransference in psychoanalytic therapy. *Psychoanal. Rev.*, 38:158-171.

Gitelson, M. (1952), The emotional position of the analyst in the psychoanalytic situation. *Internat. J. Psycho-Anal.*, 33:1-10.

Heimann, P. (1950), On countertransference. *Internat. J. Psycho-Anal.*, 31:81-84.

Little, M. (1951), Countertransference and the patient's response to it. *Internat. J. Psycho-Anal.*, 32:32-40.

Reich, A. (1951), On countertransference. *Internat. J. Psycho-Anal.*, 32:25-31.

Reik, T. (1949), *Listening with the Third Ear*. New York: Farrar, Straus.

Thompson, C. (1945), Transference as a therapeutic instrument. *Psychiatry*, 8:273.

Weigert, E. (1952), Contribution to the problem of terminating psychoanalysis. *Psychoanal. Quart.*, 21:465-480.

6

THE DEVELOPMENT OF FOCAL ATTENTION AND THE EMERGENCE OF REALITY

ERNEST SCHACHTEL

[1954]

INTRODUCTION

Jerome L. Singer

I had the opportunity to know Ernest G. Schachtel only in a professional way. We both served on the original advisory committee for the founding of *Contemporary Psychoanalysis* and also had some opportunities for primarily intellectual conversations. I was honored when he told me, after reviewing the paper that follows, that I had grasped the basic thrust of his efforts. My own research, which has sought to develop a variety of empirically testable methods for studying imagination, daydreaming, children's play, and related phenomena of private experience drew again and again on his sweeping, flexible approach to human experience in contrast to the rigidities of orthodox psychoanalysis as it had crystallized by mid-century.

Ernest Schachtel had undertaken the risky but much needed task of examining the fundamental concepts needed to humanize the overly biologized, outmoded theory that was Freud's legacy. He was trying in his own quiet and deeply thoughtful way to find metaphors or scientific images that could preserve the value of the great clinical observations of psychoanalysis, and somehow bring theory in closer touch with how humans actually think, feel, and talk. In his articles and books, published over several decades, he addressed again and again the question of how we develop a set of basic assumptions that can help us grasp more fully the special humanity of the individual. If a single book can be said to make a difference in lives, his great *Metamorphosis* (1959) can be appraised as such a one. Rarely in art or science have wisdom and beauty of language come together so well in one work.

Jerome L. Singer, Ph.D. is Professor of Psychology, Yale University.

The task that Schachtel set for himself was no less than the formulation of a fundamental psychological model for the interpersonal theory of Sullivan, Fromm, Horney, and various other clinicians who adhere to some phase of the increasingly convergent neo-Freudian, object relations, and existential positions in contemporary psychiatry and clinical psychology. As one delves deeper into the crucial issues of a clinical theory, one is confronted with the necessity for a more precise statement of its underlying premises. Ultimately any theory rests on how it treats basic processes such as attention, perception, memory, learning, affect, and drive. Freud (1895) recognized this quite early and his long voluntarily unpublished "Project for a Scientific Psychology" represents from our modern perspective a remarkable effort to build a model for thought, perception, and attention out of the properties of the simplest neural network.

What Freud failed to do for psychoanalysis is what Schachtel proposed to accomplish in his own work. Examining the fundaments of sensory experience and then of the relations of sensation to emotion or affect, he began to develop a framework for perception, memory, and thought. In scope and purpose this effort bears comparison with the sadly unfinished efforts of David Rapaport (1960), who was attempting an integration of "orthodox" Freudian psychoanalysis within one all-encompassing theoretical structure. Mention of Rapaport in juxtaposition with Schachtel points up some of the major defining characteristics of each man's efforts. Indeed, next to Freud, Rapaport is cited by Schachtel much more than anyone else, and the references usually involve a comparison of or differentiation between each man's position on a given point. For Rapaport, the central notion upon which the psychoanalytic theory rested was the "appetitive" drive. Even with the broadening of the concept of motivation introduced by Hartmann's (1958) notion of ego-autonomy, he persisted in emphasizing the biological drives as man's primary motives. The term "appetitive," so linked to orality and to a hunger sequence, exemplifies the primary model of psychoanalysis: the infant lacks food—restlessness—mother arrives with food—subsidence of restlessness (Rapaport, 1960).

The concepts of drive-reduction and pleasure-unpleasure lie at the heart of Freudian theory, according to Schachtel (1959). Indeed, one might add that even Sullivan's notion of satisfactions and securities or of the self emerging out of efforts to reduce anxiety, involves a drive or fear-reduction model. Schachtel analyzed the implications of such a model and showed how limited it is in dealing with the activity and restlessness of the young infant as well as the older child. By introducing the importance of affect, rather than drive, as a primary motivational condition, Schachtel was able to account for the important child-developmental evidence of Jean Piaget (1962), Heinz Werner (1948), and of the comparative psychologists. Such findings suggest that curiosity, environmental stimulation, and exploratory activity or competence are all key features of the human behavioral repertoire. In his tying of "embeddedness-affect" to experiences of need satisfaction, and "activity-affect" to positive experiences of joy and excitement, Schachtel's conceptual scheme proves to be closer to important recent neurophysiological research on the separation of "joy" and "distress" centers in the brain. Indeed, the embeddedness-activity dimension is also in accord with the arousal and activation phenomena being studied now in work on the reticular formation.

One might also see in the use of the term "embeddedness" an "other"-orientation, surely a forerunner of current emphases on our intrinsic human need for attachment (Blatt, 1990; Singer and Bonanno, 1990).

Having laid the foundation for an intrinsic conception of positive and negative affects as primary motivators, Schachtel freed the psychoanalytic structure from an excessive dependence on specific drives for their explanatory concepts. As Tomkins (1962, 1963, 1991) has also pointed out in his analysis of the relations of affect and drives, the greater flexibility of the affect system, its lack of specific satisfying objects makes it more useful in conceptualizing the great variety of human patterns. Indeed, as Schachtel noted, the more creative behavior of a child is apparent only after he or she has been fed or after some great fear has been allayed. *The effects of intense drive pressure do not increase learning but interfere with it.* The relatively biological-need-satisfied child does not curl up and do nothing—he or she starts exploring and trying out effectiveness in dealing with the many fascinating objects in the environment which the child could scarcely notice previously while his or her attention was narrowed by the pangs of hunger or by the effort to inhibit urination.

Theorists who have earlier emphasized the classical psychoanalytic model have recently moved closer to the position of Schachtel. Klein (1967) in his examination of peremptory ideation was forced to recognize the greater role of information-processing and cognitive-feedback loops and to question the traditional biological-drive principle. Holt (1976) carried out a lucid analysis of the drive model that underlies psychoanalytic theory and points out that even hunger as a body system doesn't conform to the drive concept. Indeed only urination comes at all close biologically to the way Freud spoke of the drive-discharge system. Holt urges a revival of the earlier term Freud used, *wish,* and in doing so moves the theory much closer to Schachtel's humanistic, experiential emphasis. Finally, Schafer (1976) has been proposing in effect that psychoanalysts junk once and for all the tedious theoretical terminology such as *cathexis, neutralized aggressive energy,* or *ego-libido* in favor of an *action* language that conveys more directly what humans say and do to each other.

Carrying his view of affect further, Schachtel examined the role of sensory experience in relation to both affect and cognition. He analyzed the major sense modalities, taste, smell, touch, audition, and vision, from the standpoint of their relationship to affect and to objective "reality." Indeed, this scrutiny of the degree to which the sensory experience is linked to a pleasure-pain emotion and its potential for consensual validation or common-language descriptions is one of Schachtel's most illuminating contributions. He showed that we may describe our sensory or perceptual experiences along an allocentric-autocentric dimension, the latter pole representing the so-called more "primitive" sensory modalities such as taste or smell which are much harder to objectify in verbal descriptions to others. All normal perception demands both types of experience, the relatively objective, easily encoded allocentric, and the more emotional, individualized autocentric. In this analysis Schachtel appeared again to penetrate more deeply into the nature of the human being's sensuality than the vague constructs such as "erogenous zones" or "mucous-membrane pleasure areas" one finds in classic psychoanalysis.

Schachtel pointed out that part of socialization involves increased reliance on the more allocentric visual and auditory modalities, often to the extent of developing such pat verbal labels for these experiences that the ties between sensory and affective experiences are almost totally lost. This extreme is the kind of coldness, deadness, or detachment that characterizes the ultra-machine man against whom Fromm, the Zen teachers, and others inveigh. Schachtel spelled out the basis for this malaise, which many analysts describe in their patients in a more precise fashion. Indeed, it can be argued that the ability to develop both poles of the perceptual response is a great art of living. The differentiated capacity for sensory experience with its close link to emotion enriches without weakening the significant cognitive hold on reality. Schachtel's examination of this problem provided a much more useful alternative to the concept of *regression in the service of the ego* and to the distinction between *primary* and *secondary process*. The notion of regression has never been entirely satisfactory and Schachtel showed that it is not only unnecessary but does violence to important capacities of the mature adult.

Schachtel's delineation of the hierarchy of sensory modalities and of the significance of both autocentric and allocentric capacities was not only theoretically interesting but sufficiently specific to be formulated in operational terms for empirical study. Certainly it appears more parsimonious to regard the poetic achievements of Keats in *The Eve of Saint Agnes* or of Joyce in *Ulysses* as consequences of a remarkable preservation and further development in these writers of the capacity for differentiated sensory experience, particularly in the gustatory, olfactory, or tactile modalities, rather than as a "regression." The analysis of Shakespeare's imagery by Caroline Spurgeon (1955) makes it clear that he towered over his contemporaries not only in the sheer quantity of poetic images but in the diversity of the sensory modalities involved. By comparison with Marlowe, for example, most of whose metaphors are visual or involve abstract concepts, Shakespeare employs many words from "town life," the taste, touch, and smell of the daily objects of experience. Recall the vividness of Falstaff's language—we can almost smell and taste the tavern scenes in which that knavish old "tub of guts" cavorts. And even the noble Hamlet communicates through autocentric imagery—recall his comment about the hidden corpse of Polonious: "But indeed if you find him not within this month, you shall nose him as you go up the stairs into the lobby."

Bonanno and I (Singer and Bonanno, 1990) conducted an experimental study that examined some of the implications of the theory of hierarchical sensory structure. Tests of discrimination in taste, olfaction, touch, audition, and vision were administered to persons who also filled out a scale that would ascertain the extent of their dogmatism and inability to tolerate ambiguity in opinions. It was found that the largest individual differences in discrimination on these relatively simple sensory tasks occurred for the more autocentric modalities, taste, smell, and touch, with few differences between respondents in audition and vision. In addition, those subjects who were high in dogmatism showed less sensory discrimination than those low in dogmatism, particularly on the autocentric modalities. In effect, it would appear that persons capable of making careful distinctions in their attitudes and opinions are also likely to show sharper distinctions in their smell, touch, and taste experiences—in a sense they are open in general to more differentiated experience.

From the examination of sensory experience and the basis of perception, Schachtel moved to a consideration of attention and memory. He delved more deeply than Sullivan into the nature of the "prototaxic" mode and demonstrated that memory changes and the so-called repression of childhood events are a consequence of the fundamentally different cognitive and affective capacities and degree of differentiation in schematic structure of the child and adult. In his analysis of the different consequences of early and later learning, of learning under different degrees of need, and of the role of varied environmental stimuli on attention and activity, Schachtel came close to the work of cognitive theorists in comparative psychology, such as Harlow (1953) and Tolman (1949) or the neurophysiological concepts of Hebb (1960). His consideration of the repetitive games or story-reading demands of children (for which Freud had to rely on the awkward notion of repetition compulsion) was both charming and enlightening. For the child's undifferentiated cognitive structure, each successive reading of "The Three Bears" contains considerable novelty, while for the weary parent the story is "old hat," grasped at first reading and miniaturized and encoded in a few short phrases. In the same way, the child's play may be regarded not only as a working-out of anxieties but as a positive affective response aroused by the novelty of as yet new structures or by the pleasure in integration of the new into familiar structures. Here Schachtel's work verged close to concepts such as Piaget's (1962) accommodation and assimilation, but whereas Piaget limits his examination chiefly to the child's relation to the physical environment, Schachtel is more sensitive to the interpersonal milieu. Recent studies of the development of imaginative play in children further support Schachtel's approach (Singer and Singer, 1990).

Psychology and psychoanalysis are today in a period of most exciting transition and productive convergence after years of self-defeating, snobbish, and elitist separation. The work of Hebb, White, Tomkins, Holt, and many others has forced psychology to accept the significance of inner experience, of imagery, consciousness, and emotion as phenomena that make a difference. The research on activation, on central mediation in learning, on the generation of imagery or fantasy during sensory deprivation or during information-processing tasks all point to a greater need for psychoanalysts to take note of the person's spontaneously generated cognitive and affective responses. Schachtel's theoretical model, based on sensory experience as well as affect, bridged these two poles of stimulus-origin. His approach served as a useful link between the frequent vagueness of psychoanalytic theory in the area of fundamental externally-generated experience and the increasingly greater precision of the experimental investigators who work in the realm of perception and attention. At the same time, by his sensitivity to clinical data, by his commitment to a humanistic philosophy, and by his deep awareness of the meaningful features of human interaction, Schachtel provided a valuable corrective to the excessively dry, object- rather than person-oriented aspects of psychological research in the cognitive functions. Some day, historians may write of the year 1959 as a turning point in modern psychology—it was in that year that both Schactel's (1959) *Metamorphosis* and R. W. White's (1959) *Motivation Reconsidered: The Concept of Competence* appeared and changed the direction of both psychology and psychoanalysis.

The deathblow was given to the drive concept, and clinicians suddenly were free to examine the whole panoply of human behavior without the constraints of an artificial reductionism. All clinicians can profit from an examination of their own working assumptions in the light of Schachtel's model of the fundamental dimensions of human experience.

T he theory of attention is crucial for an understanding of both consciousness and repression. In developing a dynamic theory of attention, Freud (1918) formulated this insight by saying that "the act of becoming conscious depends upon a definite psychic function—attention—being brought to bear" (p. 529).[1] Not all acts of attention, however, shed the full light of consciousness on the matter attended. For instance, something that strikes one's attention may lead to flight, to a turning away, if it arouses anxiety; and it may lead to an act of *focal attention* if it arouses one's curiosity. By "focal attention," as distinguished from other forms of attention, I designate man's capacity to *center* his attention on an object fully, so that he can perceive or understand it from *many sides,* as clearly as possible. In this presentation, I shall attempt to show (1) that focal attention is the main instrument which, as it gradually develops, enables man to progress from the primitive mental activity of wishing or wanting (primary-process thought) to a grasp of reality (secondary-process thought); and (2) that man's grasp of reality is not merely based on his wish to satisfy primary, biological needs—is not merely, as Freud assumed, a detour on the path to wish fulfillment—but that it also has as a prerequisite an autonomous interest in the environment. Focal attention is the tool of this interest; it appears first in the child's exploratory play and requires relative freedom from need and anxiety. In discussing these topics, I shall describe the structure of acts of focal attention, briefly sketch the development of focal attention, discuss the bearing of this development on Freud's theory of repetition compulsion, and examine the basis of man's grasp of reality, reviewing critically Freud's theory of the origin and nature of thought.

THE STRUCTURE OF FOCAL ATTENTION

Acts of focal attention are distinguished from developmentally earlier forms of experience by a number of factors which bring about a change

---

Metamorphosis. New York: Basic Books, 1959, pp. 251–278.

[1]William James's concise formulation, "My experience is what I agree to attend to," also stresses the dynamic, motivational character of attention and experience. See especially Vol. I, p. 402.

in the nature of consciousness and of experience. The emergence of acts of focal attention does not, however, prevent the survival and continued significance of these developmentally earlier forms throughout man's life. Focal attention superimposes a new kind of experience on them; it also changes the earlier forms of experience. But it does not extinguish or replace them completely, and it is, in its turn, affected by them.

The most important of the distinguishing characteristics of focal attention are these: (1) Acts of focal attention are *directional;* they do not concern the total field[2]—that is, they are not global, as the most primitive forms of experience are, but focus attention in a particular direction. (2) They are directed at a *particular object,* which may be an external object or an internal object, such as a thought or a feeling.[3] They take hold of the object and aim at its active mental grasp. (4) Each focal act, as a rule, consists of not just *one* sustained approach to the object to which it is directed but *several renewed* approaches. These approaches explore different aspects and relations of the object. Not only are they made from different angles, as it were, but often they are made repeatedly from the same angle and directed at the same facet of the object in an attempt to assimilate it more thoroughly. They also usually—probably always— alternate or oscillate between a more passive, receptive, reactive phase and a more active, taking-hold, structuring, integrating phase. The relation of these two phases to each other and their relative predominance vary considerably both inter- and intra-individually. (5) Acts of focal attention *exclude* the rest of the field (environmental and internal) from that form of consciousness which is designated as focal awareness.

These factors are essential for an understanding of the change of consciousness and experience brought about by the gradual development and maturation of the capacity for focal attention in infancy and child- hood. It is a change from (1) a diffuse total awareness of well- or ill-being, in which at first there is no distinction between the infant and the environment, through (2) a diffuse, more or less global awareness of an impinging environment, to (3) a state in which distinct needs and feelings become increasingly differentiated and discrete objects emerge from the environment. Ultimately, these objects are conceived by the child to have an existence of their own that continues even when the object does not

---

[2]By "field," I designate, in this context, both the external and internal fields in their interaction—that is, the environment as well as the thoughts, feelings, impulses, tensions, and needs of the person.

[3]The object-directedness of attention has often been described. See, for example, Koffka (1935, p. 358). Phenomenologists have discussed this problem in terms of intentionality of acts. Intentionality (*Intentionalitat*) does not mean purposiveness or purposefulness. It refers to an essential aspect of consciousness—namely, that every act of consciousness has an object, that an object is "given" in every act of consciousness (cf. Husserl, 1913, esp. Vol. 2, part 1, pp. 343–507).

impinge on the child's receptors. In this way focal attention plays a most important role in the gradual emergence and constitution of the object world (reality) and of the sense of self. It plays an equally decisive role in the development of the capacity for delay and drive control, by virtue of its *exclusion mechanism*. This mechanism excludes, for the duration of the focal act, the rest of the field from focal awareness. Thereby it delays the discharge of all those impulses which are motivated by the rest of the field and require focal attention for their execution. It also delays and/or mitigates the impact of the rest of the impinging field—which is excluded from focal awareness—by reducing vigilance, diffuse awareness, and fringe awareness. The degree of such mitigation depends on, among other factors, the intensity of the act of focal attention and the strength of the need *not* to become aware of the rest of the field—that is, the distribution of hypercathectic and countercathectic energies during any particular act of focal attention. This implies that the temporary exclusion mechanism of focal attention often, perhaps always, is structurally and dynamically similar to repression. It is distinguished from repression by its brief duration and by the fact that the person is able to terminate it, whereupon attention can be directed to that which before had been excluded from focal awareness.

The temporary shutting-out of the rest of the field during acts of focal attention directed at a particular object is not the only relation between focal attention and repression. With the full development of focal attention, focal awareness becomes the highest and the predominating form of consciousness in the waking life of man. What is not focally perceived is not in full awareness. What is not accessible to focal awareness for reason of man's limited horizon remains unknown to him. If the inaccessibility is due not to the general limitations of man, but to anxieties rooted in the individual life experience, it constitutes repression proper.

THE DEVELOPMENT OF FOCAL ATTENTION

The first change in man's life—and the most profound, comprehensive, and abrupt one—occurs at birth, and consists of the transition from a fetal, prenatal existence to a separate, post-natal one. Before birth all of the embryo's needs for food, liquid, and oxygen are supplied by the mother's blood stream through the placenta. The fetus lives in the moist, nurturing, evenly warm interior of the mother's body. This form of existence, as Ferenczi (1924) especially has pointed out, resembles in many ways that of the sea animals, particularly the lower ones such as the protozoa, whose needs for oxygen and nourishing minerals are supplied by the sea water, and whose existence may be characterized as predominantly drifting, receptive, without active motility, without direction, passive. In fetal existence, because of the constant supply from the mother's body of all food and oxygen needs and of warmth, relatively few need tensions arise, and probably there is no differentiation of needs, or at least no felt differentiation.

Only after birth does the marked and constant alternation begin between rising need tension and satisfaction of the need which continues throughout life. It is probably the experience of this alternation and of variations in it which gradually produces an awareness in the infant of his own body as different from the mother who satisfies the needs (Benedek, 1938). The emergence of mother or mother's breast as something different and separate from the infant cannot be pictured as the full-blown and distinct idea of mother as a separate person. This idea comes much later, after the capacity for focal attention has matured. At first, the infant probably has only the vaguest feeling, like: "There is something out there which has to happen, which has to come, to make me feel good." This is different from fetal existence in which there was no *there*—no outside, separate from the fetus. The *something*, at this first, postnatal stage, must not be understood as an "object," or a "person," but is entirely vague and nondescript. The something is characterized only by the fact that it has to happen in order to make the infant comfortable and that the infant wants it to happen; there is a first glimmering of the notion that this something that has to come from somewhere *outside* the baby's body will then produce, for example, the satisfying state of "nipple-in-lips."[4] At the same time, the change from continuous gratification of all needs *in utero* to a state in which need-tensions mount until they are satisfied, at intervals, also leads to a *differentiation of needs and of the felt experience of these needs*. Being hungry feels different from being cold and from being sleepy, and so on. Furthermore, discomfort felt in different regions of the body leads to further differentiation. Thus, in addition to global feelings of comfort and discomfort, there arise increasingly differentiated feelings of *particular* need tensions, vague awareness of different body regions, and strivings *directed* toward satisfaction of the *particular* needs and alleviation of the particular discomforts, mainly by means of crying, which calls forth the mother's need-satisfying activity.

In this stage of the infant's development, *vaguely directional* (that is, not sharply focused, but not completely global) experiences assume increasing importance. They can also be observed in the reaction to impinging light and noises. While not yet being able to *look at* anything or to *listen* to anything, the infant does experience the coming of light or noises from a

---

[4] Compare Sullivan, 1953, pp. 66–73, 80–91, 110–122. His analysis of the nursing situation and of the emergence of "good mother" and "bad mother" personifications conveys an idea of the complexity and significance of the processes going on *before* the idea of the mother as *one, separate* person is eventually developed by the child.

vaguely perceived, general direction. At four weeks, a vacant, diffuse stare is still the most typical behavior. In the fifth and sixth weeks, although the infant still stares vaguely, he stares in a certain direction— for example, at the window or at the wall—and for the first time he also occasionally focuses his eyes and looks at people and objects in his environment. Following the fifth week, this focused looking at people and objects is an increasingly frequent behavior; at first the infant focuses only for brief moments, but from approximately ten weeks on he focuses on the same object for a prolonged period. Together with the development of focal regard, the infant starts to follow a moving object with his eyes—that is, to hold on to it and *keep* it in focus.[5] The infant now no longer depends entirely on what happens to fall into his line of vision. An object no longer necessarily disappears—ceases to exist for the infant— when it moves, but the infant begins to be able to keep hold of the object by following it with his eyes and turning his head. Toward the end of the first year (from approximately the seventh or eighth month on), the infant also becomes increasingly capable of, and interested in, focusing on very small objects. In the period of vague directional staring, only large areas impressed the infant's vision; and in the early stages of focal vision, he focused only on objects which were relatively large or which loomed large directly in front of his eyes—especially if they also impinged upon his attention in some other way, as a rattle might impinge by producing a noise, or as an object might impinge which was moved back and forth in front of his eyes. Attention to very small objects is another important step—a change from attending only reactively to what impinges, to attending actively to an object which arouses curiosity and interest. It is at about the same period, between the ages of nine and twelve months, that another decisive step in the development of focal attention takes place: the birth of the idea that an object may continue to exist even if it ceases to impinge on the baby's receptors, and that this object may be made to appear again by means of appropriate motor behavior. This is in contrast to the way in which he has made the experience of being nursed, the nipple-in-mouth situation, recur by means of crying. Between the ages of five and eight months the child

[5]The age levels given above are taken from Gesell and Thompson, 1938, pp. 170–172. There a detailed description of the development of focal regard during the first year is given for different types of objects. According to a personal communication from Lois B. Murphy of the Menninger Foundation, the baby starts to look at things with interest even before the ability to focus has fully matured. This looking takes place only when the baby is neither hungry nor sleepy, as described later in this chapter. She has observed it already on the ninth day and describes it as involving "a comprehensive bodily effort; the whole body is still and the energy is concentrated in holding the head up for a moment or two and the baby keeps its gaze or stare steadily on one object, something bright generally, for some seconds." Similarly, Stirnimann (1940) reports interested, attentive looking of some infants from the first or second week on.

grasps an object which he sees, but he immediately loses interest in it and does not seek for it if, in front of his eyes, one covers it with a cloth or places a screen in front of it. But from eight months on the child will seek the object underneath the cloth which covers it (Piaget, 1951).[6]

Beginning with this first glimmering of the idea of object constancy, focal attention gradually during the next years becomes increasingly capable of being used in *thought,* instead of being tied completely to focal perception. The first step in this development is that the child not only becomes able to focus attention via the senses on an object seen, touched, and so on, but also becomes able to focus attention on the *idea of an object.* This focal attention to thoughts develops in the second year, together with the learning of speech—without which the capacity to have ideas of objects could not go beyond an extremely primitive stage. Gradually not only objects but also their *relationships,* real or fancied, to the child and to each other become the objects of focal attention in thought. The child's reflective focusing on his own feelings and experiences constitutes the last step in the development of focal attention and accompanies the development of the idea of "I" and the autobiographical memory—that is, the concept of the continuity of the self. During the time when the instrument of focal attention is developing, and also after it has reached maturation, the object world and the person's inner world are explored and assimilated so that they become part of the consciously known world of man, part of the sphere of his focal awareness. This work, which takes place through ever repeated acts of focal attention, is of truly staggering proportions during childhood. No later period in life compares, in the scope and variety of exploration by means of focal attention, to the age of discovery—the age of early childhood; for children, unless they are very disturbed and succumb to apathy, always show great curiosity and desire for exploration.[7] People vary considerably, however, in the degree to which they retain this desire in later life, ranging from those

---

[6]While the behavior described above may be conceived of as the birth of the idea of an object's continuing to exist even if not impinging on the receptors, at this stage the object still remains very closely tied to the child's motor activity, as Piaget shows. Just as crying produced mother's nipple, so now diving underneath the pillow produces the object hidden under it. Piaget describes how, between nine and ten months, the baby who has succeeded in finding an object hidden under a pillow to his right, if the next time it is placed, in front of his eyes, under a pillow to his left, will continue to seek it under the pillow to his right. The baby's experience at this time seems to be *diving under pillow to right will produce the object that I can't see,* rather than the experience of realizing that the object has an autonomous place in space, which is independent of the repetition of a particular action such as crying or diving under the pillow to the right.

[7]The degree and quality of exploratory curiosity and play vary considerably in children because of hereditary and congenital factors as well as the child's early interpersonal experiences. However, in spite of these variations there is no doubt that the drive to explore is much stronger, as a rule, in children than it is in adults. The same seems to hold true for young monkeys as compared with adult monkeys (see Butler, 1954).

for whom there is nothing new and who are incapable especially of seeing the new in the familiar, to those who are always interested and to whom even the familiar is full of unexplored aspects, of hidden depths, of surprising facets.

FOCAL EXPLORATION AND REPETITION COMPULSION

The structure and development of focal attention, as described here, shed new light on certain phenomena in the child's behavior which Freud looked upon as early manifestations of the repetition compulsion. Although Freud (1922) states that the repetition compulsion can serve as an instrument for the active mastery of experiences, he characterizes it mainly by its conservative nature and considers it to be the expression of an inertia principle, of a drive to return to an earlier state, and, in the final analysis, of the death instinct.

I want to discuss briefly here only one often observed fact: a child's pleasure in, and insistence on, being read or told the same story over and over again. This discussion will (1) serve as an example for a more detailed description of the exploratory function of focal attention, and (2) show that the child's insistence on repetition is not due primarily to an inertia principle but, on the contrary, is essential for the productive work of exploring and assimilating the objects of the environment—in this case, an object of the cultural environment.

Adult observers have often been struck by the disturbance a child may show at the slightest change—even one word—in a story which has been repeated for the child. This disturbance does not seem to make much sense to the adult mind. What is the difference if a minor episode or a mere word is changed, as long as the main drift of events is retained in the story? This viewpoint overlooks the enormous difference in meaning which the repetition of a story has for the child who listens to it with absorption and for the adult who is bored by it. One tries in vain to encompass the child's experience with categories of the adult mind which are not suitable for grasping the meaning of the situation for the child.

What are the decisive differences between the child's and the adult's experience in listening to the same story over and over again? The age at which such repetition is desired, and enjoyed by the child is roughly from two to five years, with considerable individual variation. At the beginning of this period, the child has already learned to perceive distinct and concrete objects, but this learning must necessarily continue, for the object world of the child is constantly and rapidly expanding, and increasingly includes such complicated objects as words and pictures which

denote or represent other objects. However, the manner in which discrete objects are perceived by the young child differs a great deal from
the manner in which they are perceived by the older child and the adult.
The young child perceives objects much more globally and concretely
than the older child or adult. This implies that "any phenomenon known
in terms of qualities-of-the-whole, rather than in terms of strictly articu-
lated qualities, is apt to be seen by the young child as undergoing a
complete change, even if no more than minor details in the situation are
altered." From the young child's viewpoint, none of the many elements
making up the global situation "need be more essential than any other,
since all of them contribute to the characteristic coloration, or tone, of
the situational totality" (Werner, 1948).

Since a story contains not only many different objects but also many
different relationships among these objects, which unfold in a definite
sequence of events, it is much more complex than even the most complex
objects in the child's environment. For the young child to grasp and digest
a story requires an amount of attention and of effort at understanding
which the adult is incapable of imagining, since his grasp of a story rests
not only on years of training but also on a quite different, much more
abstractive kind of perception and understanding. Only by repeated acts
of focal attention, which at one time turn more to one part, at other times
to other parts, can the child very gradually come to understand and
assimilate a story. A particular part of the story may become something to
wonder about even if on some other day it seemed already familiar or not
worthy of special attention. To encompass all of it is no small achievement.
What if the story should change as the child tries to get hold of it? Any
change makes it elusive and frustrates the child's effort to master it. The
attempt to assimilate a particular story requires a complex labor of attention and thought; in fact, it usually involves the child's learning the story by
heart. This learning-by-heart is a by-product of the child's innumerable acts
of focal attention toward the story as a whole and toward its different parts,
and of the child's feelings about the story. The fact that this learning-by-
heart comes as a by-product—much in contrast to later learning-by-heart in
school—indicates the difference in degree and quality of attention between the young child's and the older child's or adult's listening to a story.

The young child who listens to the story not only is engaged in assimilating its complex fabric but, in addition to that, is confronted with the
equally or even more difficult problem of finding his way in the puzzl-
ing distinctions between reality, representations of reality, possibility,
and sheer fantasy. Just as the task of learning that a picture can represent a real object but that it is different from the real object is not an easy
one and takes considerable time and effort to master, so it is a difficult task
to learn about the various possible relations between a story and reality.

Furthermore, it is of great importance to the child that he can *rely* on a story—that it does not suddenly disappear, that it is still there. This is just as important as to be able to rely on the fact that a toy in which the child is interested will not vanish overnight. Before the child can read, the only way to be sure that he can rely on a story is by having it reread or retold to him and making quite sure that it is really the same story.

A change in the story is about as upsetting to the child as it might be to an adult to discover that overnight the table in the living room had changed its shape. The idea that one can *make* a story, hence also *change* it, dawns much later on the child than the earlier implicit conviction that a story is a piece of reality on which one can rely, so that any change of it interferes drastically with the important task of getting thoroughly acquainted with this particular piece of reality.

When Freud says that the child's need to hear the same story over and over again is a trait which disappears in the adult, he refers, probably without being aware of it, to a phenomenon which is characteristic only of large segments of the adult population in modern Western civilization, but which is not true of all men or of all times. For the greater part of man's history, people read or listened to the same stories many times. This is as true of the Bible as it is of *The Arabian Nights;* and it is equally true of the sermons of Buddha, which employ in a most impressive way literal repetition of the same stories and phrases—a device which is frequent in Oriental poetry. The modern need to read the latest best-seller, to look at a new movie or television show, to consume enormous amounts of always new mysteries, magazines, and comic strips, is peculiar to our time and culture.

Moreover, a proper comparison, I believe, of a child's attitude toward a story can be made only with an adult's attitude toward an object of *similar significance.* The story, to the child, is at first strange country which he gradually explores and in which new discoveries are always possible. A comparable relationship exists in our culture between the appreciative adult and a work of art, a piece of music, or a poem. One does not tire easily of looking again and again at a cherished painting, of listening many times over to a beloved piece of music or a poem. Every renewed encounter may reveal new aspects and lead to deeper understanding. Any change in the poem, the painting, the music would destroy it. Because of the quasi-organic, lifelike character of the real work of art, such a change would indeed make it into something very different.

In other words if the adult matures to a stage where he is capable of meaningful encounter with a significant human creation, then his relationship to this creation is likely to require many contacts with it, just as the child's relationship to the story does. The meaning of such significant encounters is very different from the kind of reading or listening which has the purpose of killing time, or being entertained passively or thrilled and titillated. For inherent in every real encounter with a work of art, a myth, a fairy tale is an active effort of the total personality, which is also inherent—in a somewhat different way—in the child's attempt to gradually assimilate the story. The motive of inertia seems to be considerably stronger in the adult who wants to see a new movie or read a new mystery every night than in the child who wants to hear the same story retold. The former avoids meaningful and enriching experience; the latter seeks it.

That the child's insistence on repetition of the same story serves primarily the purpose of assimilating it, of getting fully acquainted with all its aspects by many acts of focal attention,[8] and of making quite sure that it is still there and can be explored and enjoyed with some measure of dependability.

The story as an object is different from other objects, such as the baby's own body and toys, in that it is not available without a cooperating adult who reads or tells it. Exploring the story, thus, depends on such cooperation. The same holds true of all those *play* experiences in which the child plays *with* an adult. These experiences, too, require many repetitions in order to be fully explored and assimilated. For these repetitions, the child is dependent on the cooperating adult. Such interpersonal play has special significance since it is perhaps the most important situation experienced by the young child in which his own contribution is as important as the adult's; in other words, it is a situation in which he and the adult integrate as partners, rather than as one person who is in need and helpless and another who is powerful and can satisfy the need. While the emphasis in rehearing a story is on the exploration of the story, which only *incidentally* requires the cooperation of the adult, the emphasis in interpersonal play is on the give and take of the play situation, which *essentially* consists of the participation of two people, the child and the adult.[9]

Once the infant no longer lives in the primitive world of fetal and neonatal existence, it becomes of vital importance to him that the world outside, especially the mothering one, can be *depended on* and does not suddenly disappear without returning. Because of the infant's helplessness, the only way in which he can assimilate and accept the at first painful realization that the mothering one is not always present when needed is by realizing that he can depend upon her reappearance.[10] Similarly, it would be well nigh impossible for him to become oriented in

---

[8]For a related viewpoint with regard to other repetition phenomena, compare Piaget (1951).

[9]The significance of the bedtime story very often lies more in the reassuring integration of an interpersonal situation than in the story as something which the child wants to explore.

[10]If the infant cannot depend on the reappearance of the mothering one, his development very often will suffer and pathology may develop.

the environment, which assumes increasing importance during the periods of late infancy and early childhood, if he could not rely on the fact that the more significant objects of the environment continue to exist and remain identical—that is, *do not change*—even when they are not visible or touchable. Learning about object constancy, thus, is probably closely linked emotionally with the degree to which the infant experiences the constancy—that is, dependability—of the most important object, the mother. The more helpless a person feels, the more likely he is to require an extreme degree of object constancy, and the less able he is to tolerate any change in the environment. This can be observed not only in the emotionally disturbed child who cannot tolerate his mother's absence or the absence of a toy, but also in many neurotic patients and especially some patients with brain lesions, (cf. Goldstein, 1947, pp. 103–104), who are frightened by change and, to reassure themselves, insist on a rigid constancy of environmental conditions.

In the play described by Freud (1922) of a boy of one and a half who made a spool fastened to a thread disappear behind the curtains of his bed in order to pull it out again and joyfully greet its reappearance, the mastery of the experience of the disappearing and reappearing mother was a decisive factor. Since it is highly probable that the infant's first inkling of the fact that the objects of reality are separate from his body comes about through the painful realization that his mother is not always present when needed, the gradual development of the important insight that objects continue to exist, even though they disappear, may well remain closely linked in many children, for a considerable time, with the experience of the absence of the mothering one.

Thus manifold interrelations exist between the following: (a) the discovery of object constancy; (b) the power to make an object reappear—be it mother, by crying, or the spool, by pulling at the thread; (c) the capacity to recover an object by going after it and finding it in reality; (d) the confidence that an object will continue to exist and eventually will be available again even if, for the time being, one can neither make it reappear nor go and look for it; and (e) the capacity to keep hold of an object in *thought*—that is, to develop focal attention to the idea of an object even when the object is not available for present need satisfaction, manipulation, perception, and exploration. Not all of these interrelations can be explored here, but I want to emphasize that even quite apart from the need for, and confidence in, the reappearance of the mother, the importance for reality orientation of learning about object constancy leads the child to quite extensive and often repeated experimentation with disappearing and reappearing objects. Such experimentation is likely to proceed the more productively, the less the child is worried about the dependability of the mothering one.

Thus, much of what impressed Freud as repetition compulsion in the child's need to repeat a story or play activity over and over again turns out to be neither the result of a desire to return to an earlier state nor the effect of the principle of inertia, but an essential requirement for the gradual exploration of the environment, the world of reality, and the child's relations to it. Exploration by many acts of focal attention is possible only if the object of exploration is repeatedly available and is unchanged; and orientation in the environment would become quite impossible if one could not depend on its relative constancy. This does not mean that no other motives are present in the child's need for repetition of experiences. The enjoyment in doing that which one already masters, as compared with the hazards of any new venture, are ever present competitors in man's life. Their relative strength may result in an empty, fear-conditioned inertia which dreads the new and prefers the familiar, or in the victory of the desire to explore something new and to have significant experiences. Already in the child the tendency to prefer the safe mastery of the familiar to the challenge of the unknown often plays a role, especially if his natural curiosity and desire to venture have been inhibited or stifled by an over-anxious or forbidding parent. In the child's insistence that not a single word be changed in a story, there may also be the desire, born of anxiety, to control the situation and the reading adult. But the possible presence of such other motivations must not blind one to the fact that exploration and discovery of unknown aspects are constantly going on in what may ostensibly impress one as mere repetition.

THE EMERGENCE OF THE OBJECT WORLD (REALITY)

The child's exploration of the object world depends not only on the continued availability of the objects but also on the child's relative freedom from too strong need or anxiety tensions. The emergence of the object world is inseparably linked to the temporary *abeyance* of needs. In the infant, this abeyance is brought about by the satisfaction of needs through the mothering one. But, in the course of development, it is also increasingly brought about by the child's capacity to *delay* need satisfaction. The more secure the infant or child feels in being able to *depend* on the mother for eventual need satisfaction—and, later, on his own capacity to satisfy his needs—the more adequately this capacity to delay need satisfaction is likely to develop. Focal attention is the instrument which plays a decisive role both in the development of the capacity for delay and in the grasp of reality, of the object world. Only by means of focal attention do distinct objects emerge from the impinging environment so that they can be perceived and understood as independent of human needs. This is possible only because the rest of the field is excluded for the duration of the act of focal attention—that is, the claim of all other needs and impulses for attention is delayed or abated.

The understanding of this development has suffered from a semantic difficulty arising from the different meanings of the word "object" in psychoanalytic and general usage. Originally, object was that which is *objectum*—that is, the thing thrown before the mind, the thing which one encounters. Derived from this original meaning is the general meaning of object as anything presented to the eye, the senses, or the mind—anything which is objective and not merely subjective. But object means also that which is one's purpose, goal, or aim. Psychoanalytic terminology has made use only of this latter meaning and has further restricted it to include only the need-satisfying object—primarily the object of libido, of sexual desire. Here, the word *object* is used only for the objective object, for the object that exists independent of man's needs.[11] This object is more than just something which satisfies a particular need; it has aspects other than the one which makes it suitable to satisfy the need. It has an existence of its own. It does not come into existence because the need which it may satisfy is in tension, nor does it cease to exist because the need has been satisfied (unless it is swallowed because it satisfies hunger or is killed because it arouses fear). The reverse is true of perception of the "object" in a field characterized by high need tension. That is, the hungry animal sees only the prey, and as soon as the hunger is satisfied, the field completely changes its character, and the animal no longer pays any attention to what before was the outstanding "object." In contrast to the temporary and single-aspect-dominated character of the need-satisfying object, the emergence of the real object is predicated on two characteristics of the process of focal attention: (a) focal attention permits one to hold on to the object in one's mind while excluding need tensions from focal awareness, so that one is not propelled by a need in high tension, and (b) it permits one, in holding on to the object, to approach it from a variety of angles and repeatedly, so that many other aspects of it become apparent besides those which make it suitable to satisfy a need. In the world of biological needs, the "object" arises with the need and disappears or perishes with its satisfaction. In the world of focal attention, the object can be seen from all sides and obtains constancy—that is, it is perceived as continuing to exist even though the interest in it may slacken. The perceiver or thinker knows that the object may be contemplated again, perceptually or in thought, if he wishes to do so; it continues to exist. Indeed, it may be said that the object arises only when strong need tension subsides, for one cannot see the independent,

---

[11]Whenever the psychoanalytic meaning is referred to, "object" will be put in quotation marks or specifically designated as a need-satisfying object.

objective object as long as one is driven by a strong need. The primary, biological needs, especially when they are strong—that is, in a state of high tension—prevent the experience of the object because they produce an overwhelming pressure toward need satisfaction. Thus the object merges when the need tension is relaxed.

These considerations cast some doubt on the adequacy of Freud's theory of the origin and nature of thought, especially of the relation of secondary-process (reality) thought to primary-process thought. According to Freud, thought has only one ancestor, the attempt at hallucinatory need satisfaction. Thought, thus, is the child of want, of an id drive in tension which clamors for satisfaction and obeys only the pleasure principle. It originates in the hallucinatory perception of the need-satisfying object, such as food, when satisfaction is delayed and the need tension rises. Since this attempt at hallucinatory need satisfaction succeeds only to a very limited degree and does not really satisfy the need, a more reality-oriented thinking develops—secondary-process thought. But Freud (1918) makes it quite clear that secondary-process thought "merely represents a roundabout way to which fulfillment made necessary by experience" and that "thinking is nothing but a substitute for the hallucinatory wish."[12]

In contrast to Freud's view, I believe that thought has two ancestors rather than one—namely, motivating needs *and* a distinctively human capacity, the relatively autonomous capacity for object interest. Focal attention is the tool, the distinctively human equipment, by means of which the capacity for object interest can be realized.[13] There is no proof that the wish for need satisfaction alone would ever lead to object perception and to object-oriented thought—that is, to a relatively objective view of reality. On the other hand, it can be shown that the more urgently need-driven perception and thought are, the less able they are to grasp and understand the object.

---

[12]Also compare Freud (1959, pp. 13–16). Freud's view that thought is nothing but a substitute for hallucinatory wish fulfillment parallels his view that the ego is merely an offshoot of the id—a part of the id which, under the influence of the environment via the perception system has been gradually differentiated from the id. Compare Freud (1923).

This view has been opposed by Hartmann, Kris, and Loewenstein (1946), who assume that the ego and the id both arise from a common, undifferentiated phase, thus emphasizing a relatively greater autonomy of the ego. The views presented in this chapter lend support to their assumption rather than to Freud's.

[13]I shall not attempt at this point to give a detailed analysis of the meaning of object interest in man, which perhaps parallels the meaning of love, although a brief analysis is made later in the chapter. It is likely that this human capacity, too, has one of its evolutionary ancestors in the animal world—namely, in the *curiosity* of monkeys. The work of Harlow, Butler, and Walker has shown that the monkey's curiosity is not motivated by a desire for food or other rewards, but is a primary motivation containing its own reward. For a summary of this work, see Butler, (1954); compare also Tolman's (1954) observations on rats. Tolman, starting from a quite different approach, arrives at conclusions similar to mine, regarding the incompatibility of strong need- or fear-pressure and the pursuit of truth.

One of the main proofs offered for the assumption that hallucinatory need satisfaction is the cradle of object representation in thought is the observation of the dream process, of the illusions of people suffering hunger or thirst, and of the hallucinations of cases of Meynert's amentia. (cf. Rapaport) However, this argument overlooks the fact that all of these examples are taken from people in whom the capacity for focal attention has been fully developed. And once the world has been perceived by means of focal attention—that is, structure in terms of objects—objects will continue to be seen as such, regardless of whether their perception follows the drive or the reality organization of thought, whether the objects are evoked by the needs or fears of a hallucinating psychotic patient or by a motivating dream impulse, or whether they are seen by a person idly glancing out of the window. The drive organization of thought, the primary process at this stage, uses imagery which, in its turn, has developed only *after* focal attention has matured, after the world of objects has emerged, after secondary-process thought has furnished the raw material out of which this imagery is built.

Freud assumes that the *perception of food is an essential constituent* of the infant's experience of the satisfaction of hunger, and that, therefore, when the infant again is hungry, a psychic impulse which may be called a wish will re-evoke the former food-percept (Freud, 1918; see also A. Freud, 1953). This is highly improbable. The available evidence shows that at the earliest stages, specifically before focal attention develops, no objects are perceived by the infant. He perceives neither the milk, nor the mother, nor the mother's breast as a separate and distinct object. All the infant "perceives" at this stage are global feelings of well- or ill-being, of satisfaction or need tension, of the disturbing or pleasant impact of an environment which is as yet neither clearly differentiated from the infant nor structured in itself. And even after there slowly dawns on the infant the distinction between his own body sphere and the something "out there"—from which pleasant or unpleasant things seem to impinge on or happen to the body—there is no differentiation of the environment into distinct objects, such as food, or mother's body, or blanket. Sullivan (1951) refers to this primitive, egocentric, global stage of experience as "prototaxic," and describes it as consisting of "instantaneous records of total situations" (p. 252). While the psychic activity going on at this stage is largely a matter of conjecture and inference, there is definite evidence that no objects are perceived at this stage.[14] How can one picture, then, the mental activity of the infant when need tension arises, when he longs for satisfaction of the need? One can picture it only as a longing for the

---

[14]See the section on "The Development of Focal Attention" and the data presented there which show that no visual perception of objects takes place.

return of the total state of the former need-satisfying experiences. If one can speak of hallucinatory activity at all, it must be a kind of hallucination which is different from that known to us from dreams or psychotic hallucinations. It cannot consist of the hallucination of visual images of objects or of distinct sounds. It can only be a reactivation of the memory traces of the "total situation"—for example, of the total feeling of well-being while being nursed. It is a longing for, and, perhaps, a hallucinatory reactivation of, an "instantaneous record of a total situation," and this situation is not to be conceived as consisting of differentiated objects, but of how it feels to be comfortable, to be nursed, and so on.

That the infant does not long for or hallucinate food, but, rather, longs for or hallucinates the recurrence of a total situation of well-being is consistent also with the modern concept of instinct and instinctual action. Konrad Lorenz (1937) has shown that it is not the "object"—such as the prey or the mating partner—but the instinctual action itself which is the goal of the animal; the "object" merely releases this action and is its environmental substrate. Similarly, the "goal" of the infant is not mother's breast or the milk, but the repetition of the total experience of being nursed or, in terms of the parallel to the biological concept of instinctual action, the satisfying sucking and being held experience.

The ancestral role of hallucinatory experience in relation to thought, then, is merely that it constitutes primitive mental activity of a wishing or longing character. It is the cradle of primary-process thought, but there is no path that leads from it to secondary-process thought, to the emergence of the object world. Indeed, Freud does not indicate any steps which lead from primary-process to secondary-process thought, but merely states that another type of thought has to develop, since the primary-process thought is not equipped to bring about the satisfaction, but merely to evoke the hallucinatory image of the need-satisfying object or, as I would prefer to say, of the diffuse, global need-satisfying experience.

Where, then, must one seek for other ancestors of thought, especially of object- or reality-centered thought, of secondary-process thought? Objects become distinct parts of experience only when they are encountered in a field sufficiently relaxed from need tension to permit the infant to approach and explore the object *playfully*—that is, without having to incorporate it as nourishment. In exploratory "play" (which is at this stage, and for a long time to come, the most important way of *learning*) the infant or child approaches, grasps the object, and lets it go again, in ever renewed encounters and from different angles. That infants like to put objects in their mouths and sometimes will even swallow them does not mean that they do this because the need tension of hunger drives them. It means that of the great variety of exploratory, playful contacts which can be had with an object, contact through the mouth is the earliest and therefore for some time the most important one, which later is equaled and then superseded in importance by contact with the hands. The object gradually emerges as the thing which can be felt, touched, teased, seen, let go, recaptured, patted, squeezed, hit, pulled, and so on—which not only is known as satisfying hunger but also can be experienced in a great many different ways, from different angles, and which remains the focus of all these different experiences and makes them possible.

In the need-dominated approach, the whole field receives its character from the need, and the "objects" in the field are perceived only as signals pointing toward food, prey, danger, or escape, as the case may be. The action is completely directional: toward or away from. In the *play* of young dogs or cats the object is approached and then let go, approached again and released again, turned around, chased, abandoned, watched, picked up again, in ever repeated and ever varied approaches. The playing child discovers that different kinds of actions can be performed and different kinds of contacts had with the toy-object and with his own body. These varied actions become possible only when the object is *not* approached or fled from under the overriding impact of need or fear. The great variety of the playful approach, as contrasted with the narrow directedness of the need-driven approach, lets the child perceive many aspects, facets, qualities of the object which would never be revealed to him if he used it only for the gratification of a basic biological need. Urgent desire and fear make one blind rather than able to see; they alert one to the immediate possibilities of need satisfaction and to danger; but they do not lead to knowledge and appreciation of the object. Gustav Bally has shown that only the tension-relaxed field permits play, and that only play permits the recognition of an object world. Only those animals which, because of a prolonged period of parental protection and care, experience relative security from too great need tension show the beginnings of play; and man, in whom the parental satisfaction of the young's vital needs is most prolonged and who therefore is least exposed to overwhelming need tension, has developed play to an extent unknown in the animal world. His relative freedom from urgent need tension is the basis of the richness of his object world, which could not have developed if he had not been free, in play and thought, to explore objects without having to use them for immediate need satisfaction (Bally, 1945).[15]

In the brief outline I have presented of the main structural aspects of focal attention, I mentioned the fact that focal acts usually consist of several approaches from different angles to the object and/or renewed approaches from the same angle, and that these approaches oscillate between receptive exposure to the object and active taking hold of it. This

---

[15]It is regrettable that this excellent and thoughtful study has not yet been translated.

aspect has essentially the same character as the back and forth of the child's playful exploration of the world around him. It can be observed as easily in focal attention to something visually perceived as in focal attention to a thought or feeling. In attentively looking at an object, such as the pencil lying in front of me on my desk, my glance does not remain fixed on any one point of the pencil for any long period of time. It wanders, goes back and forth, sometimes slowly, sometimes quickly shifting from one point to another, and then returning again to a point looked at before. Thus I receive a variety of impressions, each of which is then integrated more or less completely into my total experience of the pencil. This behavior takes place in *all* acts of focal, visual attention. When the glance remains fixed on only one point for any length of time, it very soon turns into an unseeing stare which no longer has the character of active visual exploration but of passively being held by the point stared at.[16] If maintained long enough, this kind of stare may lead to a trancelike experience, which is the reason why many hypnotists use a very small, bright object to help in inducing a trance. The person looking at a small, bright metal disk very soon stares unseeingly at the bright spot; his glance becomes fixed on the brightness. An object showing many features would be unsuitable for inducing a trance, because it would invite the eye to explore it, to circumnavigate it actively, and to wander over it. The exploring, wandering-back-and-forth nature of focal, visual attention is also characteristic of focal attention to a thought. The object of thought is viewed from many different angles and in repeated approaches; it is considered in its various real or possible relations to other objects, in different contexts, and so on. Without this back-and-forth movement, thought becomes sterile and fruitless. Just as the completely need- or fear-governed action (and the instinctual action) never really encounters the object, so the thought which is under the pressure of either too much fear or anxiety, or under the pressure of too urgent or narrow a goal, does not do justice to its object. Only thought which is sufficiently free from the pressure of urgent needs or fears can contemplate its object fully and recognize it in relative independence from the thinker's needs and fears—that is, as something objective. Thus focal attention is incompatible with severe anxiety. The starving person does not think about what he eats, but grabs at anything.

But even outside the sphere of urgent biological needs, it can be shown that too strong need pressure interferes with productive thought. In

---

[16]This unseeing stare plays a considerable role in difficulties in concentration and thinking. The blind, unmoving, fixed mental "staring" at a word or a thought is one of the ways in which active and productive thought is interrupted. The passive "stare" replaces active thought when other needs or anxiety interfere with the thought process—that is, when one experiences "working difficulties."

thinking about a problem one is usually successful only if one does not press too hard for a solution; that is, one is more likely to be successful if the thought is truly object-centered, free to contemplate the object from all sides, than if the thought is goal-centered, under the pressure of *having* to produce a solution immediately. In teaching diagnostic testing, I have been impressed many times with the fact that the students who feel under the pressure of having to know, at all cost, whether this person is schizophrenic or that person is hysterical are much less likely to learn something about either the person, or schizophrenia, or hysteria than are the students who are able to take in and contemplate the data in front of them, without the pressure of the narrow goal idea of having to find a diagnostic label.

The development of focal attention and the emergence of the object world presuppose relative freedom from basic need tension, so that the object can be perceived under many different aspects, rather than apprehended merely as something that will satisfy hunger or that arouses fear and has to be fled from. And even after focal attention is fully developed and the environment is perceived as consisting of distinct objects, the need-driven (as opposed to the object-interested) perceiver or thinker will not see the object as fully in its own right as will the person who contemplates it in relative freedom from acute need tension. Curiosity, the desire for knowledge, the wish to orient oneself in the world one lives in—and finally the posing of man's eternal questions, "Who am I?" "What is this world around me?" "What can I hope for?" "What should I do?"—all these do not develop under the pressure of relentless need or of fear for one's life. They develop when man can pause to think, when the child is free to wonder and to explore. They are not, as Freud would have us believe, merely detours on the path to gratification of basic biological needs, any more than thought is only a substitute for hallucinatory wish fulfillment. They represent man's distinctive capacity to develop *interest*—the autonomous interest which alone permits the full encounter with the object. That man is capable of autonomous interest does not, of course, rule out the fact that he also remains subject to his biological and other needs, and that these may interfere with his quest for truth, or may further it, as the case may be. Just as the infant first encounters the object *not* when he is hungry or afraid, but when he is free to play and explore, so does man, on each successively higher level of understanding, discover new aspects of the object world and of himself when he is not driven by consuming need or fear, but when he can devote himself to the object. The relation of autonomous interest to need-dominated interest is similar to the relation of love to sexual desire, and to neurotic need of the "love-object." Like love, autonomous object interest is potentially inexhaustible and lasting, while need-dominated interest subsides with the satisfaction of the need, and revives only when the need tension, such as hunger or sexual desire, rises again. Moreover, while need satisfaction, according to Freud, is related to tension discharge, both love and object interest find their fulfillment not in a discharge of tension but, rather, in the maintenance of it, in sustained and ever renewed acts of relating to the beloved person or to the object of interest.[17]

Focal attention to people is slower and longer in developing than focal attention to other objects of the environment. Even after the child has developed the capacity of object-centered focal attention with regard to his peers or to some adults, his own parents still may not be seen focally— that is, from all sides and in all their aspects. The reason for this is, of course, that the parents, especially the mother, are of such overwhelming significance as the need-satisfying and also as the anxiety-arousing "objects" that they are relatively slow in emerging for the child as people with an existence of their own, independent of the child's needs and fears. To this is added another factor: Many parents prevent the child from seeing them in all their different aspects, focally, as they really are. They do this out of their own needs and anxieties, in order to perpetuate the child's dependence on them, or in order to maintain in their own and their children's minds an idealized image of themselves as the good or model parents. To this end they discourage, consciously as well as unconsciously, the child's focally attentive and explorative approach. The parents must not have any weaknesses or shortcomings; the child must not be critical of them, they must be exempt from the realistic curiosity of the child. Thus the idea that parents are people about whom one may have opinions and whom one may critically judge—that they are people like other people—may come as a shock to the child, or, indeed, may never occur to him. If the parent, by forbidding gestures or other manifestations of the parental tabu on focal attention to the parent as a person, arouses sufficiently severe and pervasive anxiety in the child, such anxiety will interfere effectively with any focal attention toward the parent and, possibly, toward people in general. Thus people will continue to be experienced predominantly as anxiety-arousing and need-satisfying "objects" by the person whose focal attention to the parents has been disrupted and diverted by anxiety. Actually, this is the case, to a greater or lesser extent, in most neurotic and psychotic patients. This same strategy of arousing fear in order to discourage focal attention toward a person, a problem, a situation—to discourage exploring them from all angles, objectively—has always been and continues to be favored as an instrument of *social power;* it is used by all those who have a stake in hindering or

---

[17]The capacity for autonomous interest, or object-centered focal attention, is the basis of what Fromm (1947) has called productive thought, which in his view, too, parallels love (pp. 96–107).

preventing man's search for truth and freedom, who thereby maintain their own irrational authority unquestioned.

The psychoanalytic patient-therapist relationship shows clearly the difference between perception in a need-dominated field and in a field sufficiently relaxed from tension to permit the emergence of the object and the development of autonomous interest. First, the relationship is designed to lessen anxiety to the point where focal attention, rather than need- or fear-driven alertness, can develop sufficiently to enable the patient to see himself. Second, in the transference relationship the patient uses and sees the therapist at first largely as a need-satisfying object and/or as a danger against which he has to protect himself. This perception changes gradually, and to the extent that the patient no longer sees the therapist as a need-satisfying or as a threatening object, the patient becomes able to see the therapist objectively as a person. Similarly, the therapist's perception of the patient will be an objective one only to the extent to which the therapist has autonomous interest in the patient and is not blinded by his own needs and anxieties.

Autonomous object interest and object-centered focal attention in man are everywhere and at all times closely interwoven with need-driven perception and thought. Man's capacity for autonomous, object-centered interest—and with it, his search for truth—has forever to disentangle itself from his fears and needs. This constitutes one of man's limitations. It also makes it difficult to keep clearly in mind the essential difference between these modes of relating to the world. Yet, without recognizing the emergence of this capacity which is not to be found in the animal world, it is not possible to understand man, to understand his relation to others and to the objects in the world around him.

The viewpoint presented here does not imply that man's capacity for object interest and his desire for truth are not the results of evolution. No doubt these capacities have developed because they enable man to know more about his environment, to adapt more effectively to it, and to change it, which he could not do were his behavior dominated by instinctive needs and fears to the extent characteristic of animals. But one would succumb to what Julian Huxley has termed the "nothing but" fallacy if one assumed that because these capacities have developed in the service of more effective adaptation, they have remained nothing but servants of man's biological needs.

The "nothing but" view of man permeates Freud's work. It underlies the theory of the pleasure principle as well as that of the death instinct, just as it underlies the libido theory, the concept of sublimation, and the theory of thought as being nothing but a detour toward instinctual need-gratification. It sounds like a distant echo of God's angry words after man had eaten from the tree of knowledge, "For dust thou art and unto dust

shalt thou return," and of the bitter and pessimistic pathos of Eccle-
siastes, "The thing that has been, it is that which shall be; and that which
is done is that which shall be done; and there is no new thing under the
sun." If one views the revolutionary discoveries of Freud in the context of
the nineteenth century's image of man, then the strength of his genius—
in this respect similar to Nietzsche's—lies in the destruction of a shallow
and self-satisfied optimism which believed that man was an entirely
rational being and that if he had not achieved the best and most reasonable of all worlds, he had come close to achieving it. Freud showed the
dark, powerful, and complex subterranean forces which give the lie to
such a soporific view of mankind. But in emphasizing these forces, in the
course of discovering man's individual prehistory and its tremendous
impact on his life, Freud tended to overlook the fact that the movement of
evolution as well as of history does create "new things under the sun,"
and that man is not only the slave of his past, but, with all his limitations,
also the potential master of his future.

Freud has been accused of being too biologically oriented. And his
view of man as "homo natura,"[18] with its relative disregard of social and
historical factors, supports this criticism. But the biological view of man,
if aware of its own limitations, is a legitimate and fruitful one. What
seems to me a more basic criticism of Freud is that *within* the biological
framework he was more impressed by death than by life, more impressed
by the return of all organisms to the inorganic than by the miracle of life
developing from inorganic matter. His penetrating glance was turned
toward the frustrating and tragic spectacle of man's being bound by his
phylogenetic, his ontogenetic, and his biographical past. But the discov-
erer of a method of therapy which did more than any other method so far
to free the individual from these shackles, averted his eye from the
perhaps even more wondrous sight—which can be seen in biology and
evolution as well as in history and in individual development—of the
creative powers of life.

REFERENCES

Bally, G. (1945), *Vom Ursprung und von den Grenzen der Freiheit: Eine Deutung des Spiels bei Tier
    und Mensch*. Basel: Benno Schwabe.
Benedek, T. (1938), Adaptation to reality in early infancy. *Psychoanal. Quart.*, 7:200–215.
Binswanger, L. (1947), Freuds Auffassung des Menschen im Lichte der Anthropologie.
    Austgewählte Vorträge und Aufsätze, Vol. 1. Bern: A. Francke A. G., pp. 159–189.
Butler, R. A. (1954), Curiosity in monkeys. *Sci. Amer.*, Feb:70–75.
Ferenczi, S. (1924), *Versuch einter Genitaltheorie*. Leipzig: Internationaler Psychoanalytischer.
Freud, A. (1953), Some remarks on infant observations. *The Psychoanalytic Study of the Child*,
    8:12–13. New York: International Universities Press.

[18]Compare Binswanger's (1947) essay on this aspect of Freud's work.

Freud, S. (1918), The interpretation of dreams. *Basic Writings.* New York: Random House.

—— (1922), *Beyond the Pleasure Principle.* London: International Psychoanalytic Press.

—— (1923) *The Ego and the Id.* London: Hogarth Press.

—— (1959), Formulations regarding the two principles in mental functioning. *Collected Papers.* New York: Basic Books.

Fromm, E. (1947), *Man for Himself.* New York: Rinehart.

Gesell, A. & Thompson, H. (1938), *The Psychology of Early Growth.* New York: Macmillan.

Goldstein, K. (1947), *Human Nature in the Light of Psychopathology.* Cambridge, MA: Harvard University Press.

Hartmann, E., Kris, E. & Lowenstein, R. M. (1946), Comments on the formation of psychic structure. *The Psychoanalytic Study of the Child,* Vol. 2. New York: International Universities Press.

Husserl, E. (1913), *Logische Untersuchungen.* Halle: Max Niemeyer.

James, W. (1931), *The Principles of Psychology.* New York: Henry Holt.

Koffka, K. (1935), *Principles of Gestalt Psychology.* New York: Harcourt, Brace.

Lorenz, K. (1937), Ueber den Begriff der Instinkthandlung. *Folia Biotheoretica,* 2:18–50.

Piaget, J. (1951), Principal factors determining intellectual evolution from childhood to adult life. In: *Organization and Pathology of Thought,* ed. D. Rapaport. New York: Columbia University Press, pp. 161–164.

Schilder, R. (n.d.), Studies concerning the psychology and symptomatology of general paresis. *Pathology of Thought,* 574–575, n.285.

Stirnimann, F. (1940), *Psychologie des neugeborenen Kindes.* Zurich: Rascher.

Sullivan, H. S. (1953), *The Interpersonal Theory of Psychiatry.* New York: Norton.

Tolman, E. C. (1954), Freedom and the cognitive need. *Amer. Psycholog.,* 9:536–538.

Werner, H. (1948), *Comparative Psychology of Mental Development* (rev.). Chicago: Follett.

7

EXPLORING THE THERAPEUTIC USE OF COUNTERTRANSFERENCE DATA

EDWARD S. TAUBER

[1954]

INTRODUCTION

Edgar A. Levenson

I trust it is not unseemly of me if I consider myself particularly qualified to introduce Tauber's article. In 1952, when this article was published, I was a candidate at the William Alanson White Psychoanalytic Institute, where Tauber was affiliated and taught, and I was consequently directly exposed to his concepts and writings, as well as to those of Fromm, who also lectured and supervised at the Institute. But of far greater pertinence to this discussion, I was an analysand of Tauber's during that time and thus directly participated in his clinical explorations. Indeed, in my treatment with him, he told me several of his dreams and free associations. For the moment, suffice it to say that I have not only read about his use of his own countertransferential data but also *experienced* it.

Seminal psychoanalytic concepts do not spring full grown from the ear of Zeus. Psychoanalysts have antecedents and progeny—a lineage of intellectual inheritance—and our concepts come more from our analysts than from academic exposure. Tauber's two analysts were first Clara Thompson and then Erich Fromm. Thompson's line of development was directly from Ferenczi (her analyst) and Sullivan, her friend and mentor and briefly her analysand. Fromm was analyzed by Hanns Sachs and Frieda Fromm-Reichmann, both in Berlin, and was by background a Marxist and social scientist. So, Ferenczi's experimentations with democratizing the analytic

Edgar A. Levenson, M. D. is Faculty, Training and Supervising Analyst, William Alanson White Institute; Clinical Professor of Psychology, New York University, Postdoctoral Program in Psychotherapy and Psychoanalysis.

process, Sullivan's concepts of anxiety, Thompson's very American pragmatism, and Fromm's very active confrontational style may all be seen as the antecedents of Tauber's position, as developed in this paper. He later developed and expanded this inquiry into the larger field of "prelogical" (read "intuitive") processes in therapy in his and M. Green's book (Tauber and Green, 1959).

In our current atmosphere of ecumenism—with its growing disenchantment with the plausability of the "neutral" analyst concept; and with its acceptance of the inevitability and usefulness of the therapist's activity—it is hard to imagine how utterly radical and outrageous Tauber's position seemed to the psychoanalytic establishment. Even at the White Institute, for all its well-deserved reputation for intellectual tolerance, his free-ranging explorations were considered by some as a bit too much. Although Tauber continued to experiment with using his own dreams, free-associations, and fantasies in therapy, and although he continued to write, he was, at least as I saw it, discouraged by the criticism and, in the latter part of his career, turned increasingly to hard research in eye movement and dream research. He achieved an enviable reputation in this second field, publishing extensively. He seemed happiest with his lizards, lasers, and complicated recording devices. It was about as far as one could get from the audacious, poetic, ground-breaking experiments with intersubjectivity that this paper epitomizes. I believe that had he continued to extend and elaborate his ideas, he would have explicitly anticipated much of what we presently consider to be the cutting edge of interpersonal theory. Tauber amalgamated the confluence of influences bearing on him, and pointed a seminal direction.

The idea of making one's self available to the patient for his or her inquiry; the democratization of a heretofore quite authoritarian psychoanalysis; the use of one's own "countertransference" as valuable grist for the analytic mill rather than as an obstacle to the treatment and a confession of one's own shortcomings; the use of one's free associations and dreams without being clear what might be revealed—all this was an audacious attempt to create a contemporary psychoanalysis. It should have worked—after all, it was (similar to) what we are doing now. To a considerable extent it worked, but it was before its time.

I don't believe that patients, forty years ago, were able to view the analytic process in such an egalitarian light. They were not comfortable with assessing the analyst, or disrespecting analytic authority. One remembers that, in those days, psychoanalysts were revered as magicians and pundits. Virtually every dimension of social life was imbued with psychoanalytic concepts and jargon. Most patients would have as soon looked into the countenance of God as confront their analysts. Nor were analysts so comfortable being confronted by their patients. Even if the analyst did his/her very best to be open to the patient's observations, who is to say that an analyst doesn't have an unconscious? According to the precept of Harry Stack Sullivan, everyone learns not to make other people anxious. Anxiety provokes defenses and the threat of desertion or retaliation by the caretaker; thus running the serious risk of loss of necessary satisfactions (Sullivan, 1953a).

To minimize this frightening possibility, everyone monitors very closely the other's peace of mind and backs away from disruptive experiences. This "dew-line" of defense reaches down to the unconscious anxiety of the other. Patients are no different from anyone else, and the patient *qua* patient learns the first cardinal rule of survival—don't make your analyst so anxious that the anxiety is totally dissociated and disowned. Unconscious retaliation will surely follow.

At least, that was my experience. Perhaps I was more wary than some analysands, but certainly if Tauber's pioneer effort foundered at all, it was around this issue. I remember being quite uneasy when Tauber told me his dreams or his associations. Since I was not on the couch, I had a pretty good view of him and his inadvertent movements and expressions, and had some idea of when I was heading for trouble; so I avoided it, sometimes consciously, sometimes well out of my own awareness. I must emphasize that this was not an inevitable outcome. A more comfortable analysand may have felt freer to confront him, and would have, I am sure, been greeted with encouragement and enthusiasm. This is, however, a great deal to expect of both participants in the process.

Contemporary interpersonal psychoanalysis has come a long way, and patients and therapists alike are far more at ease with the flexible and egalitarian participation Tauber prescribed. The problem lay not in the concept, but in its application. I don't think the field was quite ready for it, and although he was not as savaged as Ferenczi, neither did he receive the acceptance he richly deserved. It is still not a comfortable or risk-free process, and, as Tauber warns in the article, it behooves the analyst employing it to maintain a high degree of vigilance and integrity. Nevertheless, for most of us, it is integral to the therapeutic process.

It gives me great pleasure to introduce this paper. It is a milestone in the development of psychoanalytic thinking, by no means limited to "interpersonal" psychoanalysis. The entire field is struggling with the issues of transference "enactment"; that is, the presence of the analyst as a real participant in the intersubjective field. This paper is certainly germane to the topic. In addition to its theoretical significance, it communicates something of the vitality, respectful good will, colorfulness, and curiosity, both about himself and others, that characterized the man and his work.

T his paper is designed to illustrate the fact that countertransference phenomena may under certain circumstances afford an opportunity to evoke new material about the patient, the analyst, or the relationship, and that they may be used therapeutically to increase mutual spontaneity. The author believes that there is a real need for developing a scientific method to utilize constructively the negative components introduced by the therapist in the treatment situation and to determine which of

Psychiatry, 17:332-336.

This paper was originally given before a postgraduate seminar at the Medical School of the University of Mexico on November 30, 1952.

these components are worthy of mutual exploration. According to classical psychoanalytic theory, countertransference reactions represent unanalyzed portions of the therapist's personality that either transparently or unwittingly interfere with the treatment situation. These reactions may be due to blind spots, private needs, irrelevant attitudes, biases, or moral prejudices; and they call for a change to a more productive orientation, necessitating their analysis. This is the basis in psychoanalytic theory for recognizing that any person engaged in intensive psychotherapeutic work with others needs a training analysis—a recognition that represents one of the most valuable discoveries in psychoanalysis.

It seems to me, however, that this emphasis on the negative value of countertransference reactions, important as it is, has tended to preclude the possibility of using these very reactions for achieving therapeutic goals. That is, the analyst may be so concerned with avoiding countertransference reactions that he does not take time to examine the content of the reaction fully. In this way, for instance, he may deliberately try to forget a dream he has had about a patient; or he may fail to mention to a supervisor some fleeting thought he has had about the patient. In other words, there is a taboo on anything that vaguely resembles countertransference reactions, and only the grossest type are explored even in supervision. Eventually the gross countertransference phenomena tend to diminish; the more subtle ones remain, but are probably handled by selective inattention. This taboo has the harmful effect of inhibiting the analyst from recognizing the creative spontaneous insights that may occur to him in a dream, or in making use of a marginal thought or a slip of the tongue.

It is my impression that the analyst takes in more about the patient than he realizes; that there may be special reasons for the analyst's inability to bring some of his unconscious grasp of the patient into his own conscious awareness; and that by discussing some of the countertransference fragments, both the analyst and the patient may find out that the analyst has a richer understanding of the patient that can be put to good use in the exploratory process of analysis.

The very nature of the analytic setting is such that the analyst plays a relatively passive role and maintains an incognito. Many patients seem to respond to this setting by presenting an incognito of their own. Such a patient may give the analyst no clues even for suspecting that his behavior in therapy really represents only a small part of his total functioning and way of living. As a result, both the analyst's taboo on countertransference attitudes and the patient's subtle incognito limit the amount of potentially useful information available for analytic progress. Thus the analytic procedure seems to require a constant infusion of new materials, fresh appraisals, and a challenging reconsideration of issues in the light of provocative data. Otherwise the analysis can become stagnant, and the so-called standardization of the procedure and the established scientific postulates can themselves become targets of the patient's resistance. This, of course, does not imply that the countertransference reactions should be construed as license for acting out with the patient, but only that mutual exploration of their significance can open up more areas of development in the therapeutic situation.

With this as a hypothesis, I have discussed openly with several patients for mutual clarification, dream material of mine that involved them, and also some fleeting fragments of an intrusive nature. I shall illustrate this by three different instances.

ILLUSTRATION 1

Over a period of several weeks, the analyst has two successive dreams about patient A. In presenting his first dream, the analyst pointed out that he thought it might throw some light on his attitude toward the patient and he asked the patient for his impression of the dream:

The patient and the analyst are sitting at a small table in a sidewalk café, perhaps in Paris. The patient is saying very little, but has a very troubled expression on his face. He appears worried. The analyst says to him, "Why not try to tell me what is the matter?"

The patient seemed to respond to this dream in a very meager fashion. Except for a polite nod, he indicated no particular interest in giving his impressions and seemed to have something else he wished to talk about. Thus an analysis of the dream was not pursued. The analyst's second dream about the patient occurred several weeks later and was reported to the patient:

The patient and the analyst are sitting at a table in an expensive bar, having a drink. They are talking casually, but the content of the conversation is not recalled. Suddenly as they are about to leave the bar, two men not previously noticed jump on the patient. The situation develops swiftly, and the analyst cannot tell if the patient is really being attacked, or if these are just old college chums who are taking the patient by surprise, and roughhousing with him. The dream ends as the analyst quickly goes to the patient to ask him if this is serious and if he needs help, or if they are all joking.

At first the patient made no comments about the dream, except to say that it expressed the analyst's belief that the patient was withholding data and at the same time seemed in need of help. The analyst asked the patient, "Do you think that I believe that you are in need of help?" The patient responded in equivocal fashion, indicating that perhaps he thought the analyst had this feeling about him.

But later in the hour, the patient showed by his manner that the dream had something to say to him that was worth considering. His associations implied that the patient-doctor relationship had always been satisfactory and that he felt it was essential to keep it that way, that his experience in life had led him to believe that it was best to let sleeping dogs lie, that one can never work out a satisfactory solution by getting too deeply involved or by making one's ultimate position known. He then went on to make the important suggestion that both dreams had a hoax like quality: although they manifestly indicated the analyst's concern for him, at the same time he suspected that the analyst was perfectly happy with the friendly, unstressed quality of the relationship; and although the analyst was trying to indicate that he believed they should go deeper into these issues, he had some private reasons for avoiding the challenge.

The analyst found this latter comment thought-provoking, and he could not answer it with either a flat denial or an affirmation. The analyst seriously asked himself whether he was guilty of wanting to avoid difficulties. The analyst's association to this was to remember information from outside sources about the patient that was not too favorable. He did not feel free under the circumstances to communicate this information to the patient. The analyst then made some comments about the dream in which he indicated that in one sense he believed it implied that he was having some difficulty obtaining the maximum degree of participation from the patient, and that possibly the dream was an indirect method of conveying to the patient the analyst's desire for deeper collaboration.

The analyst's first verbalized association was that the dream was an attempt to provoke the patient to reveal more clearly the transference picture. The analyst acknowledged the possibility that he might have an unconscious fear of knowing something inauspicious about the patient; although he was not aware of the nature of this fear, it might become apparent later. The analyst pointed out that the dream, in its manifest content, contained a rather obvious message, which could be known to both participants. But he reminded the patient that he, the analyst, could easily have some blind spots about the meaning of the dream, and the patient should develop his own ideas about the dream.

The next session was an extremely fruitful one, because it conveyed to both of them—more strikingly than perhaps at any other time—the essence of the patient's real fear of closeness. It had always been difficult for the patient to convey the emotional atmosphere of his home situation; although he had previously made sensible statements about his home situation, they often lacked the affect that is so essential in the analytic setting. In this particular instance, however, the patient's usual nonchalance was lacking, and his distress at an impending social engagement was touchingly revealed. After the patient had expressed this distress, the analyst was able to tell the patient about a previous occasion when he had sensed the patient's deep fear of his closeness to his mother. They both then realized that the issue had been hit upon—namely, that the analyst had been afraid to push this particular point for fear of a panic reaction in the patient. In other words, the dreams seemed to have revealed a pleasant but timid coaxing of the patient, as if the analyst were saying, *"One can still go about this matter of his problems, even while having a drink."* Stated in other terms, the dreams were expressions of the analyst's ambivalence, in that he both urged the patient to greater activity, and had some reservations himself about the safety of it.

ILLUSTRATION 2

The analyst had the following dream about patient B, a young married woman who had been in analysis for a few months:

The dream takes place on an island in the Mediterranean. The patient and the analyst are walking together, and there is no conversation. It seems to be dusk. The atmosphere has a romantic quality. The analyst is trying to understand something, although nothing has been said. That is all there is to the dream.

When the analyst reported the dream to the patient, she made no comment. Prior to the analytic session, the analyst decided to report the dream to the patient although he had not considered the dream carefully. When she failed to say anything about it, the analyst noted on the spur of the moment that the patient did not seem to feel that the romantic components of her marriage were satisfactory, although there had been no mention of it in their work together. He admitted that there was no significant information to justify this association, but it had come to him anyway, and he wondered whether it had any validity. Subsequently the patient went into the subject of her marriage, revealing that the analyst's association had a rather pertinent bearing on her problem. The analyst wondered why this would have to come up in a dream. The patient seemed to have no thoughts on the matter. It occurred to the analyst, however, that he had been deliberately avoiding the subject of the patient's marriage since she had had so much distress in the analysis and had seemed to have a need to believe that her marriage at least was sound. The dream came to his assistance, however, and prevented his employing some further useless philanthropic attitudes toward the patient, which could only have delayed the handling of a problem of importance to her. It turned out that her relationship with her husband was not as happy as she wished to believe.

ILLUSTRATION 3

This illustration has to do with a fleeting thought that came to the analyst's mind during an analytic session. The analyst revealed this thought to the patient, saying at the same time that ordinarily he would not have done so, because it seemed to be out of order and to have nothing to do with the mutual inquiry. The analyst asked the patient for his reaction to this thought, and stated that he would also contribute his own associations. Here is the setting in which the thought occurred:

The patient was describing some details of his marriage. Having had occasional temporary episodes of sexual impotence prior to marriage, he was remarking that he hoped that under the stress of his present marital problem he would not again have the same disturbance. He added that because he anticipated that his wife would react adversely, such a disturbance would be extremely frightening to him. The analyst had this sudden, unaccounted-for thought, which he revealed to the patient: "Send your wife here to me. I can explain the situation to her in such a way that she won't be disturbed."

The patient quickly reacted to this remark. He said that it revealed to him that the analyst really had a lack of confidence in him and did not believe that if he became impotent, he would be able to work out the problem with his wife. While the patient was talking, the analyst had the fleeting thought that what he, the analyst, had said seemed to be an expression of ambition, as if he were trying to prove to the patient that he had the power to straighten out the matter—a kind of credit-taking fantasy. The analyst communicated this to the patient; the patient reacted by looking pale and angry, and by insisting that it proved that the analyst was merely trying to deny admitting his deeper feeling of the patient's inadequacy by accusing himself of ambition.

The patient was silent at the beginning of the next day's session. The analyst urged the patient to say what was on his mind, but the patient was still uncommunicative and seemed slightly uneasy and uncomfortable. Prior to this session, the analyst had had some thoughts about his remarks of the session before, and he now proceeded to communicate them to the patient:

The analyst explained that he suspected that his behavior of the day before represented an unconscious mimicking of the patient's mother or identification with her, and that it was motivated in order to recapture with the patient a relationship the patient had with his mother that had never come out strongly in the analysis. In other words, the analyst believed that this unconscious device was aimed at forcing the patient to reveal a sensitive area that could have remained concealed in the ordinary conditions of analysis.

The patient reacted to this latter comment by blushing and saying, with some anger, "You are trying to get off the hook." By this the patient meant that the analyst had originally indicated a lack of confidence in the patient, and had first attempted to deny this by explaining his comment as an expression of his own ambition. Then, when that was not satisfactory, the analyst tried a new tactic—namely, to explain his behavior as an unconscious therapeutic maneuver. But the patient did not believe that the analyst's associations had explained away his lack of confidence in the patient.

At the next session the patient was quite eager to relate a dream that he had had the night before:

There is a huge ballroom filled with couples dancing. A doctor, whom the patient has known for many years and has regarded as an ally of his from early childhood, is dancing with his wife. The dance steps are elaborate, with the partners' stepping away from each other and coming together again. Suddenly the patient's mother, standing alone on the sidelines, gets into the doctor's arms before the patient's wife can complete the steps necessary to return her into his arms. Apparently the doctor showed no objection to the swift change in partners, and willingly continued to dance with the patient's mother. The patient, who observed all this, said nothing, but was disappointed in the doctor's behavior.

The patient's associations were that the doctor and the analyst were the same person, and that the analyst had betrayed him. The patient felt that this dream was his way of expressing what he believed the analyst had meant about their relationship at the time the analyst had commented on the patient's anticipated potency problem. The analyst's interpretation of the patient's dream was in line with the patient's comments. In effect, the dream indicated that the patient felt that the analyst had turned away from him after having had a satisfactory relationship with him, and had now become an ally of his mother. It indicated that the patient did feel disappointed in the analyst's earlier remarks on the grounds that the analyst had later suspected—namely, that the analyst had unconsciously simulated the patient's mother. In other words, the analyst believed that his remarks represented an unconscious attempt to stimulate or provoke emotional data in an area that was important but still insufficiently explored. The matter was left with the patient, however, who was urged to attempt to clarify in the analytic work the important critical problem of whether or not the analyst's attitude was genuinely hostile. These analytic hours had emphasized for the patient the necessity to be concerned with the real and assumed attitudes of the analyst, and also that he could not and should not be satisfied with an uncritical acceptance of the analyst's appraisal of his own attitudes.

It seemed to the analyst that two important points were brought out clearly through this incident. First, the patient was obliged to move away from a somewhat artificially arrived at conception of the analyst's attitude toward him; and he was forced to consider the analyst as a human being with whom he was working rather than a special category of person who fitted his defensive needs. Second, the analyst's experiment of expressing a private thought—which was out of order at first glance—provoked material reflecting quite genuinely the patient's strong doubt about his mother's alleged faith in him, a point that he had previously indicated with relatively unimpressive affect.

Sometimes it is useful to enter into the parataxis with the patient in order to recapture more vividly the quality of the memory, or to simulate in some way the significant parent or other figure in order to illuminate the history of the current distortion. The romantic dream reported in Illustration 2 is also an example of the analyst's unconsciously entering the parataxic field of the patient. That is, the therapist responds to the patient's irrational needs in an inappropriate fashion—namely, with his own irrational reveries or dreams. Yet the question must be raised as to whether the therapist does not enter the parataxic areas of the patient's life much more often than he realizes, if he dares to recognize this. The distinction as to when this unconscious operation is of value or not has to be explored further. One point that seems indisputable is that once the intrusion is made, the therapist must be able to assume responsibility for his actions and thoughts with honesty and without defensiveness. Furthermore, it is my opinion that the therapist probably avoids burdening the patient as long as the solution of his own problems of living is in good measure meaningful.

In this paper, I have tried to identify more clearly certain issues inherent in the procedure of utilizing countertransference data in the treatment setting. From my observations, I would say that countertransference reactions are more likely to occur during fallow or lengthy resistant periods. They function at such times to provoke contact with the patient, to break into the resistance by surprise. The surprise is not a random jiggling of the controls to see what will happen, but occurs in a setting of deep concentration, in which the analyst is trying to reach the patient. The surprise is an expression of spontaneity, and as such can have constructive and unconstructive implications. The analyst must be free to follow through and participate in the truest sense of the word—there is no time at that point for sophistical defensive operations. The special responsibility of the therapist at such a time is to recognize that he may be making irrational demands on the patient and that he must be able to handle this. It is not the patient's job to support him if his spontaneity creates tensions. Thus the utilization of countertransference reactions in the treatment setting is not license to carry on wildcat, irresponsible experimentation. If the therapist feels he is playing with fire, he should not deal with countertransference reactions with his patient; in other words, the optimal conditions for such exploration are not at hand.

If one wishes to appraise the possibly injurious effects of exploring countertransference reactions in the therapeutic situation, the only injury that I believe requires serious consideration is that which could be imposed on the patient by the therapist's own attitudes. If the therapist, however, is serious, responsible, competent and resourceful, it seems highly improbable that the patient will react with panic or a depression, or that he will suddenly leave treatment. It is, moveover, significant that in my own experience the examination of countertransference reactions has not led to further bogging down and resistance. The more usual result has been the re-establishment of varying degrees of contact, further activity, and more hopefulness.

8

REMARKS ON THE PROBLEM OF FREE ASSOCIATION

ERICH FROMM

[1955]

INTRODUCTION

Marianne Horney Eckardt

Ideally, psychoanalysis is an interdisciplinary science. Many scholars, distinguished by their varied backgrounds, have enriched our field. Outstanding among this company is Erich Fromm, known as a Talmudic scholar, a moral philosopher, a sociologist, a social critic, a writer, and, of course, a psychoanalyst. His contributions uniquely reflect the scholarly roads he traveled. But foremost we think of him as a humanist. He himself referred to his pursuits as developing a humanistic science of man, or a humanistic view of the world, or humanistic ethics. This orientation developed at an early date, as he was born into a family deeply rooted in rabbinical tradition. Fromm became, as mentioned, a Talmudic scholar, and all his life was fascinated by the teachings of the prophets. One of my favorite books by Fromm (1966) is *You Shall Be As Gods,* in which he presents his humanistic beliefs as evolved in the Bible and by the prophets. His interest in man led him to the study of sociology and philosophy. The writings of Aristotle, Spinoza, and the young Karl Marx proved to be particularly meaningful. Psychoanalysis fascinated him by the deepened insight into human activity and motivation it offered, and by its discovery of the dynamic unconscious and personality formation.

Fromm was born in 1900 in Frankfurt, Germany. He received his psychoanalytic training in Berlin. He worked with, and was briefly married to, Frieda Fromm-Reichman. His associates then and later were creative,

---

Marianne Horney Eckardt, M.D. is a member of the American Academy of Psychoanalysis.

independent thinkers who forged their own paths. His friends Georg Grod-
dek and Wilhelm Reich opened up new debates. Later, after arriving in
the United States, Fromm, Harry Stack Sullivan, Karen Horney, Clara
Thompson, and Abraham Kardiner met regularly to challenge, debate, and
clarify the mysteries of psychoanalysis and contributed immeasurably to
each other's creative productiveness. This group became known as the neo-
Freudians, as they began to question the libidinal roots of all neurotic
pathology and in many different ways emphasized the impact of culture,
family, early environment, and society on normal and neurotic personality
development. Fromm (1941) was then at work on his first book, *Escape from
Freedom*. He was ever aware of the fact that man is a social animal, that society
has formative influences on him, and that he in turn shapes society.

Fromm's activities were rarely limited solely to the practice of psychoanalysis. He participated in a sociopolitical research study on the authoritarian character of workers in Germany. He taught at the New School for
Social Research, at Yale, and at Bennington. He lectured all over the world.
Above all, he authored more than 25 books and numerous essays and papers.
He wrote about the theory of psychoanalysis, though never about individual
case histories. He wrote as a social psychologist, as a moral philosopher, and
as a social critic. He wrote for a worldwide public and with a mission.

A few more facts about his life should be mentioned before some of his
contributions are described. He participated in the founding of the William
Alanson White Psychoanalytic Society and Institute in 1944. He met and
married Henny Gurland, a photographer. Her illness caused them to move to
Mexico City in 1949, and here Fromm established a psychoanalytic institute
at the University of Mexico City. Henny died in 1952. The following year
Fromm married Annis Freeman. A wonderful companionship enriched
their life together. They moved to Cuernavaca and later, because his health
demanded it, to Locarno, Switzerland. While Fromm helped found societies
and institutes, he did not wish to be a leader nor to have followers. He was,
however, a teacher with a vision and a mission.

I will select and emphasize just some of Fromm's contributions and concepts. Fromm believed in evolution. Man has the potential for good or
evil. Fromm's (1941) vision pertains to man's humanistic potential as expressed in these lines by Pico della Mirandola, with which Fromm begins his
Escape from Freedom:

> Neither heavenly nor earthly, neither mortal nor immortal have we
> created thee, so that thou mightest be free according to thy own will and
> honor, to be thy own creator and builder. To thee alone we gave growth
> and development depending on thy own free will. Thou bearest in thee
> the germs of a universal life.

We also encounter this vision in Fromm's notions of the biophilic person who
loves life, is productive, and relates caringly to his fellow man. We can
understand his mission only if we grasp his concept of the essence of man.
Man evolved out of animal existence. Our essence consists in the contradiction of being part of nature yet transcending it, as we are endowed with
reason and self-awareness. Man has to act to find solutions. No absolute
answers exist. Human beings, of course, find a myriad of solutions of many

different qualities. Fromm pointed to regressive and progressive solutions. His life long mission aimed at making people aware of bad solutions, those that do not serve the welfare and growth of man, and pointing to existing alternatives and their consequences. Fromm (1962) wrote, "Confrontation with true alternatives may awaken all the hidden energies in a person, and enable him to choose life. No one else can breathe life into him" (p. 146).

Man is a social animal. He has to live in groups and cooperate with others. He must have a frame of orientation that permits him to grasp reality and to communicate with others. This frame of orientation is acquired by learning, but to a large extent it comes about by way of social character formation. Fromm is not referring here to individual character but to social character, that is, to predominant traits that are common to a group. The concept of social character is to Fromm a key concept for the understanding of the social process. "Character," writes Fromm (1992), "is the form in which human energy is channeled during the process of 'socialization' and 'assimilation.' Character is, in fact, a substitute for instincts" (p. 7). In *Escape from Freedom* Fromm (1941) describes the influence of the modern industrialized state on character development. Old family and social bonds are weakened. People feel increasingly powerless and insignificant, and crave an authority that will promise salvation or security. Thus they can become victims of dictatorships.

Fromm's (1947) book, *Man for Himself,* depicts various character orientations and their consequences. These character orientations have definite ethical implications. Fromm is emphatic in his belief that psychology cannot be divorced from ethics. He writes:

> My experience as a practicing psychoanalyst has confirmed my conviction that problems of ethics cannot be omitted from the study of personality, either theoretically or therapeutically. The value judgment we make determines our actions, and upon their validity rests our mental health and happiness. . . . Neurosis itself is, in the last analysis, a symptom of moral failure [p. v].

In contrast to Freud, Fromm sees character not as an outgrowth of various types of libido organizations, but as specific kinds of relatedness to the world. He describes the following nonproductive character orientations: (a) The receptive orientation is at its core organized around the idea of being given love, nourishment, security. Persons seem amiable but become anxious when their "source of supply" is threatened. (b) The exploitative orientation is centered around the necessity of taking what one needs as it will not be given voluntarily. (c) The hoarding orientation relies on safety by saving and hoarding. (d) The marketing orientation revolves around experiencing oneself as a commodity, the value of which depends solely on the forces of the market. There exists no solid sense of self, no integrity, as behavior is designed to go with the prevailing winds. In contrast to these orientations, Fromm projects the productive orientation arising out of a capacity of relatedness in all realms of human experiences. Productiveness is man's ability to use his powers for love, caring, and creativity, and to realize the potentialities inherent in him. Every human being is capable of developing this attitude, unless he is mentally and emotionally crippled. Fromm believed in the existence of an inherent striving for health and happiness. His books *The Sane Society* (1955), *The Art of Loving* (1956), and *You Shall Be As Gods* (1966) give us a sense of what we and society could be, a goal to strive for.

The Fromm article on free association that is presented here is remarkable and unique. It could serve as a classic model for how technical issues in psychoanalysis ought to be discussed, though rarely are. What makes the essay so refreshingly readable is Fromm's language. All concepts are immediately translated into everyday experience and everyday language. He demystifies all jargon. His style may give the impression of addressing an audience unfamiliar with psychoanalysis, but this would fail to recognize Fromm's goal of conveying his thoughts in as clear a manner as possible and not hiding behind abstractions.

Fromm places his comments on free association into the context of the great discoveries of Freud: the unconscious, the mechanism of repression, and how to make this unconscious accessible. Freud taught his patients to bypass their rational conventional mode of thought and to allow thoughts or feelings to arise from somewhere inside them, maybe the belly or the heart. Memories or thoughts were thus revealed which proved amazingly relevant. But methods can deteriorate. They have to retain their meaning and vitality to be effective and this is where Fromm points to the problem. Obedience to the technical rituals of psychoanalysis can take the heart out of the methods and thus rob them of effectiveness. This is particularly true of free associations, which were heralded as the royal road to the unconscious.

To fully appreciate Fromm's criticisms, it is important to understand some core themes of his writings. Most important is his reaffirmation of the old biblical injunction against idolatry. Even in the Bible, the emphasis was not on the worship of one God versus the worship of many gods, but on the worship of one unknowable God in contrast to the worship of images or objects that could be seen, touched, and possessed. Fromm's concern is not with God, but with idols, that is, with what should not be worshiped. Fromm finds that the source of our pervasive human inclination to look for a powerful omniscient person to guide us and promise protection is in our evolutionary emergence from the animal kingdom into human beings with self-awareness. Our instincts alone did not guide us any more; we had to make decisions. We were aware of our vulnerability and helplessness. Thus religions and institutions were born to respond to a deep-seated longing in us to believe in an all-powerful, omniscient, all-caring person or social body, a longing that is ever ready to form an intense affective bond with this magic helper. It resembles the attachment of the child to mother and father in being essentially passive, hoping, and trusting. Fromm calls all these longed-for figures by the generic name of idols. The person transfers his own strength and power to the particular idol, and in so doing curtails his own creativity and individuality. Fromm plays this theme in many different ways. He contrasts two differing approaches to life, the mode of "having," or possessing, and that of "being," which does not rely on what one has, be it power, money, fame, status, or the certainty of knowledge. We find it again in his contrasting the necrophilic person, who wants to possess and takes pleasure in destroying, to the biophilic person who loves life, spontaneity, creativity, affectionate caring, and is open to hope. Hope replaces certainty. We can hope for and strive for but we do not possess the answers for tomorrow.

Fromm sees the possibility of lessening the tendency to believe in idols. Fromm (1992) writes:

> I am led to the conclusion that the sense of powerlessness, and hence the need for idols, becomes less intense the more a person succeeds in attributing his existence to his own active efforts; the more he develops his powers of love and reason; the more he acquires a sense of identity, not mediated by his social role but rooted in the authenticity of his self; the more he can give and is related to others, without losing his freedom and integrity; and the more he is aware of his unconscious, so that nothing human within himself and in others is alien to him [p. 52].

Before elaborating on the relevance of the theme of idol worship to the Fromm article on free association presented here, I want to convey some of Fromm's descriptions of the unconscious. In the article he likens it to our being two people, the rational, conventional person, what C. G. Jung called our persona, and the other, the dissociated person, the child in us, be it of one or three or fourteen years of age. Both these personalities determine our feelings and actions. Unconsciousness is a function, not a place. We can be more or less unconscious. The concept of the "social filter," consisting of the language, logic, and mores of the world around us, appealed to Fromm. We are raised to think, speak, and behave in certain ways, and to adapt to our sociocultural environment. Yet our subjective being coexists, though it may remain private, or secret, or may just appear in our dreams. Fromm equates unconsciousness with the unawareness of truth; becoming aware means discovering the truth. What is not allowed into consciousness is not just what is bad, like hate and feeling murderous; it can be a whole range of perceptions that happen not to blend easily into conventional perceptions. Psychoanalytic therapy is not the only road to truth or to being awakened. New experiences brought about by changes in the environment, be it in the workplace or in new relationships or artistic endeavors, can radically change our perspective and allow a new outlook to emerge.

All of the above does have relevance to the Fromm article you are about to read. The process of deterioration in the manner in which the tool of free association is used is an illustration of how we regard prescribed analytic techniques as sacrosanct, that is, as idols. If you are an obedient, conscientious analyst and routinely tell your patient to obey the rules and say what comes to mind, then all should be well. If all is not well, the assumption arises that the patient's resistance may be causing the trouble. In the article, Fromm restores meaning by offering suggestions as to how to retain pertinence, aliveness, and effectiveness in using this procedure. These are meant only as illustrations. Do not make them into prescriptions to follow! In my own practice, however, I have found very helpful his suggestion to make occasional but deliberately timed intervention by asking for free associations. I want to stress also the importance of Fromm's distinction between requests for information or requests for a rational discussion and requests for free associations. Many analysts do not feel free to ask questions for their own enlightenment because they believe that their patients know their world, take most of it for granted, and will not mention important details unless they have become emotionally charged. I remember a time when an accidental question of mine revealed that the family never ate together, and in another instance that talk at the dinner table was minimal because the father, or perhaps it was the husband, read the newspaper while eating his meal. Details are important. They enliven the information for us, and thus permit some meaningful empathy. While we listen, our imagination replays the scenarios the patient is presenting to us. We notice gaps and vagueness in our under-standing and we inquire. We have to be alert and create an atmosphere of aliveness. Fromm (1976) writes: "The essential factor in psychoanalytic treat-ment is this alivening quality in the therapist. No amount of psychoanalytic interpretation will have an effect if the therapeutic atmosphere is heavy, unalive, and boring" (p. 34).

The article is a good example of what Fromm means by aliveness. It speaks to the reader in direct language. Its critical analysis is alert to all nuances of concepts and practicalities. It informs and aims to be helpful by giving perspectives rather than rules. His hope that man has the possibility for a more creative, active, caring existence reaches out to us. Read the article and enjoy it!

The great discovery of Freud lies in two directions: one is of sub-stance, and the other is of method. I would say that, as far as the first part of Freud's discovery is concerned, the most lasting and fundamental discovery is that of the unconscious. And, as far as method is concerned, it is the discovery of a method to recognize the unconscious, that is, to see something which usually cannot be seen. What Freud showed was that everyone of us is two persons. One is the adult, rational, conventional person, the official person, so to speak, which we all are when we are awake, when we behave conventionally, when we go about our business. Then there is this other personality, the little child in us; or several children, one of six months, and one of one year, and one of three years, perhaps, and one of fourteen; all together being alive, acting, determin-ing our feelings and actions; yet never directly observable, never directly visible. Our behavior, our feeling, our thought, is always a mixture, always a blend of the "day personality," and that other personality which you might call the unconscious or the dissociated personality in us. Actually, this dissociated personality can be observed directly only in several instances: in psychosis, under hypnosis, under the influence of drugs, or during sleep, in our dreams, which Freud described as a transitory psychosis. We are listening in our sleep to this dissociated personality; it comes to the fore, talks, thinks, and sees things; the day personality is

Psychiatric Research Reports, No. 2, pp. 1–6. Washington, DC: American Psychiatric Association.

relegated to the background and speaks only with a very small voice, by distorting and embellishing certain things that the dissociated personality says. Indeed, among psychoanalysts there are differences about what is the essence of that dissociated personality. Freud thought it was centered around a core of infantile sexual desires. For other psychoanalysts, the concept of the dissociated personality is a broader one and not essentially centered around this sexual core. But, in spite of such differences, they too define the dissociated personality in terms of the child which has not yet fully emerged from his mother's womb, or which has not yet been fully separated from mother's breasts, or which has not yet fully separated from obedient attachment to father's authority, and emerged into an active, productive life of his own. These differences do not matter, from the standpoint of our discussion here, because the essential point and the greatness of Freud's discovery was that there is this secret, hidden, dissociated personality, and that this personality has a tremendous effect on everything we do, and everything we think. If there is any definition of psychoanalysis, whatever school of psychoanalysis we are talking about, then it is based on this concept of the unconscious, and psychoanalysis has to be described as a method which tries to uncover the dissociated part of a person's personality.

Now as to the method, I would say again that it is one of the great achievements of Freud to have overcome the seemingly unanswerable logical objection to a method of discovering the unconscious. The logical objection being: If something is unconscious, we cannot become aware of it, therefore there is no method by which we can arrive with any degree of certainty at a picture of that which is dissociated; by its very nature, it is not open to inspection. Freud did find ways for the observation of the unconscious. One was the interpretation of dreams; the other was the analysis of transference; the third was free association.

How could we describe in general terms the meaning of free association according to Freud? What Freud discovered was that a person, even if he is not asleep and dreaming, even if he is not insane, even if he is not in a hypnotic trance, nevertheless, can hear the voice of his unconscious, provided that he does something which seems very simple: namely, that he leave the realm of conventional, rational thought, and permit himself to voice ideas which are not determined by the rules of normal, conventional thinking. If he does this, ideas emerge, not from his head but, as the Chinese would say, from his belly; ideas which are not part of his official personality, but which are the language of this dissociated, hidden personality. Furthermore, Freud discovered the fact that if I permit myself to associate freely, then these very thoughts which come from this dissociated realm attract other relevant and germane thoughts from the realm of the unconscious.

Originally Freud thought it to be necessary for the stimulation of free association to touch the forehead of his patient, after having given him the instruction that, when he touched his forehead, the patient should say what was on his mind at that very moment. Later, Freud found that one did not even need to touch the forehead, that one could give the patient the general instruction that throughout the whole analytic session he should "free associate." Freud tried to help the effectiveness of this idea by the technical arrangement which he chose for the treatment, that is, the "use of the couch." The idea was brilliant, and seemed to be very promising. But actually what happened was, I think, a deterioration of the whole method of free association. In orthodox Freudian analysis (not always, but in many instances), free association has become an empty ritual. The patient lies on the couch, he is instructed not to hide anything, to say everything that comes to his mind. That is fine. Let us assume that the patient does that, and is conscientious and honest, and says whatever comes to his mind. What guarantee do we have that the things that do come to his mind have any meaning in the sense of the dissociated personality? That in speaking without restriction he is saying things which are relevant? In many instances free association has deteriorated into meaningless chatter, into "free talk," into uncontrolled complaining, and sterile thinking. All that passes for free association because the formal rule is observed: namely, not to omit anything which is on one's mind. The original meaning of free association was to be spontaneous association; the deteriorated free association is not spontaneous at all; it is free only in the negative sense that no thought is omitted. The patient comes in, and he says for the twentieth time what he has said to his wife, what his wife has said to him, what happened in his business, and this and the other, and the analyst sits there and listens and does not say anything. The hour ends, and both are satisfied because everything has happened according to the ritual.

My criticism of free association is not at all meant to be criticism only of orthodox psychoanalysis. I, myself, am not an orthodox psychoanalyst. But I must admit that in observing what goes on in non-orthodox analysis, I conclude that free association has deteriorated there just as much as it has in orthodox psychoanalysis, except in a different way. Instead of the ritualistic priest-like, authoritarian attitude with which the patient is confronted, you find a tolerant, reasonable, friendly attitude. The analyst does not sit behind the couch. He is not so silent. He also instructs his patient to say anything that comes to his mind. But there is often the danger of transforming the situation into a friendly dialogue, instead of the more austere Freudian monologue.

Often several approaches are confused with the request for free association, particularly (a) the request for more information, and (b) the question as to what the patient *thinks about* a dream, or an occurrence. One should strictly differentiate between these three approaches: quest for information, for opinion, and for free association. In the quest for more information the analyst asks the patient questions in order to clarify what he is saying, in order to bring out contradictions, in order to see, perhaps, where the patient is omitting something or distorting something. Such questions should be as precise, concrete, detailed, and clear as possible. Secondly, it is something else again if the analyst invites the patient to join him in rational thought about the meaning of certain things. To ask him, "What do you think this could mean?" "What is your idea about this or that behavior, or this or that incident?" This also is not free association. It does not make any difference whether it is phrased in the form of a question, or whether it is phrased in the form of a hypothesis. If I invite the patient to join me in reasonable thought about an object matter, then this is thinking, and not free association. And thirdly, there is free association in the sense of spontaneous association. We should indeed separate the latter from the former two, and be aware when we use free association as a tool, and when we do not use it.

What can the analyst do to avoid the deterioration of free association?

First of all, I believe he must convince himself that it is not enough to explain to the patient the basic rule of analysis, not even to begin each session by using the ritualistic formula and saying to the patient: "Tell me what comes to mind." Rather than doing this, I find it helpful to stimulate free association at various times during the session by asking the patient in a definite way: "Tell me what is in your mind *right now*." The difference sounds small, yet it is considerable. What matters is the *now*, the urgency of the request. Usually the patient will answer this request more spontaneously than the general question, "What comes to mind?" When he has said what is in his mind, one can go on requesting further association with the ideas expressed. In the tone of voice, the definiteness, the suddenness in which the question is asked, lies a factor similar to Freud's original touching of the forehead.

There are other active methods to stimulate free association. Let us assume you have analyzed the patient's relationship to his father, but want more unconscious material than he has offered in his associations; you tell the patient: "Now, concentrate on the picture of your father, and tell me what is the first thing that comes to your mind." I might draw your attention to the fact that there is a certain difference between asking the patient, "What comes to your mind about your father?" and the second way of telling him: "Now, concentrate, focus on your father." Or, "Visualize your father now, and tell me what is on your mind." There seems to be only a slight difference in wording. However, there is a very great difference in the effect.

Another way of stimulating free association lies in giving the patient the picture of a certain situation, then asking what comes to his mind. For instance, you tell the patient: "Assume tomorrow morning your telephone rings and the person calling tells you I have died. What comes to mind?" Well, you will find that there are very interesting free associations which come up.

There is one technique which the late Augusta Slesinger developed, which goes just a little further along these lines. She used what you might call concentration techniques to further increase the possibility of free association. She would tell a patient: "Now close your eyes. Try to think of nothing. Try to make your mind completely blank. Try to do this by imagining a white movie screen with no pictures on it. After a few minutes, I shall give you a sign. Let us say, I shall say 'now.' Keep your eyes closed, but tell me what goes through your mind at this very moment." The advantage of this technique is that by this short period of concentration the patient's conventional thought process is by-passed, as it were, and usually the associations come from a deeper level of the unconscious. You can use this concentration technique in various ways. One experiment, for instance, also suggested by Mrs. Slesinger, is to give the patient the instruction: "Try after this period of concentration to form the experience 'I,' and then to say what comes up in your mind at the very moment when you try to feel 'I,' 'I, myself.' " Now if you do it (you can also do it yourself when alone), you find all sorts of interesting things. You discover how terribly difficult it is for most people to have a clear experience "I." At this very moment, when they try to feel "I," other thoughts come to their minds which, however, usually are indicative of that which is a substitute of their sense of self. Let me give you an example of free association with this kind of technique. One is of a man who was a very good teacher and a very good speaker; when he was supposed to say what came up in his mind, he saw himself in a beautifully cut suit, standing on the platform and lecturing, with everybody looking at him. This is his concept of "I,"; he experiences himself as himself inasmuch as he is this good-looking, elegantly dressed lecturer. Another patient saw himself as a prisoner of war, completely alone and abandoned by everybody, crying for help. And in the next picture he saw himself leading a regiment into battle on a white charger. Now actually, this was a patient whose whole personality was split between a person who, in his social relations or in his love relations, was a helpless person feeling lonely and powerless; in his professional relations as a surgeon, he was sure of his authority, fearless and competent with an element of grandiosity.

You can use this concentration technique for other purposes too. You can say, for instance, after the concentration, "What comes to your mind about me, the analyst?" or your father, your mother, or any other person.

Or you can use it by asking the question, "What comes to mind when you think of the thing you like least in yourself, or are ashamed of, or are most proud of?" The use of it is varied; the principle is simply to reinforce the purpose of free association by this concentration technique. These are just a few examples by way of emphasizing that free association must not become a ritual. It must be something which is pursued intentionally, with a certain suggestive and stimulating attitude by the analyst. While it is one of the most important tools in the understanding of the dissoci-ated personality, it is at the same time a tool which must not be taken for granted.

I should like to raise another question which is also related to free association. Namely, the question that there is not only the problem of free association for the patient, but there is also the problem of free association for the analyst. Should the analyst free associate too? In order to understand a patient, you must make the fullest use of your own imagination. Your own imagination must be mobilized to the highest extent. We all are crazy, we all are neurotic, we all are children, and the difference between us is only of degree. But unless we can mobilize in ourselves the very same irrational fantasy which exists in patients, we certainly cannot understand them. And we must have the courage to do it. If we, as analysts, consider ourselves to be the "normal" person, *here,* and the patient the "irrational" person, *there,* then we shall never under-stand the patient. Then communication is indeed a fraud; then nothing goes on between two persons except words and chatter.

To understand means to respond, to answer, to be in touch. To inter-pret means to react with one's own imagination and free associations to the patient's utterances. It does not mean to apply the patient's associa-tions to the theory. The analyst's function is to a large extent not think-ing, but free associating, and often helping the patient in his free associations by presenting him with his (the analyst's) own. All this means that the analyst is, as Sullivan put it, a "participant observer," not a blank mirror, a detached observer. The process of analysis may well be described in this way. Two people communicate. The one says whatever goes through his mind. The other listens, and says what reactions (asso-ciations) the patient's utterances have produced in him. His, the analyst's, ideas are not said with the claim that they are right, but only because they indicate how one person's imagination reacts to the patient's imagina-tion. The only claim the analyst can make is that he has been concentrat-ing on what the patient was saying, and that his imagination is trained by experience and appropriate theoretical thoughts. The patient then reacts with new associations to the analyst's, who in turn reacts again, and so on, until some clarification and change is reached. (It must not be under-stood that I mean there is continuous dialogue; in my concept of analysis the patient does, quantitatively speaking, most of the talking, but what matters is that the analyst's "interpretations," when they are given, are essentially his free associations.)

To sum up: The analytic relationship is a unique reality of communication, based on mutual freedom and spontaneity. Free association is one of the most important tools. However, it must be cultivated, furthered, and stimulated, and prevented from deteriorating into a sterile ritual.

9

THE INTER-PERSONAL AND THE INTRA-PERSONAL

HARRY BONE

[1959]

INTRODUCTION

Benjamin Wolstein

Even though I did not know Harry Bone's therapeutic approach through direct experience, nor learn about it from him in supervision or seminar, I welcome this occasion to comment on his paper, an early effort to probe the interpersonal underground and uncover intrapersonal psychic resources, in order to extend the scope of therapeutic inquiry. The post-Sullivanian direction of Bone's paper, an early statement of diversity at the White Institute, makes it a fitting addition to this gathering of papers by the first generation of pioneers in American interpersonal relations. Bone's paper became part of the clinical and conceptual backdrop against which he and others, such as Fromm, Fromm-Reichmann, Mullahy, J. Rioch, and Thompson, were stretching the interpersonal perspective beyond the uniquely constructed, and constricted, operational frame that Sullivan built to define the experiential field of therapy.

There is a number of things Bone and I would have to discuss: for example, his unqualified appeal to the principle of determinism; or his weak reference to the unconscious therapeutic present—"the here and now"—a therapist and patient coparticipate; or the absence of the psychic center of the self that he might term both intrapersonal and interpersonal; and finally, while I sense what he means by "the auto-therapeutic force of the individual," I will not use the notion of "force" in the psychic domain until its assertability is

Benjamin Wolstein, Ph.D. is a Training and Supervising Analyst, William Alanson White Institute; and Clinical Professor of Psychology, New York University, Postdoctoral Program in Psychotherapy and Psychoanalysis.

duly warranted by laboratory experiment and/or clarified in direct clinical experience. I have no serious reservation about his "auto-therapeutic" emphasis—it calls to mind Anna O's autohypnotic procedure carried out under Breuer's theory of hypnoid states that launched the new psychoanalytic therapy of unconscious psychic experience.

When compared with the strength of Bone's pointed enlargement of the scope of interpersonal relations beyond Sullivan's exclusionary operational statement, my differences with Bone pale into relative insignificance. There is probably general agreement all around, today, with the heart of his argument: "Therapeutic creativity, like all respectful creativity in relation to persons, is not directed toward changing the person. That would make an object of a subject". Worth noting here is the notion of "person" itself (Latin: *persona*), which, taken literally, denotes the mask a therapist and patient put on their subjective psychic interaction. The mask of their psyches is interpersonal: both come to know their intermask, so to speak, by, as Sullivan believed, consensual validation, without ever gaining access to its subinterpersonal origins within them both.

On reading Bone, one quickly encounters the egregious difficulty of hard-edged interpersonal relations: there is no way to get through the outer interpersonal edge and into the intrapersonal resources. Yet therapist and patient both bring such inner psychic resources to their therapeutic field, each from a dynamic, uniquely configured, interpersonal underground. Because therapist and patient are uniquely individual, so is the experiential field of therapy they cocreate. This factor of psychic uniqueness continues, without letup, to disturb the closed clarity of Sullivan's approach. His form of operationism did not allow for the clinical room needed to address both the interpersonal self and its dynamic center in one and the same field of therapy. Here again, the experience of psychic life is, in the analysis, always stronger than the narrative of its metapsychic interpretation. Shared interpersonal relations, however constructed, no more sustain themselves without unique psychic origins than do unique psychic origins, however experienced, without shared interpersonal relations. And that is the centripetal point of Bone's effort: to supplement interpersonal with intrapersonal relations. Otherwise, if Sullivan thought unique individuality without interpersonal relations was an illusion, what, from the other side, would become of interpersonal relations without unique individuality? Would they be delusions which are a series of social and cultural patterns arbitrarily dissociated from their roots in psychic reality? That is to ask, more generally, whether the human psyche, both in its unique and in its shared features, depends for its existence on Sullivan's, or anyone else's, interpretive construction. Or are other constructions logically possible, and infinitely so? About perspectives in psychoanalytic metapsychology, it comes down to the old line: "Are you going to believe what I say you see, or are you going to believe your own eyes?"

In Crowley's reading of him,[1] Sullivan accepted the existence of unique individuality itself, arguing only that it is beyond inquiry within the frame of

---

[1]Readers who are interested in a detailed response to Bone, built around direct citations from Sullivan's writings, I refer to Crowley (1975). Bone unfortunately, could no longer respond in turn. In my reading of the exchange, Crowley did not successfully answer Bone, yet his restatement of Sullivan may enable some undecided readers to make up their own minds, and enable others already decided to reconsider the matter in a fresh light.

his interpersonal field operationally defined. That holds true in the context of his writings, of course, but certain unavoidable questions remain. If unique individuality really transcends the limits of his clinical knowledge, how could Sullivan know it well enough to term it illusion? Yet, if it does exist, why did he work as though it does not, especially with those therapists and patients for whom the direct awareness of its existence makes a difference in the unfolding direction of their interpersonal work?

It is when Bone moved the focus away from interpretive metapsychology and over to actual therapeutic inquiry that his theme becomes clearer. It becomes, in sum, more epistemological: whether to follow the empirical psychology of patient and therapist or to uphold the therapist's interpretive metapsychology against the patient's. Therapist and patient may, obviously, each exercise the freedom to choose between whatever is empirically observable and whatever fits interpretable expectations. It takes the two unique selves who seek the experience of this interpersonal therapy to make it, and they must each be pluralistic enough to hear the other's interpretive point of view.

To what extent, now, should therapist and patient coparticipate their unspun immediate experience, lived and worked through as it happens, explained as natural process and patterning, and interpreted from diverse perspectives, and do all these things, as Bone sees it, "auto-therapeutically?" As widely and deeply, that means, as any two coparticipants are each willing and able to do.

———————————————

A s everyone who has been an analyst for a quarter of a century, I have acquired conceptions and ways of working that are more or less my own. I have borrowed freely, and freely modified what I have borrowed. Each listener may judge for himself whether I have borrowed the best ideas, and whether my modifications are creatively inventive or blindly autistic. In any case, I have coined few if any neologisms!

Most of the items in my frame of reference for psychotherapy will not get into the picture this evening. (Incidentally, the term "psychotherapy," or simple "therapy," will refer indiscriminately to "psychoanalysis," "intensive psychotherapy," "deep psychotherapy," "analysis of the total personality," and so forth.) What I shall discuss are several topics which I believe can be clarified by the combined use of the two concepts, the "inter-personal" and the "intra-personal".

Inter-personal refers to cause and effect relations between individuals. *Intra-personal* refers to cause and effect relations between parts of a single individual. For instance, "Bill hates John" is an inter-personal statement;

Contemporary Psychoanalysis, 11:46–65 [1975]. This paper was the Presidential address by Dr. Bone to the William Alanson White Psychoanalytic Society, May 26, 1959. It is published here with the gracious permission of Mrs. Harry Bone. This was the first in a series of presentations of unpublished presidential addresses with critical commentary.

"John hates himself" is an intra-personal statement. John's intra-personal self-hatred is, of course, a result of previous inter-personal relationships. But it may outlive the relationships which caused it by becoming part of the structure of John's personality, and hence the cause of further effects, both intra- and inter-personal. These two kinds of processes originate and develop concomitantly. Either may be causal (or partly causal) with respect to the other and, pari passu, either may be an effect (or part of an effect) of the other.

Let me say a few words about three contemporary issues in the history of ideas which I believe may be approached with this duality of concepts. The first of these is the conflict between the Lockean and the Leibnitzian modes of thought in psychological matters. (Incidentally, when I use the terms *psychology* and *psychological* I refer to the psychological aspect of psychiatry and of all other professions and disciplines that have a psychological aspect.) Gordon Allport has written,

> Virtually all modern psychological theories seem oriented toward one of two polar conceptions, which, at the risk of some historical oversimplification, I shall call the Lockean and the Leibnitzian traditions respectively. It is not the total philosophy of Locke or of Leibnitz that is here in question. Rather it is their views on one aspect of man's mind—its essentially passive nature (Locke) or its active nature (Leibnitz)—that I wish to contrast.

He goes on to show that most current theories are either one or the other—that in the last analysis they either interpret individuality in social terms, or social processes in terms of individual motives. It all boils down to the old debate of heredity versus environment, or nature versus nurture. It is past time for a restatement of the issue and many are attempting it. For instance, Cattell and his colleagues have conducted ingenious studies of the *ratio* of hereditary and environmental factors in various aspects of personality and behavior.

Now most therapists believe that the personality is profoundly determined, in its very structure, by social—that is, inter-personal—influences. Most of us, I think, also believe that the plasticity of the human organism is limited, and that the imposition upon it of patterns incongruent with its nature result in reactive formations—covert or overt—and that the resultant conflict in the personality is the source of stultification or criminality or neurosis or psychosis, as the case may be. Since both nature and nurture, in some ratio, are inherent in all psychological structures and functions it would seem that personality should be studied with concepts that do not prejudge the issue. One way of doing this would seem to lie in assuming that the two distinguishable processes,

social or inter-personal and individual or intra-personal, are, in principle, on an equal basis conceptually. This permits their inter-relations to
be studied. It also permits either to be focused upon, at a given time, as
long as the other is retained as *ground.* In this way the values of the
Lockean and the Leibnitzian perspectives may both be retained. *But,*
neither may be reduced to the other, or absorbed by the other, or
adequately described in the language of the other.

A second issue concerns the application of field theory to psychology.
It is generally recognized that the interaction that takes place among
entities may be thought of as a field of force. It seems to be equally
necessary to recognize that the interaction between *parts* of an organized
entity may also be thought of as a field of force. This gives us, at various
levels, the inter- and intra-atomic, the inter- and intra-organismic, and
the inter- and intra-group concepts. At the psychological level it gives us
the inter- and intra-personal.

This brings me to the last of the three contemporary issues in psychology which initiated the present study—the issue presented by Sullivan's
Inter-personal Theory of Psychiatry. It lies in his constricted way of
dealing with intra-personal events. For, of course, he *did* deal with them.
He called individual personality a myth, but this alleged myth emerges
from his writings with a full-bodied human realism that is rare in
technical treatises. In his vivid descriptions of individuals, however, he
confined himself as much as possible to inter-personal language. To him
the *self system* was a relatively enduring pattern of inter-personal relations—*not* a pattern of inter- and intra-personal relations. It is true that
he did not deny the existence of a "private" personality; he merely stated
that it is not open to observation and study, as are inter-personal events.
The fact is, it seems to me, that it is this "private" personality which
determines, and is revealed in, inter-personal relations. It is also, as Ernst
Schachtel has shown, the "private" personality of the observer which is
the source of his understanding of any other person.

I cannot go into the vicissitudes which the self-concept has undergone
in the past hundred years. I will merely remind you that it was largely
rejected during the rise of scientific psychology, and that it has been reaccepted, in a new form, in the psychological theories of Lewin, Goldstein, Angyal, Murphy, and many others. Most of the new concepts which
have replaced the historic religious and philosophical self concepts have
many characteristics in common. In them, generally, the self is not a
homunculus, it is not reified, it is dynamic rather than static, more of a
process than a structure, its boundaries are fluid and indefinite and
constantly changing, it extends beyond the confines of the physical
organism—in brief, it is conceptionalized in a manner that takes account
of both its separate uniqueness and its embeddedness in inter-personal

processes. Thus the death of the self-concept and its resurrection in a revised form were both good, in my opinion. Now Sullivan played up the social and played down the individual because he was applying a new way of thinking in a field which was dominated by unfruitful atomistic assumptions regarding personality. It is precisely because he was highly successful in his aim that we do not need to do the same thing today. Our task is, rather, to free ourselves from the early exploratory and polemical aspects of his work, and to extend its usefulness by continuing the development of its essential aspects. I believe that inter-personal theory will lose nothing and perhaps gain much by an explicit affirmation of the reality of the individual and his right to a concept of his own—such as, for instance, the *intra-personal.*

I will now describe several areas of personality study in terms of the two concepts. These areas are: the origin and development of personality; the structure of personality disorder; and psychotherapy, or the conditions of personality change. I will have to do this rather abstractly, with broad, swift strokes, in order to have time, finally, for clinical examples.

Lewin and others use the term *actualization* for the process by which personality originates and grows—the process by which the pure biology of the newly born infant is transformed into a psychological being. It is a good term because it refers equally and without prejudice to the two aspects of the process: *socialization,* on the one hand, and *maturation* or *individualization* on the other. The use of any one of these latter terms for the total process represents a Lockean or a Leibnitzian bias and distorts psychological thinking. The term socialization, however, is useful for referring to the inter-personal *aspect* of actualization, while individualization is useful for referring to the intra-personal *aspect.* Socialization may be thought of as the actualization of the culture in the biological raw material represented by the infant. This is a Lockean perspective. (More specifically, socialization is the actualization of the parent personalities in the child's personality.) Individualization, on the other hand, may be thought of as the actualization of an infant's biological individuality in a congenial psychological individuality through the collaboration of the social environment. This is a Leibnitzian perspective.

Thus *actualization* consists of *individualization* and *socialization.* The former is the intra-personal aspect of personality development; the latter is its inter-personal aspect. This simple terminology makes it possible to define personality structures and functions in terms of their most essential and most general characteristics. I will define and then briefly discuss several of these topics of personality study. If the gobbledegook of the technical definitions is not immediately clear, it may become so as they are discussed.

Actualization is the process by which a biological fetus gradually becomes a bio-social being, and eventually an adult personality.

Actualization is *hygienic* when its two aspects, individualization and
socialization, take place in free and open inter-relation with each other,
so that the resulting personality will be able to satisfy its individual and
social needs harmoniously.

Actualization is *pathogenic* when its two aspects, individualization and
socialization, take place in relative isolation from each other, so that the
resulting personality is structurally unable to satisfy its individual needs
without frustrating its social needs, or its social needs without frustrating
its individual needs.

Personality disorder is that condition of personality structure which is
characterized by incongruence between its intra-personal and interpersonal aspects, and incongruence within each of these two aspects.

The *aim* of personality *therapy* is congruence between the intra- and
interpersonal structures of the personality, and congruence within each
of these two structures. The *process* of personality *therapy* is a relationship
which is conducive to progressive congruence between its inter-personal
and its intra-personal aspects.

So much for the definitions. Let me elaborate on them a bit.

Hygienic actualization is congruence between the individualizing and
the socializing processes. Non-technically stated: healthy development
tends to occur when the child can be himself, and belong, at the same
time. Being himself individualizes him; belonging socializes him. Under
these circumstances, heredity and environment, the original intra- and
inter-personal components, tend to combine appropriately in a *joint*
determination of the personality structure. The eventual person will be
on good terms with himself and on good terms with others. He will be
uniquely individual, and intimately related, without structural conflicts
between his "inner" and "outer" selves. He will, as it were, speak the
common language, but with his individual accent. Thus his *individual
separateness* will not be isolation or loneliness, and his *social relatedness* will
not be either submission or domination. Actualization of this sort occurs
when being and belonging, individualization and socialization, take
place in free and open inter-action, so that they can mutually correct,
support, and supplement each other.

This principle, that the satisfactory development of the child depends
upon taking into account *both* the child's needs *and* social expectations in
his training, is either explicit or implicit in all the good counsel in all the
good books on infant care, child training, and how to live with your
teenager, by Ribble, Spock, Baruch, and the rest.

In contrast to the foregoing, pathogenic actualization is incongruence
between the individualizing and socializing processes. If, due to parental

attitudes, the child's individual needs come into sharp conflict with the satisfaction of his social needs, he is in a dilemma. Man is the animal that lost his instincts, and invented mores to take their place—mores, and parenthood to mediate the mores. Mere biological maturation does not provide inherent guidance for the structuring of vital functions into a human life style. For this, the individual needs intimate inter-play between his organic individuality and an already actualized Other. He needs an Other not only for physical care but in order to become a person: in order to achieve the uniquely human kind of awareness or consciousness; in order to select among, and organize, his polymorphous possibilities—in order that his autism may become autonomy and his impulsivity, spontaneity; in order that his subjectivity may be validated objectively—in brief, so that he can experience himself as both *separate* and *related* at the same time: a real person in a world of real persons.

Since the Other is indispensable, then, the child must comply—or appear to comply—with whatever requirements are imposed as the condition of acceptance. Of course, the child cannot abandon, totally, either his relations with the Other or his relations with himself. Consequently he solves his dilemmas by *compromises*. By trials, errors, and successes, the nascent personality finds, and consolidates as parts of his character structure, those compromises which maintain, as well as possible, his relations with the Other, while sacrificing as little as possible of his relations with himself. As with a tree which becomes crooked by growing around an over-hanging rock, so with a child who is dependent upon an exigent Other, the vital urge itself creates the disorder. In fact, only from the viewpoint of desirable human possibilities IS it disorder; in view of the inescapable situation it is the optimum of order, under the circumstances. It follows that the individual himself creates his "disorder"; thus it must be attributed to *him*. But he *had* to organize himself in the way he did, as the least possible evil; thus it is irrational to blame him as though he abused freedom of choice. He was not free to do otherwise even though he may believe he was. I will leave it to your clinical observations, and your autobiographies, to supply examples of the ways in which parental attitudes present the child with the alternatives of losing close relations with *himself,* or losing close relations with *them.*

I believe that all functional personality disorders originate in this dilemma. They consist of various kinds of compromise solutions of conflict between individual and social needs. The child cannot really give up either self or Other, so he partly gives up both in order partly to retain both. The partial loss of relations with himself consists of (intrapersonal) repressions and dissociations; the partial loss of relations with others consists of distrustful, insincere (inter-personal) patterns. He becomes a pseudo-self in pseudo-community with others. If it is true that personality disorders are crystallized solutions of the dilemma mentioned, it should be possible to define all psychopathological dynamisms and syndromes in terms of the two concepts. (The examples which follow are grossly oversimplified for brevity's sake.) For instance, a *compulsion* is an interference in the functioning of the accepted inter-personal self, due to autonomous activity by a rejected and repressed intra-personal self. *Inhibition* has the same definition. *Rationalization* is an attempt to satisfy disapproved intra-personal desires without losing inter-personal approval. *Projection* is experiencing relations between one's different sub-selves as relations between oneself and another individual, in other words, perceiving intra-personal processes as inter-personal processes. *Introjection* is perceiving inter-personal processes as intra-personal processes. And so forth. As for syndromes, the most clear-cut example of a compromise solution of conflict between individualization and socialization is *dual personality*. In these cases the organism solves the dilemma by developing *two* personalities: one being so actualized as to satisfy inter-personal needs; the other being so actualized as to satisfy intra-personal needs. More of this later.

I defined the process of therapy as a relationship which is conducive to progressive congruence between its inter- and intra-personal aspects. Nontechnically stated: When two persons increasingly express to each other what they subjectively think and feel, without destroying their relationship, it may be said that their inter- and intra-personal processes are progressively congruent—they are being themselves and being related at the same time. Under these circumstances personality reconstruction and growth tend to take place.

Since a person organizes himself unsatisfactorily in an unsatisfactory relationship, he may re-organize himself satisfactorily in a satisfactory relationship. Since the child got into conflict with himself because the original Other could not let him be himself and belong at the same time, he may get out of conflict with himself if the therapeutic Other *can* let him be himself and belong at the same time.

This does not mean that the therapist's task is to be the good parent that the person should have had at the beginning. It is too late for that. The person is not an unformed child but a malformed adult—or youth, or child, as the case may be. During his defective actualization his individual and his social motives both became exaggerated, distorted, and rigidified. It is this present person who must learn, through concrete experience, that he can be himself, in this relationship at least, while retaining the relationship intact. Only gradually, as he finds that every aspect of himself is acceptable to the therapist, can he become aware of all aspects of himself, and accept them. As he does this, the over-socialized and over-individualized complexes are re-differentiated and re-integrated, and constructive re-organization occurs.

A great number of procedures have been advocated by psychotherapists, and an even greater number have been practiced. Here is a partial list, in alphabetical order: admitting errors, admitting irrational reactions, advising, agreeing, being sarcastic, being silent, cajoling, combining dispersed items of data, complying, condemning, confronting, depriving, diagnosing, discussing, empathizing, encouraging, exhorting, guiding, hypnotizing, informing, interpreting, listening, loving, making anxious, mimicking, persuading, prohibiting, provoking, reassuring, receiving, reflecting, relating (one's own experiences), satiating (previously deprived maturational needs), suggesting, supporting, sympathizing, telling one's dreams, threatening, understanding, warning. Which of these (and others) are useful, and if so in what circumstances, cannot be discussed here. Suffice it to state that some of them are not inherently contradictory to essential acceptance of the person. And it is only acceptance, as I will further define it, that presently concerns us.

Acceptance by the therapist does not mean ethical *approval* of every aspect of the person. It means that nothing in the person can alienate the therapist's essential respect for him and acceptance of him. This attitude of the therapist is based on certain assumptions which I will try briefly to state. The person, because of his history, is exactly as he has to be. Also, there is nothing in him except human nature, actualized according to the circumstances of his development, in various satisfactory and unsatisfactory ways. To believe that any part of him should or could be different than it is, is to believe in the ghost of unconditioned free will, instead of in determinism. And to abandon determinism is to abandon the indispensable condition of freedom. Another assumption is this: Unless the person is accepted as he is, he cannot become what he may become. Thus the trans-moral or humanistically ethical attitude that can be taken toward a person who is in trouble with himself—or toward any other person, including oneself. What I have been saying is, I think, essentially identical with Erich Fromm's conception of "understanding what is beyond judgment."

In psychotherapeutic research—and psychotherapy is inherently a form of research—more than in any other kind of research, the attitude and activity of the researcher are highly determinative of the data that are created and that, consequently, he has the opportunity to observe. Only insofar as we therapists are able to release the auto-therapeutic force in the individual can we have convincing evidence of its existence and its potency.

Related to these views are certain assumptions regarding the distribution of therapeutic forces in psychotherapy. The primary therapeutic force is intra-personal—it resides in the person, whether he knows it or not. And, I might add, whether the therapist knows it or not. The life force in the individual which created the pathological personality in a pathogenic environment is the force which, though handicapped, will create a satisfactory personality in a satisfactory environment.

The secondary therapeutic force, secondary but also indispensable, is inter-personal—it resides in the relationship which the therapist provides for the person's renewed attempt at self-actualization. The person is the seed which has hopefully transported itself from a less to a more satisfactory environment. The therapist is the environment: soil, fertilizer, and so forth. If it seems derogatory to the dignity of our profession to liken it to fertilizer, let me remind you that to be fertilizer to a person is to be a person oneself, with all the rights, responsibilities, and opportunity for creativity that inheres in personhood. Therapeutic creativity, however, like all respectful creativity in relation to persons, is not directed toward changing the person. That would be to make an object of a subject—to make a person-to-object relationship of what should be a person-to-person relationship. Rather, the therapist's creativity is expressed in establishing the inter-personal environment which will give the person a better context in which to grow than those he had during his previous attempts.

Two reported instances of therapy bear on this matter of therapeutic forces. Frieda Fromm-Reichmann once said to a grateful patient who praised her skill as being like that of a virtuoso violinist, "But a violinist cannot play well without an excellent violin." Harry Stack Sullivan once said to a patient who expressed a warm feeling for him at the end of a clarifying hour, "Yes, when one corrects a major fiction in the presence of another person, one is apt to have warm feeling for that person." It may be that these responses were appropriate to the particular situations in which they occurred. But, in my opinion, both are misleading if taken as a general indication of the actual distribution of therapeutic forces in therapy. The former gives insufficient recognition to the conscious and unconscious contribution of the person to the therapeutic achievement; the latter gives insufficient recognition to the equally indispensable contribution of the therapist.

I will finish with some positive and negative clinical illustrations of the principles presented. Instances of therapy with multiple personalities offer one kind of opportunity for this.

Thigpen's case of Eve White, W. F. Prince's case of Doris Fischer, and Morton Prince's case of Christine Beauchamp are prime to my purpose because all were deeply studied and copiously reported. In each of them, as in most cases of multiple personality, there is a conforming self, *A*, and a non-conforming self, *B*. Eve *White* was conventionally good, dutiful, and self-abnegating; Eve *Black* was gay, pleasure-loving, bold, and irresponsible. *Doris* Fischer was sober and compliant and studied her lessons faithfully; *Margaret* Fischer was mischievous and rebellious and generally refused to do school work. *Christine* Beauchamp was prim, pious, fearful, studious, submissive, and morbidly conscientious; *Sally* Beauchamp was care-free, fun-loving, assertive, and adventuresome. The three conforming selves were obviously actualized to gain the acceptance of a rejecting parental authority and to maintain inter-personal relations with her— their histories document this over-whelmingly. Equally obviously, the three non-conforming selves were actualized in loyalty to the native self for the purpose of maintaining good intra-personal relations. In brief, the *A* personality is a means of belonging; the *B* personality is a means of being oneself. (Incidentally, the tremendous energy in the auto-therapeutic impulse is vividly manifested in these cases, for in all of them the *B* personality developed with very little inter-personal acceptance— very little objective validation.)

The materials for studying the case of Eve are: a scientific article, a sound-film of the three Eves in therapy, a book by the therapist, a generally accurate movie based on the book, and diagnostic tests, including Osgood's semantic differential, and electroencephalograms of each of the three Eves. (The technician who took the EEGs was a disbeliever in multiple personality beforehand but a believer afterwards.) Finally, there is the book by the present Evelyn herself, the fourth and final personality.

The story in outline is this. Eve was strictly raised by authoritarian parents. She suffered deprivation and several severe traumas the memory of which was dissociated until re-integrated years later by therapy. With a few exceptions, due to the breaking out of Eve Black (as was discovered in therapy) she was always a colorless "good" girl. In marriage she was a dutiful wife and a self-sacrificing mother. She entered therapy because of migraine and other ailments, and because she was mystified at her husband's accusing her of charging expensive party-girl clothes to him, and of trying to strangle her daughter. As was later found out, these acts were perpetrated by Eve Black. During the therapy Eve Black "came out," to the bewilderment of the therapist, who had to recognize her as an entirely different person from Eve White. She excoriated Eve White's "disgusting" self-abnegation, and her having married "that jerk," Ralph White. She was boldly palsy-walsy with the therapist and wanted him to go dancing with her. The therapist considered Eve White to be his patient, and was often exasperated at Eve Black's interference with his aim of curing Eve White. In time he acquired a certain sympathy for Eve Black, but continued his efforts to eliminate her. After many dramatic vicissitudes, including hospitalization, and several almost fatal incidents, *Jane,* a third personality, appeared. She seemed to the therapist to be superior to the two Eves and he now took *her* as his patient. In time he established Jane's exclusive possession of the organism by the extinction of both Eves. Having seen this much in the movie, I was dubious about Jane's stability. My theory requires acceptance of all aspects of a personality as the condition of authentic integration. It is true that neither Eve White nor Eve Black was a satisfactory personality. Nor would a merging of the two of them, were it possible, have resulted in a satisfactory person. As Gardner Murphy has said, the various selves of a multiple personality are not stereoscopic, they are not mutually supplementary, so that in combination they would constitute a balanced, adequate personality. I believe the reason for this is that the original social and organic needs which engendered, respectively, the inter- and the intra-personal selves of the personality, were actualized separately from the other. As a result, according to theoretical expectation, the first was oversocialized, in a distorted manner, and the second was over-individualized, in a distorted manner. The individual and the social sides of a personality must develop harmoniously in intimate interrelation with each other if either is to be satisfactory. Thus Eve White and Eve Black were not stereoscopic, *but* the two types of needs which, respectively, motivated the two separate directions of actualization *were* stereoscopic or mutually supplementary. That is merely to say that the individual and the social aspects of personality are supplementary. The theory is that with indiscriminate therapeutic acceptance each of the malformed and rigidified selves tends to change. It tends to soften up to "go into solution," as it were, and to be reduced sufficiently to its valid essence that the two sides, individual and social, can be re-individualized and re-socialized congruently, and so actualize a more satisfactory personality. Since, in Eve's therapy, the therapist rejected Eve White and Eve Black, and accepted Jane, I guessed that there was too little of Eve White's essence, and *much* too little of Eve Black's essence, in Jane. Also, that Jane had emerged prematurely, and would be incomplete and unstable.

Several years later a book appeared which was called, *The Final Face of Eve,* by Evelyn Lancaster, the "Final Face" herself. In it I learned that Jane, having re-married, became increasingly desperate but did not re-enter therapy, that she tried to kill herself and, in a psychological sense, did so, because she was extinguished, but the organism was saved from the poison Jane swallowed by the spontaneous emergence of Evelyn, who got rid of the poison. Three brief but eloquent items will indicate Evelyn's quality. Her little daughter said to her, "You love me *now,* Mommie." Her husband said, "My, it's good to come home to you." He also said, after making love with his formerly frigid wife, "Well, I'll be damned!"

It is ironical and most unfortunate when the intra-personal auto-therapeutic wisdom of the organism has to escape from the professed therapist in order not to be frustrated in the achievement of its aim—a healthy personality.

Now a brief glance at the two other cases, W. F. Prince hypnotized Doris Fisher and said to her "bad" self, "I am going to take away your power." The girl's pulse weakened and she turned blue. The voice of a previously unsuspected personality spoke out and said, "You must get her out of this. Walk her! Walk her!" Prince walked her and she was restored. The intra-personal therapeutic force, the wisdom of the organism, saved the patient from the therapist's mistaken therapy. Prince did not learn from this what might have been hoped. Progressively, by allowing more and more time in control of the body to Doris, and increasingly less to Margaret, he consolidated the "good" self and eliminated the "bad" one. The case report is voluminous and very complicated; dogmatic judgment about it is not called for. I believe, however, that the data presented by the therapist himself reveals that the outcome was restricted because not enough of the independent, self-affirming aspects of the Margaret self were permitted to be incorporated into it.

Finally, Morton Prince's famous case of Miss Beauchamp. The mother had been extremely rejecting toward the child. Christine reacted in the way that produces neurosis—she idealized her mother and blamed *herself* for being rejected. Sally, on the other hand, had, from early years, precisely the sort of realistic appraisal of the mother that therapy attempts to achieve. It is true that Sally was seriously incomplete as a person, but I do not believe she would have remained so if the therapist had supplied for her the validation that the mother had withheld. Instead, he took the masochistic Christine as his patient and systematically attempted to destroy the inconvenient other tenant of the same organism, the life-loving but irresponsible Sally. But let me go back. There were two splittings of Miss Beauchamp's personality. The first, which occurred very early and was not recognized before therapy, was between Christine and Sally. Call them A and B. Later, when A was a young woman, a disturbing incident split her into A-1 and A-2. It was A-2 who went for therapy. The therapist discovered A-1 (Christine) and B (Sally). He decided that the "real" Miss Beauchamp was A-1 plus A-2. He finally very cleverly synthesized them by hypnosis, and by driving Sally underground by deception, psychological coercion, and the use of ether. The new Miss Beauchamp was a great improvement over both A-1 and A-2, in mental health and in character. Unfortunately, stress would reduce her again to the three contradictory selves! I believe that the integration would have been superior and more stable if the therapist had permitted the inclusion of the self-affirming essence of Sally in it. Before her exclusion Sally had said some profound things to the therapist, such as this: "I know the difference between real people and the kind you make up. This one is made up. You forget the *willing* part." But he saw in her, not the wisdom of the intra-personal self, but "a subconscious state," and advised the reader not to take her seriously.

In the last of these three cases, the therapist gave little weight to "wisdom of the organism," in the second case somewhat more, in the first case, that of Eve, very much more. This indicates encouraging progress in therapy during the last fifty years, since Eve is a recent case while the other two occurred early in this century. But I believe, for the reasons given, that even in the case of Eve the intra-personal wisdom was neglected, to the detriment of the therapy.

Multiple personality can illuminate all functional personality disorders because the psychodynamics are essentially identical. Every personality is a multiple unity, or a more or less unified multiplicity. All personality conflict is conflict between contradictory selves, or parts of selves. This similarity between multiple personality and other disorders is a most intriguing subject but we cannot pursue it at present.

The therapists in the three cases I have reviewed tried to force change by accepting some parts of the total personality and rejecting others. We therapists generally are tempted to induce change by trying to eliminate, by rejection, what we consider undesirable in the person. When we yield to this temptation we either ruin or truncate the therapy. Or, if the person's intra-personal resources are strong, we merely increase "resistance." In other words, we provoke the autotherapeutic urge to desperate resurgence, as in the case of Margaret against W. F. Prince. In such instances a sort of "homeopathic cure" *may* result, the person may integrate himself by opposing us, but he must overcome us or, as in the case of Evelyn, escape from the therapist, in order to do it. The clinical excerpts which follow are taken from more ordinary therapeutic experience (where the conflicting aspects of the personality have not become completely mutually exclusive as is the case with multiple personalities). These excerpts illustrate the positive consequences of acceptance, and the negative consequences of rejection, by the therapist, of "rejectable" expressions of the person.

Virgil was in a dilemma over whether to marry a girl of a different religion. It seemed established that he loved his fiancée, that neither the churches nor their parents would interfere in the marriage, and so forth. The therapist said, "I don't see any problem in your marrying Dorothy." This reassurance didn't reassure. Virgil believed he was crazy to feel he had a problem since the authority saw no reason for his feeling. He didn't return, and his daily functioning was worse than before. He had a similar experience with another therapist and stayed away from therapists for six months. In a third try the new therapist said after hearing his story, "Your marrying Dorothy is a dilemma, obviously, though we don't see the reason why." Virgil was inexpressibly relieved, no longer felt hopeless, and made rapid progress in therapy.

Leonore, after two months of therapy, wondered if she was not told to free-associate because the therapist considered her too sick for "real" analysis. He pointed out to her that she had frequently had illuminating memories pop into her head while wrestling with some issue. Her face lighted up and she quoted the "bourgeois gentilhomme" in Molière, "I've been speaking prose all my life without knowing it!"

The urge for *self-determined* growth and change may be blocked by the most imperceptible *outside* pressure toward change. The most vivid illustration of this truth, to my knowledge, is an incident related by Frieda Fromm-Reichmann. After an extended period of therapy the person had manifested no progress whatever. The hospital staff decided on terminating the therapeutic effort. However, the therapist was granted her request to continue the interviews for purely research purposes. Thereafter there was some movement!

Vera was disgusted with herself because she did not either terminate or accept her marriage but only complained about it continually. "I ought to do one or the other," she said, "but I have no right to do neither and then complain about my situation." The therapist said, "Obviously you can neither leave nor comfortably remain. Since all you can do is complain why not do that—as much as you want to?" She did complain, and with less self-imposed restraint than ever before. The resulting complete picture of the destructiveness of the relationship, side by side with her inability to get out of it, shocked her into realizing that she was literally two selves. With this self-confrontation she forgot about the question, "To leave or not to leave," and concentrated on what manner of person she was, and why. When she finally integrated herself she returned to the practical problem with little difficulty.

At the beginning of the hour Jim did something that was unprecedented with him. He was silent for twenty minutes. The therapist was with him in spirit, willing to listen but quite relaxed and free from impatience. To his own complete surprise Jim suddenly began to sob. Almost immediately he knew what it was about. He had not been doing what he was "supposed" to do—*talk*—and yet he was fully accepted. He then realized in his belly, what he had long known in his head, that all his life he had been inconsolable because he had never been able to relate to his father while doing what he wanted to do.

Henry, in his second year of therapy, once became convinced, after a discussion, that a certain suspicion he had had of the therapist's motives was groundless. He blamed himself for doubting the therapist who had given many proofs of dependability. The therapist said, "Obviously some facet of your distrust had not been tested out."

Martha came to realize that her childhood preference for the mother of a friend, over her own mother, was not wicked but good judgment. Progressively, she realized that time and again during her life she had made sound judgments but could not fully believe in them because they were denied the necessary inter-personal confirmation. Her self-esteem increased enormously when she recognized that *all* her life she had been trying to find her way—*not* just from the time that she secured the therapist's help.

During analysis Harold recalled vividly the exact time and place when he had given up and run from life. He had consciously decided not to have feelings any more because it was too painful. Study of his life situation at the time revealed that for Harold to have had feelings, under the circumstances, would have been futile and intolerably frustrating. He ceased feeling that he was an incurable coward and utterly worthless.

Burt, at an emergency appointment, said he was crazy and wanted to be hospitalized. When in his apartment, though he *knew* he was alone, he could not escape the *feeling* that someone was there with hostile intentions toward him. He was compelled to search everywhere, despising himself the whole time. The therapist, remembering Burt's practices when alone, and his fear of their consequence, said, "I think your perception was essentially correct: There *was* an enemy in your apartment—as soon as you entered it." Burt's sense of the situation had been right, but he localized the intra-personal process in the inter-personal field.

Sam had been in analysis several months with an analyst who believed that he needed her guidance. He had always been scared stiff of girls and had a girlfriend at the time only because the girl initiated and carried the relationship. In spite of the handicap of the therapist's idea of what he needed from her, a grass-blade of self-confidence had sprouted in him. He toyed with the daring idea of approaching a girl and trying to have sex with her. When he timidly let the therapist in on this she said, "Why do you want to risk your relationship with Greta?" There were several years of appointments after that but no fundamental therapy. Later, with an analyst who confined himself to analyzing instead of being a sage, Sam achieved a basic change in himself. In the course of it he discovered that he could never do anything that was frowned on by his mother, or a mother figure.

During Hal's analysis, he came to see that his daughter's restrained responsiveness to him was due to his own detachment. He tried for some months, and in various ways, to establish closer relations with her. She seemed unaffected by his efforts and he got angry. He told his analyst, "I'm going to tell her that if she wants to have a father she's got to be a daughter." The therapist perked up from his customary taciturnity and said, "That would threaten her terribly." The so-called therapy continued several years longer but that was the end, with *that* analyst, of Hal "Black"—Hal "White," the half-artificial "good father" held the field alone.

During two years of analysis Nora's analyst had at various times pointed out to her how and why her idea of the unfair position of women was exaggerated and irrational. She made no real progress. After several weeks with another analyst, she said to him, "I feel that you're soil that I can grow in." She also said, "You don't get in my way." She finally got to the point of violently venting, without contradiction, every absurd detail of her fantastic delusion. This hour was a turning point. Later she realized that throughout the first analysis she had experienced the analyst in terms of an aunt—the most important person in her development. The slight tendency of the analyst to mold her was enough to prevent the uncovering of the parataxic illusion—for it was not completely an illusion! The aftermath was that after ten years of wedlock, marriage took place. Also, she had a child. Later she had a second child.

Donald had had seven years of analysis during which his success in the world had been phenomenal. But he was neither secure nor happy, and he and his therapist were in agreement that no basic change had occurred. During several months with another analyst Donald became able to talk rather freely. He was full of criticism of the former analyst, and of praise of the current one. Suddenly, in the full glow of this rosy atmosphere, he turned vicious. Everything the therapist did or did not do was harshly criticized. After two weeks this suddenly ceased and Donald said, "I feel I like you and I feel like crying." The therapist, for whom the strain had been considerable and who, at these last words of Donald, felt a catch in his throat, said, "So do I." Donald couldn't take that on, at the time, but later he came back to it. "Why did *you* feel weepy?" he asked. Then, fear overtaking him and being expressed in aggression, he added, "And it better be good!" The therapist said, "The fact is, I always feel that way when someone begins to get over his fear of liking and being liked." At a later date, after significant progress had been made, Donald once said to the therapist, "I think you're wonderful." Before the therapist could respond he went on, "I know what's in your mind—*transference*." The therapist asked whether he wanted to know what was actually in his mind, and being invited to speak by an affirmative nod, he said, "I was thinking how good it is that at last you can feel that way about somebody."

The clinical excerpts have illustrated a few of the innumerable ways in which the therapist may provide, by acceptance, or fail to provide, by nonacceptance, a context in which the person may fully belong while being fully himself. In these incidents the therapists were faced with the following frequent forms of self-expression: doubt about one's belief in the existence of a problem; desire for imposition of the "Basic Rule"; resistance to pressure for change; inaction and complaining; not talking; persistent distortion of the therapist's attitudes; unrecognized insight appearing as unqualified pathology; immoral intentions; aggressive intentions; complete expression of irrational convictions; hatred for the therapist; and love for the therapist.

I have tried to show that by means of the two concepts, the interpersonal and the intra-personal, one may transcend the Lockean-Leibnitzian dualism, and also extend the use of field theory in psychology. I have also tried to show that the value of inter-personal theory is not diminished, but enhanced, by being expanded so as to include explicit intra-personal theory.

10

THE PATIENT AIDS THE ANALYST: SOME CLINICAL AND THEORETICAL OBSERVATIONS

ERWIN SINGER

[1971]

INTRODUCTION

Arthur H. Feiner

Erwin Singer was a teacher of mine in graduate school. He was one of the more imaginative, clinically oriented faculty members. At that time, he was also a candidate in psychoanalytic training at the William Alanson White Institute. It showed. He provided a dynamic clinical perspective that was as scientific and stimulating as it was humanistic.

I first read this piece by Singer 24 years ago when it was published in a *Festschrift* for Eric Fromm. When I reread it for this volume I was pleasantly surprised to realize how completely I had absorbed its central thesis. My semantics and rhetoric may be different—I use words like influence, dismissiveness, impact, and mattering, but it is really the same. Erwin has it all in these pages. Moreover, this essay is powerfully interpersonal in that it takes two-person participation in psychoanalysis for granted and is written with that in mind. In fact, it has initiated a large body of literature from like-minded analysts. It was bold in 1971, and it was original. It still is.

Sometimes the queasy feeling analysts get when listening to patients' curiosity about them is a proxy experience of the patient's own feelings. These may have derived from feelings about the lack of boundaries within their invasive or intrusive families, or the dysphoric quality of their connectedness which made the patients feel that their feelings, desires, and needs were irrelevant, subject to continuous dismissal, or worse, disavowal.

Arthur H. Feiner, Ph.D. is a Training and Supervising Analyst and former Chairman of the Council of Fellows, William Alanson White Institute; and former Editor, *Contemporary Psychoanalysis*.

Still, patients' suggestions to their analysts may have nothing at all to do with the pathological aspects of their histories. They may be implying that in their families of origin one way of showing connectedness had (or should have had) to do with being useful, helpful, or generous.

Singer sees patients as desirous of helping their therapists when it is appropriate. His hypothesis is that there are among humans powerful strivings toward others that begin in the earliest years or even earliest months of life that have an essentially altruistic aim. Like Searles, he claims that patients may be ill because these so-called therapeutic strivings have been frustrated, perhaps never acknowledged. Consequently, they can become mixed with destructive components of hate, envy, and competitiveness.

In his paper, which follows, Singer starts with the traditional, Cartesianinfluenced view of the analytic setting. Whether it is based on the medical model or Old World authoritarianism is of no matter. What is pertinent is that the early—and to this day, still common in some circles—attitude toward the analytic situation is that the doctor's superior interpretive skills are actively applied to "a relatively passive patient" [read: inferior] and that this results in cure (p. 56).

Singer points out that this is a one-sided picture of the patient and the therapy. With this assumption, we get to see the patient's pathology with the likelihood that a picture of the patient's strengths, "his constructive reactions to life's realities" (p. 58) is lost.

Singer's goal is humanistic. While his association of transference with the patient's pathology seems dated, it does not detract from his aim to present "a naturalistic microcosm of the patient's life" (p. 58).

What initiated this paper was Singer's growing awareness that a painful situation in his family was having a negative influence in his practice. He shared his reality with his patients, but not before he wrestled with his possible motives. The response was rewarding, since in addition to the patients' genuine concern and eagerness to be helpful, they expressed their desires in their own particular styles.

One patient's manipulative and domineering efforts were seen as a negative expression of her capacity to take charge and be helpful; another's necessity for depriving others of genuine satisfactions seemed to be a perverse manifestation of a capacity to preserve and gather resources for moments of real need. Singer also discovered that the mutual experience itself in the analytic session became the springboard for further self-scrutiny on the part of the patient. So Singer came to the conclusion that much of his patients' distress in living was associated with a profound sense of uselessness. Patients believed that they had failed as human beings because their contributions were embodied in nonconstructive behavior, which were their responses to nonconstructive demands. Implied in this is the idea that, as Singer puts it, "anxiety does not emanate from . . . *fear* of disapproval, but in (one's) horrifying realization that (one) *is already* disapproved (or could be) since (one) is deemed unnecessary" (p. 65). Singer writes succinctly that since human beings cannot endure being irrelevant, they discover a pseudousefulness in neurotic or psychotic behavior.

In 1971, when this paper was written, the idea of sharing with patients the thoughts, feelings, even dreams of the analyst, was not new. But Singer gave it a new slant. It was not disclosure alone that Singer emphasized—it was the positive nature of the patient's response and its interactive value. This was a profound contribution to a burgeoning tradition in interpersonal clinical practice with a direct link to the philosophic, social, and psychoanalytic thinking of Erich Fromm. Singer alludes to his interest in the origins of psychopathology and recommends that we pay serious attention to the themes of a person's sense of uselessness, and how this fundamental issue is related to Fromm's idea that destructiveness is an alternative to failed constructive efforts.

He even goes farther in a comment about parent–child relations that may be empty and ritualistic in contrast to family situations that evoke the sharing of emotional experience: Singer suggests that when the family (and the society as well) fail to encourage an authentic expression of human potentialities such as caring, support, empathy, and tenderness, the growing individual indeed may feel useless and irrelevant. What he is saying to me is that tenderness, care, and relevance are not simply qualities of compassion. They also are standards of relatedness that we sometimes fail to observe. Singer states " . . . true permissiveness has been lacking when the child has not been permitted to experience the full range of human reactions and when he has been kept from making meaningful contributions to others" (p. 66).

Singer links all his suggestions and speculations to the analytic situation itself. In terms of Fromm's goal of ridding the analytic moment of sterile ritual, Singer indicates that psychoanalysis can be a situation in which the totality of one's inner life is heard and registered.

This paper is a classic, according to T. S. Eliot's use of the term. It is the work of a mature mind, a product of Singer's understanding of the history of psychoanalytic theory in which he appreciates its ordered, unconscious progress. He respects traditional ideas despite his originality, but moves clinical psychoanalysis toward a greater complexity and toward an increased awareness of the finer nuances of analytic interaction. Its fundamental points have been appropriated by many, since Singer makes clear the actuality of the interpersonal, analytic moment. This is not about interpersonal psychoanalysis, it is interpersonal psychoanalysis itself.

From their very beginnings most publications on psychoanalytic technique have stressed at least implicitly a dominant theme: that the analyst derives little personal satisfaction from his work other than the gratification the healer inevitably derives from the sense of a job well done and, of course, from the financial rewards attending his efforts. All other satisfactions arising in his working day have been suspect of countertransference tendencies rooted in the analyst's unresolved conflicts.

In: *In The Name of Life: Essays in Honor of Erich Fromm*, ed. B. Landis & E. S. Tauber. New York: Holt, Rhinehart & Winston, pp. 56–68.

Structuring the psychoanalytic relationship in these terms molded the process into a one-way street: the helping relationship was to be one in which the analyst aided the patient, in which he could not and should not expect any comparable aid from his client. As is well known, at least two important factors were responsible for the development of this posture: First, the basic medical model and the medical tradition under whose aegis psychoanalysis unfolded imply that the doctor's superior knowledge and skills actively applied to a relatively passive patient would bring about cure; and second, any genuine and realistic help which the patient might offer the therapist would involve the former's familiarity with the therapist's personality and with his difficulties and problems in living. Yet such knowledge, it was said, would interfere with the development and the purity of the desired transference and would therefore militate against the therapeutic process.

It is the purpose of this paper to explore the potential shortcomings of this austere stance without detracting from its merits; to outline and to illustrate with clinical material the potential therapeutic power of the analyst's revelation of his own life situation, thereby making it possible for the patient to be realistically helpful; and finally, as its main contribution, to support implications for a theory of personality development derived from these observations, implications at variance with those traditionally advanced in the psychoanalytic literature.

An analyst's willingness to be aided by his patient when it was he who was asked to be the helper may easily reflect conscious or unconscious exploitive efforts. Little could be more crippling to a presumably already badly damaged person than to be exploited. In addition, an analyst's making references to events or issues in his own life while inquiring about the patient's existence, or while reacting to the latter's utterances may well indicate self-indulgence and an attempt to ingratiate himself through flattery, since he is now treating the patient as a confidant. A host of other contratherapeutic attitudes potentially lurking behind the therapist's self-revealing comments will readily come to mind. Therefore the admonitions Freud and others offered to the analyst are well taken: to keep in mind that the central considerations in analytic therapy are the patient's emotional growth, his development of insight, his being helped to know himself, and to avoid most strenuously all extraneous material.

Without questioning these basic and admirable objectives of analytic psychotherapy, some (relatively few) authors have seriously questioned the belief that such goals are actually advanced by the analyst's maintaining strict anonymity. Among those who have expressed doubts are Jourard, Searles, and most prominently Tauber, and Tauber and Green in their book *Prelogical Experience.* The latter have cogently demonstrated how the analyst's discussion of his dreams and fleeting thoughts about his patient—clearly an expression of his willingness to reveal himself to his analysand—may, in the ensuing exchange, lead to an important under-standing of the patient-therapist relationship and the psychodynamics of both patient and therapist. By pointing to the potentially constructive, creative, and communicative use of countertransference phenomena, they make it clear that the analyst's insistence on anonymity may prove deleterious to the aims of the analytic process.

There is an additional dangerous shortcoming implicit in the analyst's anonymity and the following pages examine this danger. If the analyst maintains a one-way-street position and is simply the person who holds up the mirror in which Dorian Gray may see his image, then the analytic situation will not likely lend itself to the spontaneous sharing of the patient's authentically positive reactions and to the revelation of that which is most constructive in his makeup. A rather one-sided and cari-catured picture of the patient is likely to emerge. Certainly the anonymity of the analyst lends itself exquisitely to the development of all kinds of transference reactions. But, unbending anonymity, while furthering the denouement of hidden destructive and other primitive tendencies, does not promote and activate reality-oriented and constructive qualities. Of course, the patient may reveal his strengths in examining constructive reactions that occur outside the consultation room. But just as we are able to see the patient's pathology and its roots most pointedly in his trans-ference reactions to the analyst, it is reasonable to suggest that we are equally likely to best see his strengths—his constructive reactions to life's realities—in comparably immediate and intimate terms. Only then is the analytic situation a naturalistic microcosm of the patient's life. But such expressions of health would demand, as pointed out earlier, the patient's familiarity with at least some aspects of the analyst's life.

I will now sketch a very painful event in my life, the considerations which moved me to reveal this to my patients, and their reactions to my sharing my pain with them.

Some time ago my wife became seriously ill. Upon learning the tenta-tive diagnosis, knowing full well that I would be unwilling and unable to concentrate on my work, and in my eagerness to be at her side while further diagnostic procedures were in progress, I cancelled all appoint-ments till further notice. My patients, although they knew that I took frequent and at times suddenly announced vacations, sensed from my voice that this cancellation did not reflect a frivolous impulse and sponta-neously inquired, "What's up?" Too troubled to engage in lengthy conver-sations and hesitant about how much I wanted to say, I merely replied that I would explain when I saw them again.

I was of course preoccupied during this period. Yet I had to give the question of what to tell my patients upon my return some thought. My immediate inclination was to tell them candidly what had happened. After all, it seemed only fair that an analyst who investigated the reasons for his patient's breaking appointments be equally frank when he absented himself.

But then doubts about this course arose. Was it all that simple? Were my motives really as pure as they appeared to me? Was I perhaps looking for sympathy and a chance to talk about my pain when the patient's trials should be my legitimate concern? Was I trying to stop some of the more difficult among them from sniping at me—surely they would be less demanding if they knew the painful reality of my life? Was I trying to induce guilt or show some patients how trivial many of their complaints were by presenting to them real troubles? And would I not unduly to be burdening human beings already distressed enough? These and similar ruminations occupied my thoughts as the days passed.

Clearly one or more of such countertransference motives could lurk behind the impulse to reveal to the patients this development in my life. And now looking back I believe that these deliberations with myself were essential.

With some trepidation I decided to tell them the truth. But the uncertainty about my motivations, about the possibility of my exploiting the patients, made me, when I faced them, less sure of myself than I had hoped to be. It led me to the occasional expression of an embarrassing preamble: a statement to the effect that I regretted burdening the person with my problems. But in any case I informed all my patients about the reason for my absence.

Their responses seemed to me astonishing, and that I was astonished reflected poorly on me. Concern, genuine sympathy, eagerness to be helpful with problems likely to arise, and above all efforts to be supportive and comforting—these reactions from my patients were eye openers. As I listened, deeply moved and profoundly grateful, to the patients' efforts, it became apparent that each person expressed his desire to be helpful in his particular style, a manner which often, when occurring under different circumstances, had been identified as reflecting a pathological character orientation. I will give a few illustrations.

Mrs. N., a woman torn between her desires to be an effective domineering manager of other people's affairs (as was her socially successful mother) and her simultaneous longings for magical gratification of dependent needs for nurturance, immediately responded in terms of both facets. She eagerly informed me about the outstanding authorities on my wife's illness and intimated that she might be able to get us an entree to one of them, a man indeed quite prominent but, since he was semi-retired, difficult to reach. At the same time she insisted with great self-confidence that my wife was going to be "all right," that she knew this for a fact. Her eagerness to be comforting and encouraging, while at times expressed in childish fashion and at other times couched in unrealistic but seemingly authoritative pronouncements, was very moving.

Dr. S., a fiercely competitive physician—though he managed to obscure this tendency very well—was constantly suspicious and fearful of being exploited professionally and personally. Hearing my story immediately made him feel that he wanted to withdraw, with a sense of "Oh, my God, now I will have to take care of him, too!" Yet secretly he had always longed for the savior's role, to be the last of the just, to shoulder the burdens of the world, fearful only that he would be exploited by being denied the proper recognition. And therefore he always played the martyr. But it also became apparent that he was genuinely eager to press his considerable knowledge into the service of being helpful to me. Although he actually expressed resentment about feeling obligated to inquire about the details of the findings, he also persisted in asking about my wife's condition and encouraged me by keeping me abreast of little-known but promising research findings. By putting the many facets of the illness into proper perspective for me, he offered me genuine aid and comfort. Thus it was by no means surprising that one day, after once again ruminating about his resentment, he suddenly sat up and exclaimed: "For pity's sake, I really would like to help you and yet I always insist on feeling put upon, resentful, and suspicious. If I cannot learn here how to enjoy being helpful, what the hell am I here for?"

Mr. D. was a successful businessman in his early forties. Despite his accomplishments, his lifelong meekness and submissiveness knew no bounds, and were always accompanied by a preoccupation with finding shortcomings in others, with detecting the weak spots in precisely those whom he claimed to admire, in those whom he tended to approach in almost groveling deference. It frequently turned out that they were actually rather pathetic people, individuals whose pathos he had sensed, acquaintances whom he could flatter with his "adoration" of them, people who therefore could fall hard and easily from the heights of his esteem. In his transference reactions he had been on a constant lookout for my "hang-ups" and shortcomings and indeed he discovered quite a few of them. In any case, his approach to others, made up of a strange mixture of self-debasement and contempt, pointedly expressed itself in troublesome symptoms which caused him and those around him a good deal of grief.

One of his preferred ways of detecting the character flaws in his friends and associates was to "buy" them, to shower them with gifts and entertainment, only to look down on them if they fell for his bribes and accepted his largesse. Then, with a little deprecatory gesture of the hand, he would do away with them, feeling delighted about having found them

out as tarts of sorts, yet simultaneously feeling depressed by his conviction that he was cared for only because he had money.

Hearing about my wife's and my plight caused him deep consternation
and he cried silently for a while. Then his constructive and supportive
impulses came to the fore and characteristically expressed themselves in,
to him, familiar terms: he inquired about my financial situation, whether
I was going to be hard pressed by enormous medical expenses, and made
assurances of his readiness to lend me money. In spite of his frequent use
of affluence for manipulative purposes, this offer sounded genuine. I
thanked him with sincerity and explained that I could manage. When he
insisted, "Please don't forget if you should need it." I promised him that I
would certainly remember his offer and that I would not hesitate to call
on him if need should arise. He looked at me as if startled and once again
began to weep.

One final illustration: Dr. L., an embittered and tight-lipped young
scientist, had just gone through painful divorce proceedings. His marital
difficulties arose partly from his persistently detached manner. He had
always prized this detachment as the reflection of a calm and reasonable
disposition, of the importance he had placed on "objectivity," and of his
belief that keeping reserved, dignified, and unmindful of any turmoil
would help reason prevail. No matter what his wife did or did not do, "She
could not ruffle my cool"; and this, he thought, was all to his credit. It was
not apparent to him that his very equanimity had markedly cruel
overtones.

After I had told him what calamity had occasioned my absence, he
remained stiff and silent for quite a while. Then calmly and in contrast to
my depressed mood he inquired about the prognosis. When I told him
that the physicians were quite confident, he nodded his head in "objective" concurrence and told me about his familiarity with similar cases
and their "objectively" satisfactory outcomes. Strangely enough, his
seeming unconcern and calmness, though not congenial with my temperament, had a reassuring effect on me. It was only several sessions later
that he remarked with a good deal of sadness—and I believe this was the
first time I had seen him genuinely sad—how distressed he had been
during that session. It was not that he had pretended feeling calm, but that
he had also felt like hugging me and putting his arm around my shoulder.
This he could not do, he remarked with distress. Every fiber had fought
against it, and he regretted having remained once again outwardly
detached when inwardly he had been eager to be more involved.

I hope that these vignettes illustrate what I have learned: that the
capacity to rise to the occasion when compassion and helpfulness are
called for is part and parcel of the makeup of all human beings. Importantly, in no single instance did my disclosures have any ill effects; on the

contrary, the insights, memories, and heightened awareness which followed my self-exposure proved remarkable, and I have the deep conviction that my frankness accelerated the therapeutic process in several instances.

These observations confirm in a personal way the doubts others have expressed previously as to the validity of the position that the analyst's anonymity has universal therapeutic value. Strict psychoanalytic anonymity would have reduced my patients' opportunities to see their own strengths and certainly it would have limited my knowledge of their caring and compassionate capacities.

In addition, my observations lend support to one of Erich Fromm's hypotheses when he outlined the dialectic relationship between productive and nonproductive character facets. He suggests that in every personality we observe traits capable of being expressed in either positive or negative terms. For instance, he points out that the human trait which may express itself constructively in generosity perversely comes to the fore as wastefulness in the nonproductive marketing character. Similarly, he observes that the potentiality for man's following productively the directions of others can express itself in the nonproductive pathology of submission; or that the capacity to guide constructively can make itself felt pathologically in the tendencies to dominate. In the reactions of the people I have discussed we observe the positive manifestations of potentials and attitudes unfortunately usually expressed by them in nonproductive and pathological terms. Thus Mrs. N.'s manipulative and domineering efforts may be seen as a perverted expression of her capacity to take charge and to be helpful. Or Mr. D.'s penchant for depriving others of genuine satisfactions can be viewed as a perverse and pathological manifestation of his capacity to preserve and eventually muster his resources for moments of real need.

It is not the aim of this paper to definitively outline those of life's circumstances which make human beings "decide" to overcome life's difficulties through destructiveness rather than through constructiveness, to use Fromm's terminology. Suffice it to say—as will be seen—my disclosures and the patients' reactions to them became excellent points of departure for emotionally meaningful, instead of intellectually sterile inquiries into the origins of these decisions.

My patients' efforts to search themselves, much more seriously after my disclosures than ever before, brought to light certain themes which up to now had never emerged or had at best been mentioned only fleetingly.

Mrs. N., for instance, now genuinely attempted to grasp the truth of critical childhood experiences and of the affect associated with certain of her present-day reactions to them. She had grown up in an atmosphere dominated by a mother not only immensely resourceful and socially successful, but also vain and attractive. Her father had been equally towering in his professional, financial, and social successes, though he was severely depressed and withdrawn. With great pain Mrs. N. now began to reexperience instances of feeling totally unable to make any meaningful contributions to these all-knowing, all-successful, and seemingly "need-less" people. These feelings became particularly obvious in relation to her mother. On the other hand, she had somehow sensed the father's essential loneliness and on occasions she had caught his need for her, a tendency vigorously repressed, yet at moments betrayed by him to the girl. While his repressed needs contributed to her symptoms, they left her at least with some dim sense of being potentially useful. But in relation to mother all she could do was to sit in awe, and to hope secretly that some day she would be able to approach her mother's successes. Of course, any such success should never be attained openly, lest it represent in her eyes too much of a challenge to mother's superiority—a superiority that my patient was unwillingly substantiating through her own submissive behavior. Growth and maturity would therefore have to descend upon her magically, i.e., in ways for which she could not be held responsible, and her actual capabilities would have to be expressed in negative terms. Concern with the welfare of others was to be shown primarily through often abrasive manipulations, persistence through petulant power operations, and intimacy through pathetic helplessness.

Pointed recall of childhood events associated with the crystallization of this character orientation, together with penetrating examinations of her present behavior and affect, were now in evidence; there is little doubt in my mind that these developments and my frankness about my situation were causally related, that the admission of my pain made the vision of genuine usefulness a realistic possibility for her. In sincere bewilderment she remarked a few days after my return to work: "I feel so strange, as if it were really possible to be truly useful to you, not just being busy trying to accumulate points . . . "

Dr. S. also felt impelled by my report to search his life more thoughtfully than before. While eminently successful at a relatively early age, he often felt like a fraud, and indeed in certain ways he was just that. He frequently published manuscripts less in the hope of making a contribution than with the desire to show off and develop an impressive list of publication credits.

Several times he had discussed with some puzzlement little incidents in the hospital and his reactions to them. For instance, he was quite embarrassed when a patient praised his medical ability to others, or when he was thanked with profound gratitude for having restored health. He was honest enough not to ascribe this embarrassment to the modesty of the humanitarian physician for whom running his errands of mercy successfully is its own reward. But he did notice within himself a desire to experience the superiority "of the white man who willingly accepts his burden." Fortunately his search for such haughty exultation seemed embarrassing to him when faced with heartfelt gratitude.

My gratitude for his genuine helpfulness forced him into further self-examination. This in turn led him to pay more careful attention to daily events, his reactions to them, and memories they evoked. Thus he reported one day with great agitation that his father, feeling ill, had made an appointment to see a physician practicing the son's specialty. But he had not called the patient to inquire about the doctor—actually a prominent physician at the hospital where the patient worked—until he had made all the arrangements. The patient did feel deeply hurt about not having been consulted earlier, and about having been treated as if his training were of little consequence.

Reflection on this and similar incidents led to important insight. With shock he grasped his lifelong sense of having been incapable of making any authentic contributions to his family, that all he had ever been asked to do was to *appear* competent. The real substance of his knowledge and skills had never mattered. What was even more painful and saddening to him was his growing recognition that he had allied himself with this orientation, that he had grown up to cherish the grandstand play and had come to value form over substance. This realization became more poignant through his gradual recall of how, in quest for status within the family, he had forged silent alliances with one parent against the other. They had usually been expressed in the exchange of knowing looks and supercilious smiles. Because of this, demands for genuine relatedness now loomed as threats, as if they would interfere with old alliances and his concentration on form and style. Thus he resented them and met them with suspiciousness and self-pity about being exploited. What became obvious was that in the process he would also invite actual exploitation by others, making his self-righteous accusations and whining appear justified.

The point that I am clearly eager to make is this: much of the neurotic distress experienced by my patients seemed associated with their profound sense of personal uselessness and their sense of having failed as human beings because they knew that the only contributions they had made were embodied in nonconstructive reactions and behavior responding to equally nonconstructive demands. And so destructive interaction with others became a virtuous, alas pernicious, life-style governed by the motto: I will contribute by sham and by lack of authenticity—I will contribute by destructiveness. But, the genuineness of my distress and of my needs had disturbed the smooth operation of this style.

The sample presented is small. Nevertheless I believe that the findings point in a direction proposed occasionally during the past few years in the psychological and psychoanalytic literature. This direction suggests that those concerned with the origins of psychopathology and with efforts to rekindle emotional growth must give serious attention to the possibility that the most devastating of human experiences is the sense of uselessness. This meshes with Fromm's idea that destructiveness is an alternative in living when constructive strivings have been thwarted; with Binswanger's discussion of Ellen West's sacrifice; with Searles' view that the origins of schizophrenia can often be found in the child's pathetic effort to be useful to a pathetic parent; and with Feiner and Levenson's discussion of what they call the "compassionate sacrifice" observed by them in their young patients.

Implied is the thought that anxiety does not emanate from the *fear* of castration but from the terror of the recognition that one *is already* castrated; or that one need not look for the causes of anxiety in a man's *fear* of disapproval but in his horrifying realization that he *is already* disapproved of since he is deemed unnecessary. That is, the roots of anxiety and of emotional derangement can often be found in a person's sense of futility in living, as expressed in his feelings of isolation and uselessness culminating in his dread of loneliness. But since human beings cannot endure this nightmare of being irrelevant, they must find themselves a pseudo "usefulness" in neurotic or psychotic living.

This is not an effort to absolve the person from his real-enough guilt. For in accepting his role assignment of insignificance he becomes a collaborator with his "casting director," causing discomfort to himself and spreading it to the world around him. If this conception of neurotic and psychotic processes has merit, then the therapeutic experience must afford the patient an opportunity to grasp not only his failure to be useful but also his potential for achieving human worth and fulfillment in constructive contributions. Therefore the therapeutic encounter demands an attempt to help the patient see his difficulties in living, at least in part as the inevitable outcome of his attempt to deny justified feelings of personal insignificance.

The effort to deny this sense of personal insignificance may also be partly responsible for the enormous increase of pathology among middle- and upper-class youngsters. These strata have practiced child-rearing procedures that protect their offspring from the rough winds of emotional pain no matter how real the tragedies and the sadness around them were. The child-centered home becomes all too readily perverted into a home in which the child is shielded from psychological reality. Caring for the child became perverted into making too few significant human demands on him. Of course this assignment to the status of uselessness and inability to shoulder human burdens is easily obscured by procedures giving the impression that demands were really made. "Clean your room," "take out the garbage," "wash the dishes," "do your school work"—these are poor substitutes for "hold my hand," "dance with me in joy," or "dry my tears." The former are empty and ritualistic steps, the latter are genuine human calls and demands upon the emotional depths of others. The former are inauthentic and usually irrelevant demands because they do not offer an opportunity for giving of oneself in humanly supportive, caring, empathic, and compassionate terms. When the environment fails to make demands for the expression of these human potentialities, when in fact their very expression is precluded by sterile arrangements, then individuals cannot help but feel useless. In making these comments I am not joining the chorus of those who rail against permissiveness; on the contrary, I suggest that true permissiveness has been lacking when the child has not been permitted to experience the full range of human reactions and when he has been kept from making meaningful contributions to others. The permissiveness of Dewey and Spock was accepted by many in its form, while the substance of their thoughts has all too often been neglected.

This lack of authenticity in parent–child relations, the child's inadequate opportunities to express constructive relatedness, finds an analogue in the traditional analytic relationship. The great promise of psychoanalysis to provide a situation in which the totality of one's inner life can be heard is at least in part negated by stultifying arrangements that prevent the patient's directly experiencing and expressing his constructive tendencies. For here, too, no authentic demands are made on the person. And so, based on the experiences I have described, I believe that a marked reduction of the analyst's anonymity is essential to the therapeutic progress. This requires the analyst's willingness to share with his patient his own moods and feelings, not as a therapeutic "technique" but as a genuine expression of his concern. Fortunately this does not mean exclusively the sharing of catastrophic news. In the analyst's working day there inevitably arise innumerable "extra-therapeutic" reactions, be they fatigue or verve, joys or sorrows, excitement or irritation. To share these at least occasionally so that one's patient can be a helpful companion without intruding on the patient's life and without precluding his opportunities to express all his other reactions—this, I believe, is the road the therapist must travel.

I am aware of the possibility that my own concerns during this period in my life forced me to selectively attend to and interpret the data provided by my patients. And it is certainly conceivable that my own sense of helplessness in the face of grave illness and my eagerness to be useful by being reassuring to my wife were sensed by the people with whom I worked, causing them to respond to me in the manner I described. Worse, it is possible that I was eager to think that I was offered that for which I longed even though it was not really forthcoming.

However, I am inclined to dismiss these possibilities at this time. The patients' growth and their reflections on my and their experiences during this time support the formulations I have advanced. For some patients the events described here accelerated a process of growth well underway. But others were reached emotionally for the first time in therapy by my disclosures and willingness to accept their help. Overall some patients seemed more moved than others; to some my frankness and willingness to accept help were more meaningful than to others and consequently their therapeutic impact varied from individual to individual. I have some hunches about these individual variations. First, I told of my situation with varying degrees of comfort and I suspect that the therapeutic impact of my disclosures was less in those instances where I was most hesitant. Second, the younger the patient, and therefore the less likely to have been personally acquainted with realistic tragedies, the less likely was he to be able to empathize with me and, therefore, the less profound was his personal reaction to my situation. And finally, the longer and the more intensively we had worked together, the stronger was the positive therapeutic reaction evoked by my self-exposure.

These formulations are presented with caution. Only further investigations and reports from colleagues who had similar personal and analytical experiences will provide more definitive knowledge about the issues raised here. What I have tried to do is to point to a, to my mind, profitable direction of inquiry into the developmental aspects of a person's sense of uselessness and to the analytic issues that derive from it.

11

ATTACHMENT, DETACHMENT, AND PSYCHOANALYTIC THERAPY

DAVID E. SCHECTER

[1978]

INTRODUCTION

Philip M. Bromberg

In the solitude of our offices it is easy to hear nothing but the sound of our own theories and the acknowledgment of our personal identities. David Schecter had little of that at the core. He recognized and cherished the knowledge that personal identity is an ever-changing map of subjective reality—a uniquely evolving interplay between one's history of human relationships and the circumstances of one's stage of life. He knew that as a goal in itself, validation of personal identity is transient—a protective shield that weakens the bonds of human attachment and robs life of its inherent meaning. In that awareness and his commitment to it lay the fountainhead of his clinical artistry, his innovative contributions to analytic theory, and his interpersonal approach to infant and child development. In all of these enterprises his work was fueled by compassion and generosity, not by dogma or the echo of his own words. It was David Schecter's abiding concern with what went on between people that is the most clearly defined theme in his work. He was one of the first interpersonal psychoanalysts to study in depth the details of what takes place in mother–infant interaction and its impact on the future development of the capacity to relate to others. His sensitive portrayal of the interpersonal field and its patterning of self/other mental representation during this era of life (Schecter, 1974), stands as a major

Philip M. Bromberg, Ph.D. is a Fellow, Training and Supervising Analyst, William Alanson White Institute; and Clinical Professor of Psychology, New York University, Postdoctoral Program in Psychotherapy and Psychoanalysis.

addition to the psychoanalytic literature on the vicissitudes of human attachment and its centrality in therapeutic growth.

David Schecter's life began in Montreal, Canada in 1926 and ended in New
York City in 1980. He was 53 years old when he died, and with his passing
psychoanalysis prematurely lost one of its most searching minds and healing
clinicans. He was not an easy man to know, much less to memorialize. It should
be no surprise that what was the greatest challenge for him to change in himself
was also the source of his greatest contribution to others as a clinician and
writer—his recognition of the hidden selves in each of us for whom the pain of
being found is sometimes greater than the pain of remaining undiscovered. To
the extent that David Schecter allowed himself to be known, I loved the man I
knew—as a supervisor, a friend, and a colleague; in all of these roles he
enriched, enlivened, and emboldened me in my life.

The sample of David Schecter's work chosen for this memorial volume
(Schecter, 1978a) is a paper published two years before his death. As a piece of
writing it is a splendid choice for two reasons: first, because it represents a
convergence of several lines of thinking which he hadn't yet brought together
as richly in a single context; and second, because it reveals much about the man
himself. Schecter was a master clinician in the tradition of Winnicott, Sullivan,
Fromm-Reichmann, Balint, and Bion—analysts who had a special love and feel
for working with less accessible levels of experience, and who devoted the
largest part of their professional lives to this challenge and to writing about it.
The study of character detachment became a subject of particular interest to
Schecter during the last decade of his career, but it was his lifelong dedication
to the beauty and mystery of the human spirit's struggle to free itself from
bondage that led him there—a sensibility that is embodied, in depth, by the
present essay. This paper offers a relatively cohesive development of themes
that tended to be more unintegrated in his earlier work, but there are four
additional papers which should also be noted at this point: one on Sullivan's
concept of malevolent transformation (1978b) published concurrently with the
"detachment" paper; one on the developmental roots of anxiety (1980) published shortly before his death; and two posthumously published pieces, his
tribute to the contributions of Erich Fromm (1981), and his working notes on
the development of creativity (1983). All four are particularly pertinent to the
central thrust of the present paper and help to place it in an intellectual frame
of reference that was still evolving at the time of his death.

Schecter was, above all, experiential in his clinical work. One of his most
lyrical uses of metaphor is to be found in the present paper as he addresses the
dialectic between the experiential and the hermeneutic dimensions of psychoanalytic relatedness. He here captures the imagery of directly sharing the
patient's experience without premature conceptualization of it, and writes
(Schecter, 1978a) that if the patient's dreams, fantasies, marginal thoughts, and
free associations as a body of experience "is not foreclosed by interpretation
and 'explanation' then 'interpretive pointing' may be used to enhance the
special sense of the therapeutic dyad looking together, as in *snorkling, in
subterranean waters*" (pp. 96–97). I can't emphasize too strongly how committed
he was to being in the experience with the patient, a sensibility that was greatly
influenced by Erich Fromm and by Eastern religion, but perhaps most of all by
his love affair with infant research.

Throughout his writing, Schecter was impressed with the paradox of personality change in psychoanalytic treatment as a microcosm of a greater paradox—that of being known but still remaining private—being in the world but still separate from it. How is it possible for psychoanalysis to work? Like the hummingbird, it shouldn't be able to fly; but it does. Schecter, I think, wrote most of his papers with this issue always percolating slightly beneath the surface, sometimes clearly visible, sometimes not, but always informing the dialectical quality of his thinking about the opposing forces colliding in analytic growth. How can a therapeutic link be constructed between seemingly irreconcilable needs of the human self: stability and growth; safety and spontaneity; privacy and commonality; continuity and change; self-interest and love? Trying to come to grips with how it is possible to relate to a human being in a way that will enable him to accept dismantling the protection of his hard-won character structure in order to achieve gains that may or may not be realized, is an underlying motif in all of Schecter's writing, and is perhaps brought to its most mature point in the present paper. His use of Schopenhauer's parable of the porcupines is but one illustration of his continued fascination with the "uncanny" fact that "in a good analytic relationship both patient and analyst find the right spot to occupy in the dimensions of closeness vs. distance" (Schecter, 1978a, p. 97). He believed that analytic treatment is not an effort to cure a person of what happened to him while growing up, but an effort to help him grow beyond what he had to do to his own mind in order to cope with it. The drastic means an individual finds to protect his sense of stability, self-continuity, and psychological integrity, compromises his later ability to grow and to be fully related to others. Thus, a person enters treatment dissatisfied with his life and wanting to change it, but as he inevitably discovers, he *is* his life, and to "change" feels, paradoxically, like being "cured" of who he is—the only self he knows. "Can I risk becoming attached to this stranger and losing myself?" "Is my analyst friend or foe, and can I be certain?" Ernest Becker (1964, p. 179) considered this paradox "the basic problem of personality change" and asked trenchantly: "How is one to relinquish his world unless he first gains a new one?" The broad answer to Becker's question is that the art of psycho-analysis lies in its success as an ongoing process of negotiation, and in the main body of Schecter's work (well exemplified by the present paper) he brilliantly establishes that the aesthetics of the relationship may well be its pivotal dimension.

In what is probably one of his most important contributions, Schecter (1973) introduced the developmental inevitability that he later (Schecter, 1980, 1983) conceptualized as "strangeness anxiety"—a relatively independent source of anxiety based on the infant's "fear of the strange" that precedes and is more broadly based than the phenomenon of so-called "8-month stranger anxiety." After vividly describing this experience in infancy and explicating its effect on normal and pathological personality development, Schecter, in a powerful *coup de maître,* linked it to Sullivan's description of anxiety induced in the infant by the anxiety of the mothering one through a "not yet defined interpersonal process to which I apply the term *empathy*" (Sullivan, 1953, p. 41). Schecter (1973, pp. 31–33) suggested that the "empathic linkage" may be mediated by the fact that "when the mother is anxious or distressed she appears as both familiar and strange to her infant," and he speculated that this seemingly unfathomable form of affect transmission described by Sullivan may be concretely "the shock of strangeness." The operative dynamism that Schecter suggested, is the internalization of the feeling of badness that the child ends up with through failure of responsiveness to what is most genuine in him. *Sullivan's "anxious mother" was a mother who to Schecter is behaving in a manner that communicates to the infant that he is not giving her pleasure, and she is thus responding to her infant in a way that is going to be "strange" to the infant.* "Strangeness," to Schecter, is a phenomenon that has an impact at various levels. It is primarily an interpersonal integration, not just the perception of a quality inherent in the object (like the position of the mother's body or the shape of her mouth) when she is anxious. The "strangeness" has to do with the mother's anxiety creating a perception in the infant that is disjunctive with the infant's experience of her when she is not anxious; a total configuration of visual, kinesthetic, auditory, and interactive cues that is incompatible with the infant's self-experience as a valued participant in a relationship that feels "good."

It might be reasonably said that in this concept, particularly captured in the following statement, Schecter (1973) was foreshadowing the contemporary rediscovery of the basic significance of trauma in the shaping and reshaping of human personality. Schecter wrote:

> In the proper dosage, state, and stage of development, the infant can assimilate, and indeed seeks out, *novel experience*. The *strange experience* goes beyond the novel in the sense that the organism cannot at first adequately assimilate or cope with the new or conflicting elements. One might say that the infant then suffers from a disorder of recognition . . . which makes it difficult for him to recognize his future [p. 32].

Schecter was in effect asserting that an infant's sense of "continuity of being" can be traumatically disrupted if the mothering one fails to help render the strange into that which is engagingly novel or even familiar—a particularly important formulation insofar as it accurately defines trauma not in terms of its specific content, form, or objective magnitude, but by the degree to which it cannot be held or contained by the individual without a flooding of unintegrable interpersonal experience. Schecter observed that in order to cope with oncoming psychological disorganization the infant "freezes" (one of the hallmarks of dissociative response to trauma), leading to what he called "dys-recognition" of "me-ness" and its sense of continuity. Trauma in these terms is thus caused by the *experienced* magnitude of inconsistency—"the shock of strangeness"—in an interpersonal field upon which security depends, and is relative to the developmental tolerance of the person to accommodate the "strangeness" at that point in time. Schecter (1973) said "One of the mother's principal functions is to mediate for and with her child the new and the strange objects, sounds, and people in the environment" (p. 32).

In this same context he discussed the vicissitudes of the relational bond between patient and analyst. Psychoanalytic therapy, Schecter (1973) said, "constitutes a radical rupturing of patterns of responsive interaction that have had their fundamental structuring way back in infancy," and because of this "the patient complains that the analyst is. . . . an unfathomable stranger whom he dare not trust. How we cope with this issue in therapy is another matter" (p. 27). He was here underlining the fact that inherent to the analytic situation is a genuine "rupture" of the patient's learned patterns of social reciprocity, and the analyst must include his awareness of this into his mode of relating. In his 1980 paper, "The Developmental Roots of Anxiety", he developed a highly persuasive argument for "strangeness anxiety" being a major dimension in the process of characterological change in psychoanalysis. He spoke to the relative difficulty experienced by any person trying to accommodate into old and familiar self/other representations, new and "different" experience that doesn't precisely "fit," and he stressed "the therapeutic work of overcoming anxiety as strange and potentially creative elements are integrated into the self, thereby altering its structural identity.[1] In his final paper, his posthumously published "Notes on the Development of Creativity" (Schecter, 1983), the therapeutic relevance of "strangeness anxiety" appeared in its most clinically developed statement, with an explication of the analyst's function of repetitive "working through" to make the unfamiliar familiar as the patient attempts to cling to his old identity to give himself a sense of continuity and constancy.

The point that most influenced Schecter in his study of attachment was that the experience of futility—the loss of trust in the possibility of a good relationship—is the affective state that most often leads to character detachment. In one of his earliest papers (Schecter, 1968) he wrote of the ways in which anxiety contributes to "the walling off from awareness of the need for the care and concern of another—a phenomenon of central clinical and social significance" (p. 72). Sometimes, Schecter asserted, the chronic affect of futility can predispose the infant to *active* mistrust during early childhood and lead not to detachment per se, but to the interpersonal pattern of malevolent transformation as an alternative outcome (Schecter, 1978b). He was here emphasizing the experience of futility as the quintessential affect leading to the subsequent defensive style—character detachment, schizoid nonrelatedness, or malevolent transformation, expanding upon Sullivan's (1953) formulation of active pushing away of the other as a primary response of learned malevolence, anticipatory to the rebuff of tenderness (p. 216). Schecter believed, with Sullivan, that what is of primary importance is the infant's (and the patient's) need to get a direct response to "who he is," and, if this fails, to be safe from hopelessly exposing his most tender and real self to invalidation. But for Schecter, an infant who is characteristically not enjoyed by his parents can grow up pushing the world away as a defense against the

---

[1]The issue of structural representation is an interesting one in Schecter's writing as an interpersonal analyst. A continuing theme can be found in his effort to demonstrate that the British object relational focus on internalized "structure" (the subjective data of experience) is compatible with the emphasis on "process" in Sullivan's formulations (the characterological patterning of relationships). In one of his earliest papers (Schecter, 1971) he challenged Crowley's (1971) idea that Sullivan's theory was one of process without structure, and asserted that "a case can be made for the idea that Sullivan's conceptions imply *psychic structuralization,* for example, his "relatively enduring patterns of experience . . . We are thus offered a conceptual dialectic that includes the points of view of both *structure* and *process*" (p. 72).

painful return of futility should he ever again let himself hope for a good relationship.

In the paper presented here, Schecter (1978a) defined detachment as "the turning away from human relationship" and stated that character detach-ment "functions to protect the organism and the psyche against painful affects associated with human attachment." He then went on to say that it "can be seen as a primary and rather awesome defense against the very process of human relateness itself," and thus, with many patients, a major dimension of the analytic process itself. A patient's ability to benefit fully from an analysis often depends on the gradual surrender of his need for detachment as a primary defense, leading to increased potential for both the pleasure and pain of attachment to the analyst and the development of a fully utilized analytic process. "The final therapeutic goal," Schecter wrote, "is to bring back from dissociation all the fractured, dissociated parts of the self which can then be restructured and integrated under one roof" (pp. 81–104).

But how? The success of the treatment is based on the possibility of relatedness between patient and analyst to whatever degree is necessary for those dissociated areas to be contacted. If the patient's primary problem is itself an issue of "frozen" capacity for relatedness, how does a relationship between patient and analyst come to exist that gets beyond the essential impairment? That is the essence of the paradox that Schecter's writing addresses. The patient's determination to protect his own feeling of selfhood from being trampled on through either rejection or nonresponsiveness as it happened in infancy or childhood, leads to the felt inevitability of a disas-trous choice between being one's self or being attached to the analyst. If a patient who enters treatment is stuck with having had to make a choice between attachment or detachment, he must be able to allow himself some degree of relatedness to the analyst for the work to progress. What does the analyst contribute that enables this process to take place?

Part of the answer can be found in Schecter's unyielding belief in human potential, a quality that I feel most characterized him—his conviction that most patients, even the most detached, have what he called the "*silent growth buds* for an intimate relation" (p. 95, italics added). A concept very much his own, it describes an analyst's ability to be attuned to something in the patient that, if present, is silent and as yet undeveloped, but can be felt by the analyst intuitively. To David Schecter, the essence of being an analyst was contained in having confidence in this nascent "something" in the patient that the analyst is able to hold as a reality while still fully recognizing and relating to the patient as he is now—a full responsiveness to the person as he presents himself, while retaining the vision of potential.

I have written a series of papers on the emergence of human related-ness and the nature of human attachment. "Relatedness" here refers to a

---

Interpersonal Psychoanalysis: New Directions, ed. E. G. Witenberg. New York: Basic Books, pp. 81–104.

relationship on the level of mental representation of self and other. "Attachment" refers to the broader ethologic term that includes pre- and postrepresentational stages. My basic premise has been that observations of normal ethologic and psychic developments can contribute to the deepening of psychoanalytic theory and therapy. The time is now ripe for the integration of several fields of study: ethology, ego development, interpersonal and object relations, and psychoanalysis. The attachment of the human infant to its mother—and the reverse (Klaus and Kennel, 1976)—can be observed from these five points of view.

Detachment is the turning away from human relationship. This paper will briefly summarize the process of attachment in humans and will delineate the defense system of "character detachment" and its relevance to psychoanalytic theory and practice. Detachment will be described on both the ethologic and psychologic levels. *Character detachment* is seen as a network of defenses and coping dynamisms that become relatively stable, structuralized and chronic in the personality. *The structural network of detachment functions to protect the organism and the psyche against painful affects associated with human attachment.* In this sense character detachment can be seen as a primary and rather awesome defense against the very process of human relatedness itself.

Detachment is neither simply "good" nor simply "bad." It can be relatively adaptive or maladaptive in relation to the individual's total psychosocial situation. Significant aspects of character detachment can be found in persons bearing every psychiatric diagnosis: in the hysteric, obsessive, depressive, in character disorders, as well as, more obviously, in the "schizoid personality" or the schizophrenic individual. Character detachment can be subjectively experienced as "never again"—as far as close human relationships are concerned. The defenses are related to persistent and usually unconscious anticipation or fear of the various forms of psychic pain. The detachment defense attempts, for example, to convert the fear of being abandoned (ego-passive fear) to an *active* movement away from relationship. The greater the depth of detachment, the greater will be the sense of futility, i.e., no hope for a "good relationship." Also, the earlier in development detachment occurs, the greater will be the potential pathologic consequences.

Detachment—as used in this paper—can be observed in any stage of development. This is in contrast to the narrower concept of "schizoid detachment" which connotes a severe and lasting detachment process between mother and child beginning in the stage of infancy. We observe detachment in varying degree when a child, adolescent, or adult suffers the loss of a beloved person. To some degree the process of mourning uses aspects of detachment as part of its repertoire. Diagnostically, it is therefore crucial to observe whether the detachment is of early origin, deep and almost total (schizoid), or whether detachment is occurring in *selective areas* in a character disorder or neurotic personality. The prognosis and therapy are obviously quite different depending on the above diagnostic criteria.

Detachment as described here may at certain times be *part of healthy coping* with a difficult situation or a certain stage of development. For example, puberty-age children almost classically go "underground," and, in varying degree, may cut off their affective relationship to their parents while they intensify their bonds to their chums. Similarly, mid-life parents, whose children are on their way out into the nonfamily world, will effectively detach themselves from certain kinds of closeness to their sons and daughters. Older-age detachment may be quite adaptive, as in a kind of Oriental detachment from an anxious "over-attachment" to life itself.

In the last section of this paper we examine the psychoanalytic situation and technique appropriate for working with character detachment. The therapeutic goal, briefly stated, is to re-establish human attachment in those areas where relatedness has been "frozen" or cut off. With "re-relatedness" in these areas, dissociated aspects of the personality—including its strengths and talents—can be reintegrated, giving rise to a situation where "activity affects" can emerge over the prior defensive stance of "embeddedness affects" (Schachtel, 1959).

We must, however, be alert to periodic and perhaps necessary regression to intrapsychic fusion or symbiotic fantasies with internal objects to fill the extreme isolation of the very detached person. We must also learn to distinguish the ensuing "pseudo independence" and the "arrogant self-sufficiency" from healthy progression toward authentic autonomy and interdependency. *The final therapeutic goal is to bring back from dissociation all the fractured, dissociated parts of the self which can then be restructured and integrated under "one roof," i.e., under the roof of the total self and under control of the ego.*

Object-relations theory has helped make respectable the empathic, real relatedness of analyst to analysand (P. Bromberg, personal communication). The model of analyst as "interpretive mirror" has been replaced by the mode of participant-observation (Sullivan, 1953). Moreover, with the observation and studies of early infant-parent relationships, the analyst's empathic capacity has broadened and deepened to include preverbal and nonverbal feeling states.

ATTACHMENT AND THE CONSTANCY OF RELATIONSHIP

On the *ethologic* level of observation, an *attachment* can be defined as a unique relationship between two people that is specific and endures through time (Klaus and Kennel, 1976), though not necessarily at the level of mental representation. Attachment behaviors include fondling, kiss-ing, cuddling, prolonged gazing—behaviors that serve both to maintain contact and exhibit affection toward a specific individual. Close attach-ment can persist during long separations of time and distance even though there may be at times no visible sign of its existence, indicating the infant's "memory bank" for good relationships.

On the *psychologic* level of observation, attachment is referred to here as *relatedness* which can be said to begin when the infant shows signs of *intrapsychic representation* of the bonding between infant and parent. The observational signs of this representation include the ego's anticipation of approach by mother (second month) and increasing specific prefer-ence for mother (or mother-surrogate) over less central persons in the infant's life (second to seventh month). From the parent's side, the optimal period for bonding and attachment is seen to occur *immediately after birth*. Moreover, Klaus and Kennel (1976) note that premature in-fants who have been separated from parents show a significantly higher incidence of child battering, due in part to a failure of infant bonding. Those premature infants who were handled from birth onward by their parents thrived better and were less battered—to a significant extent—than preemies who were separated from their parents while in the hospital. These important discoveries also indicate that the parents who watch the birth of their children and handle them from birth onward are more likely to develop a specific attachment to the infant.

The process of attachment (ethologic) and the state of relatedness (psychologic) are central features of the human condition. The infant, though active, is too helpless to survive on his own. Both parents and infants are equipped with biologic and culturally given modes of form-ing a lasting bond, a bond from which all other bonds are, in part, derived. This statement applies equally to the formation of self-identity. The particular stages of formation of this bond to the level of "object constancy" have been described in detail elsewhere (Schecter, 1973, 1974). Suffice it to repeat here that the process is not based primarily on need tension-reduction. Rather is the formation of the bond organized around an evolution of bipersonal interactions where tension rises and falls in rhythmic fashion. This evolution is true for mutual smiling, eye-to-eye "choreography" (Stern, 1971), and playful interaction, including peek-a-boo (Schecter, 1973). *These processes require an interpersonal model* quite different from, for example, the reduction of oral drive tension.

In 1968, as part of a paper (Schecter, 1973) delivered at the twenty-fifth anniversary symposium of the William Alanson White Institute, I put forth several hypotheses concerning human development that were based on direct observations in natural family settings. I will summarize these briefly.

1. Social stimulation and reciprocal interaction, often playful and not necessarily "drive"-connected or tension-reducing constitute a basis for the development of specific social attachments and relationships between the infant and others.

2. We see in early reciprocal stimulation and response the precursors to *all* human communication, including eventual courtship patterns (the "invitation to dance").

3. Without adequate social stimulation, as is found in institutional infants (Province and Lipton, 1952), deficits develop in emotional and social relationships, language, abstract thinking, and inner controls. These ego functions and structures constitute the building blocks of human development and are necessary precursors to moral development and social collaboration which, in turn, constitute the fabric of our society. *It is safe to predict that until "society" and its responsible institutions take care of the needs of its infants, children, and adults, it will suffer ongoing generational family and social disorganization.*[1]

STAGES OF DEVELOPMENT OF THE CAPACITY FOR CONSTANCY OF RELATEDNESS[2]

1. *Undifferentiated stage:* Experience is not located "inside" or "outside" a self. Mother and infant form a symbiotic unit. Experience only begins to be defined as "psychologic" at stage 2.

2. *Beginning differentiation:*

   a. *A dawning self and other (mother):* There is still enough fluidity of organization for the infant's experience to oscillate between more and less differentiated states. This period overlaps the symbiotic and early separation-individuation stages (Mahler, Pine, and Bergman, 1975). If the oscillation is too rapid or too extreme the child will be forced to use detachment defenses against the disorienting, anxiety-inducing affects of oscillation.

   b. *Experience becomes organized affectively and cognitively as "good" and "bad."* These experiences precede the more differentiated experience of good-me, good-mother, etc.

---

[1] A number of observers, including Bowlby (1973) and Heinicke and Westheimer (1965), have studied the longer-term effects of separation and have shown that affects such as hopelessness and a sense of futility follow upon prolonged separation, especially with poor substitute care. Bowlby (1973) also cites a number of studies in which a surprisingly high percentage of parents—from 27 to 50 per cent—*admit* to threats of abandonment as a way of controlling or punishing a child. If to this we add more subtle abandonment or withdrawal-type of parental behavior, we see that it *is likely that a majority of children in our society realistically experience the threat of abandonment.*

[2] A somewhat parallel scheme is presented by Kernberg (1976).

3. *Further differentiation into:* (a) good-me, (b) bad-me, (c) good-mother, (d) bad-mother, (e) good relationship, (f) bad relationships: These further differentiations occur during the phases of separation-individuation. These gestalten are referred to as *personifications* by Sullivan (1953) and as *mental representations* in classical psychoanalysis.

4. The above state of affairs (2b and 3) can be described as the *normal developmental base* for the later defense mechanism of *splitting,* e.g., "mostly-good" vs. "mostly-bad mother"; "good relation" vs. "bad relation."

5. During the second and third year of life, the splits ("good" and "bad" self and mother) become integrated in their unitary wholeness in varying degrees. Mother (good-or-bad) is then *"my mother."* Self (good-or-bad) is to a great extent *"my self."* Relationship (good-or-bad) is now *"me-and-(m)other."* No longer are there simply categories of good and bad experience; rather, various levels of complexity of affect and mental representations interweave with internal and external object-persons.

6. The child not only discriminates and values his mother selectively, but also begins to represent her mentally with *qualities of increasing permanence and objectivity.* Even in the face of cruelty or frustration, or during a limited absence, the mother continues to be preferred and central to the child's life. *This centrality constitutes the achievement of "constancy of relationship" which implies "object-person constancy" as well as a growing sense of continuity and sameness in the self ("self-constancy").*

The relationship is now represented mentally (intrapsychically), invested with intense affect, and develops growing stability over the years. We tend to think that there is a "critical"—or at least, "optimal"—period for such *constancy of relationship* to be defined and maintained with growing stability and an increasing number of persons (during the second and third years and onwards). Mental health is predicated on these developments which pertain to parent as well as child. *The warps and deficits in ego and interpersonal development derive in large part from a failure to achieve a level of constancy of relationship with one or more persons early in life.*

All of the above develops in the context of increasing separation-individuation, of growing ego autonomy, and of re-relatedness on a more allocentric (Schachtel, 1959) and decreasing egocentric basis (Piaget, 1954).

The work of individual development and of therapy consists of *integrating the polar splits* of good and bad mother into the felt concept "my mother." As Sullivan suggests, the learning of language and its word symbol "mother" facilitates, and in part coerces, the integration of the good and bad polarities of experience. *The further task of both development and therapy is to be able to endure and maintain the constancy* (continuity and sameness) of the relationship, of the self (self-identity), and of the object (object constancy) despite the prevalence of ambivalent affects toward mother. *Constancy of relatedness can be defined in part as the capacity to maintain the integrated relationship (internal) to the mother in the face of the conflicting affects such as love and hate.*[3] The love object will not be exchanged and is not interchangeable even under conditions of severe cruelty.

The development of constancy of relationship is only begun in infancy. It is still highly unstable in early childhood.[4] It is really a *lifelong developmental task* to retain and modify the above described constancy under the vicissitudes of separation-individuation and of ambivalent feelings. A fresh or sharp loss or disappointment threatens to test the stability of constancy, and, clinically, we then find the splitting of parent or spouse, and/or of self into "all good" and "all bad."[5] The same is true of "the relationship" which remains potentially split into good or bad. Fairbairn (1952) describes in great detail how a splitting of the object-person is related to the splitting of the ego into (a) the "internal saboteur" and (b) the "libidinal ego"—splits from (c) the "central ego." Though each of these is interdependent, they achieve some degree of autonomy and can have separate lines of development. In Sullivan's language, the "good" and "bad" parts of the self become split off, that is, dissociated from the unity of the whole personality. In analytic therapy of deeply detached persons, a spontaneous desire develops for the various compartments of the self to be under "one roof" whose subjective expression includes "my self" or "all me." Some patients have described wanting the self "inside" instead of somewhere "outside"—a condition in which character defenses had been "inside" and false self-defenses had been experienced as the "outside" or "social" self. At this point in analysis there is a sense of momentous change and often a sense of "new beginning" (Balint, 1953). In my own work I have found this "new beginning" phenomenon occurs when the good me and the loving superego begin to predominate over the bad me and the condemning superego.

The clinical relevance of the concept of constancy of relationship is enormous. To the extent this capacity has been developed in a stable way, there will be less tendency to splitting of the object-person or of the self into all good or all bad—tendencies seen in the borderline character and in paranoid and schizophrenic persons. Moreover, such constancy anchors and centers the self during its process of separation-individuation,

---

[3]Burgner and Edgecumbe (1972) arrive at a parallel concept, the *"capacity for constant relationships"* as it develops from the more primitive *need-satisfying relationship*.

[4]See Pine (1974) on the subject of stability and liability of object constancy.

[5]This would be considered "defensive splitting" in contrast to the normal polarization into "good" and "bad" experiences. See Freud's (1938) paper on splitting of the ego.

thereby leading to increased ego autonomy and to less tendency to regression to fusion states when under stress. Also, constancy of relation protects against a sense of total loss or abandonment (e.g., when this occurs in reality with the external object) since *the internal constant relationship, if strong enough, will help mourn the loss of the external object-person.*

DETACHMENT

Having described in a general way the process of human attachment, let us turn our attention to the process of detachment. Detachment in the *ethologic* sense refers to patterns of movement away from attachment. In the *psychic* sense, detachment connotes a defense against relationship *on the level of mental representation.* Detachment can be adaptive or maladaptive depending on the total psychic situation.

Detachment has been defined as a network of defenses whose function is to undermine or sever the process of attachment in order to avoid or reduce psychic pain that is attendant on a state of relatedness. It is an attempt to anesthetize psychic pain. Detachment implies a "never again" or an "I don't care" affect as far as one's relation to specifically loved persons.[6] It attempts to neutralize the anxieties that accompany relationships, e.g., the anxiety of separation, of abandonment, of the stranger, of loss of love, or of yearning but without hope.

Detachment in its broadest sense has a biological base in development. Sullivan (1953) describes the phenomenon of "somnolent detachment" in the infant when he is overly anxious or overstimulated, as in pain. The infant's biologic defenses include both falling asleep and visual aversion, literally a turning away from a source of anxiety, e.g., the angry mother. These biologic mechanisms are seen here as the *anlagen to the psychic defense of detachment.*

My own interest in defensive detachment derives from Bowlby's (1973) description of the young child's separation reactions. Bowlby used the term "detachment" to describe the third stage of a two-year-old's reaction upon physical separation from the mother due to the child's hospitalization. After the initial stages of stormy, *angry protest* followed by *despair* (sadness, regression, loss of interest in the environment), a third stage—*detachment*—was characterized by "improved spirit' albeit with an *active avoidance of mother or by a distinct "cooling"* of the strong specific attachment behavior usually shown at this age toward the mother. Other sequelae may appear as well, such as anxious clinging, sometimes mixed

---

[6]There is a lovely children's book (age five to seven) by Maurice Sendak (1962) about Pierre who "didn't care" until he was swallowed by a lion at which point he "cared."

with aggressive detachment, serious negativism and oppositionalism may become dominant in the character (Bowlby, 1973, p. 225).

The detached child was described as committing herself less and less to succeeding figures and becoming more self-centered and more preoccupied with need satisfaction, e.g., desiring sweets and material things. The parallel—phenomenologically and etiologically—between the direct observation (by camera) of Bowlby's detachment phase following actual separation and characterologic detachment in adults is quite striking. Here I am suggesting in effect that adult detachment is a homologue to child detachment. It has occurred to me that Bowlby's description of the detachment phase needs to be understood as a process that may be conceptualized on two levels: (1) the behavioral ethologic level (pre- and postrepresentational) and (2) as intrapsychic defense.

Bowlby (1973) has observed that detachment from a parent is more frequent in relation to mother than to father and that the duration of the child's detachment correlates highly and with the length of his separation. Upon reunion, mothers complained that they were treated as strangers for the first few days. The separated children were afraid to be left alone and were far more clinging than they had been before the separation. Bowlby believes that after very long or repeated separations, detachment can persist indefinitely. *It is this aspect of detachment that I have used in my concept of character detachment.* It is true both in Bowlby's children and in partially detached characters that detachment can alternate with intense symbiosislike clinging and/or intensely ambivalent attitudes including being rejecting, hostile, or defiant toward mother. There remains of course a lingering fear in the child—and later in the adult—that he will suffer new separations should he make any new attachments. Moreover, in the attempt to make new attachments, he brings his detachment defenses with him in a way that resists the attachment process itself.

I see the intrapsychic detachment defense becoming available to the child not only after real physical separations but, on another level, ensuing upon the realization of a great sense of psychic separateness during the separation-individuation processes in childhood and in later stages of development. Mahler, Pine, and Bergman (1975) describe a change of affect of a depressive tone that comes over the child (around 18 months) when he becomes more aware of the separateness of his experience from that of his mother. This dawning realization—during the second year of life—can be seen as the developmental anlage to the later phenomenon of existential aloneness.

It is in the process of detachment and normal separation-individuation that the internal capacity for constancy of relationship becomes most critical. The more stable the constancy and the deeper the structure of the loving superego, the less traumatic will be the separation anxiety and the ensuing detachment defense.[7] In a sense we can say that a firm, healthy constancy of relationship in some degree immunizes child and adult reactions to loss, separation, and abandonment. If a good relationship is internalized in my self, I will be able to endure separation and loss without the need for extreme "schizoidlike" detachment. I will also be helped to mourn aspects of the primary relationship that are being lost, such as omnipotence and symbiosis.

CHARACTER DETACHMENT AND SCHIZOID PERSONALITY

We may now inquire into the similarities and differences between *character detachment* and the *schizoid personality*. Both to some degree may have in common the following traits described by Guntrip (1968) as "schizoid": withdrawnness, introversion, self-sufficiency, narcissism, loss of affect, loneliness, depersonalization and/or derealization, regression, and a sense of superiority (often secret). My observations in psychoanalytic practice and supervision have made clear to me that when the analysis goes deeply enough, many patients who, in psychiatric diagnostic terms, present themselves as hysteric, obsessional, or depressive character disorders are suffering as well from characterologic detachment. Some schools of thought refer to this area of depth as the basic "schizoid position" (Fairbairn, 1952) or "schizoid state" (Guntrip, 1968), but the etiologic assumption of these two views is that the patient experiences his deep craving for love as destruction (Guntrip, 1968, pp 29–31, 102). This *can* be true, but it should be kept entirely open as to whether it is *the* primary etiologic factor. This ultimate "position" smacks too much of original sin, much as does the Kleinian assumption of a primal oral destructive force—derived from the death instinct—in the three-month-old infant. Whether these basic assumptions of what amount to "evil" impulses are ascribed to a three-month-old infant or to a mother, our theory is led away from scientific observation—including interactional cognitive-affective ego development—and back to adultomorphic-blame psychologies. By staying with the concept of "character detachment," we leave open for further study how and when the future patient gets into this awesome position of having to ward off meaningful human attachment.

It is of interest here that Sullivan's notion of "malevolent transformation" implies character detachment, and is an "open system" concept, since it does not make any assumptions about "ultimate evil." Rather, the

---

[7]Defenses cannot fully regulate the ego, but they can predominate in a way that does not allow the embattled ego to gain new input and energy from its interpersonal relations. With defenses predominating, the other ego functions are not available, e.g., for object relations (internal and external).

concept addresses itself to the operational defensive function of this transformation in which there is anticipation of rebuff of the need for tenderness. Like detachment, the malevolent transformation can be found in all kinds of psychiatric diagnoses, though the extreme paranoid may reveal this dynamism in "pure culture."

Unlike the concept "schizoid position" the detachment defenses can arise and be used at *any* stage of the life cycle, and affect the personality in highly varying degrees. Naturally the earlier and more severe the etiologic trauma and psychic pain, the more severe and deep the character detachment will be—and in this instance the more it will resemble the schizoid position with its massive and permanent dissociation of large parts of the personality from a very early stage of development. Put yet another way: to the extent that detachment is predominant in the character organization, the resulting structure may approach the appearance of the so-called schizoid character. The latter usually implies a lack of capacity for intimate relatedness. A varying degree of character detachment, on the other hand, is seen in persons who are quite capable of intimate relationships.

Detachment may be observed on a number of levels and uses varying combinations of defense mechanisms: (1) stoppage of "affect flow" interpersonally and intrapsychically (*repression*);[8] (2) *isolation* of affect from idea; (3) *denial* of attachment, i.e., a disavowal of an attachment; (4) *splitting* of the internal object-person and of the ego.

Under certain optimal conditions, including a trusting psycho-analytic situation, persons with character detachment are able to develop a richness of affective responsiveness, a capacity for affective flow inter- and intropersonally, and the capacity for constancy of relatedness, including self- and object constancy. The schizoid character, in contrast, is in part defined by his severe limitation in or lack of capacity for full "relationship constancy" (Horner, 1975). Characters with strong detachment defenses may use these defenses to "shut down" relatedness or to renunciate object relations. However, their potential for and history of relatively full relatedness can be established diagnostically—in contrast to what is usually implied by the term "schizoid character."

Character detachment may be structurally discernible in certain "pockets of resistance" to relatedness. With analysis "re-relatedness" can be established in those areas associated with danger or threat. The rest of the personality may be fairly healthy and available for the analytic process and relationship. The "schizoid hollowness" is not necessarily present in someone who, nevertheless, has significant detachment defenses.

---

[8]When detachment is prominent, the affects may still be discovered as flowing between split-off dissociated parts of the self and internal object-persons, e.g., internal persecution of the "bad me" by the "internal saboteur" or "condemning superego."

Behind these defenses one often finds a strong desire to come out of the frozen-off areas of detachment (the need-fear dilemma). For the schizoid character, the experience of *affects-in-relationship* is associated with extreme psychic pain and is often ego-alien. Severe schizoid character, almost by definition, implies such a global threat to any kind of intimate relatedness that the prognosis is guarded as far as the therapeutic possibility for ego reorganization and positive growth of structures to the extent they are inherently lacking (ego deficits). For example, the structure of *relationship constancy* would have literally to be "grown" (by internalizations) in long, intensive, trusting psychoanalytic therapy.

I have seen a considerable number of persons who have lost a parent in childhood or adolescence. Many of these have defended against the painful affect of personal object loss via *partial detachment that may on the surface mimic schizoid withdrawal*. There is a danger that the presenting picture will mistakenly be diagnosed as schizoid. This would constitute a serious misdiagnosis since the prognostic course and treatment of choice would lead to a plan of treatment ill-suited to one whose detachment is in part an *unsuccessful attempt at mourning*.[9] Children and adolescents who have lost a parent will in fact present a combination of both (1) a detachment from potential painful affect associated with loss and (2) denial of the parent's death. If the latter denial were total and absolute, there would be no pain of loss. The need on the child's part for defensive detachment indicates that the denial of death is only partially effective.

Both in the schizoid personality and severe character detachment, "broken" parts of the self remain to function on their own. With reattachment, these parts of the self are rebuilt into a central self which gains increasing energy from the reverberating circuits that ensue in interpersonal relationships. "Broken" parts of the self are both the source and result of great anxiety and are, so to speak, looking for a central self and ego with which to become one (as in "getting it together").

PSYCHOANALYTIC THERAPY OF CHARACTER DETACHMENT

As mentioned above, our main goal in psychoanalytic therapy is to reestablish attachment with the patient in those detached areas that are frozen or cut off. As in all psychoanalytic therapy, we look to the healthy, nonattached areas to make a therapeutic alliance with the analysand. The alliance is largely based on the hope of relieving psychic pain through the therapeutic relationship, and the shared capacity for both therapist and patient to *look together* with their observing egos at the whole person of

---

[9]It is most difficult for children and adolescents (and even adults) to do the work of mourning. See Martha Wolfenstein's (1966) "How is Mourning Possible?"

the patient, including his interactions with the analyst and others. The analyst has the added work of keeping in touch with and analyzing his own countertransference. The latter reactions may include a sense of being drained or strained by the patient's resistance, especially in his areas of detachment. In brief, we use the patient's strengths, curiosity, and pain to set up rapport and a working alliance.

The analysand needs the therapist to be emotionally available from the beginning phase of the analysis when some detached persons may be experienced as arid, obsessional, and intellectualized in style. The analyst's attitude should be one of watchful waiting with a mobility to move in and make connections for the patient so that he can begin to see what he feels or might have felt if his detachment had not been so complete in a given area.

I am reminded of a 27-year-old patient I saw some time ago. Mr. M.'s chief complaints were chronic tension and sleepwalking. Mr. M. developed a strong loyalty to his "analytic sessions" without being able to say or feel that he was becoming attached to his analyst. Gradually, by encouraging him to talk about those experiences in which he did feel some emotion, we developed a bond of shared experience. He became expressive concerning his tastes for food, music, his boss—but almost nothing in relation to his wife. On the one hand, he indicated an attitude to his wife of "never again shall I become attached," but, on the other hand, he betrayed a quiet fondness for his wife who was sensitive to his boundaries and his need for "psychic space."

After some months of analysis I inquired about his first masturbation fantasies. He described how he had simply imaged a penis by itself unattached to any person. This extreme detachment in the sexual-emotional-interpersonal area led us into his extreme sense of isolation in childhood and adolescence. The penis fantasy remained detached from persons even after he met his wife. She was a nurse, seductive and warm, but in a way that was not threateningly intrusive. Gradually, as the therapy and the relation to his wife progressed simultaneously, the masturbation symbol of the lonely penis gave way to direct feelings of love toward his wife. This process occurred over a period of three years during which there was careful inquiry into the various threats that he experienced to any close attachment.

In the first year of analysis he retrieved a memory that was rather striking to both of us. The memory was of himself as a toddler, entrapped in a wire-mesh cage that had been placed over his bed each night when he was "put to sleep." The rationale for the use of the cage had been to prevent him from wandering and thus keep him safe. During our "looking together" at this two-year-old boy in him he became enraged at the inhumanity of his parents' attempt to control and imprison him, albeit for "his own good." This memory, now recovered with the affects of rage and of fear of being entrapped, helped us to unlock the mystery of his sleepwalking which stopped shortly after the exploration of this memory. His sleepwalking had begun around four years of age and stopped in the second year of the analysis. From the analysis of his current as well as past sleepwalking it became clear that he was searching while asleep to make contact with his parents, both of whom were cool, detached people. He had wanted especially to reach his mother. Following this insight he allowed himself to move much closer to his wife affectionately and sexually. The patient ascertained from his mother that the cage was removed after age four and that his sleepwalking began *after* that time. There was no evidence for sexual curiosity as a motive for the somnambulism.

The analytic inquiry was made in the spirit of an alliance, trying to understand and relive in the transference his deep yearning for contact, especially holding and being held. These latter two modalities were actualized with his wife, while in his analysis he described a feeling of "being held" by the analyst who had "faith" that he was not the robotlike, controlled, efficient person that he presented to the world. Later in the analysis the patient was able to express a sense of loyalty and gratitude to "the analysis" although he still staved off direct expression of feeling for the analyst. These warm feelings were brought into his marriage where intercourse, stroking, embracing, and verbalization of love became more natural for him.

In our reconstruction of his early years—partly based on his mother's information—it became clear that he had received a warm, facilitating environment during his infancy but was *restrained*—physically and emotionally—*from the exuberance of his toddler days*. The patient had felt that this had been the situation even before it was corroborated by his mother and that as a caged child he had vowed to "never again" trust someone who might be loving. The "reattachment" through his analysis and through his relationship to his wife was complete enough for him to establish "relationship constancy" with both his wife and his analyst, and later as a father to his children. Retrospectively, one of the key factors on the analyst's part was a conviction that this man had the silent "growth buds" for an intimate relation. The main signs for this included the highly intense investment he made to the analysis from early on. I have learned that commitment to the analysis is more accurate prognostically than the analysand's verbalized attachment behavior to the analyst.

I have had many patients who similarly felt emotionally imprisoned and unable to contact their loving and joyful feelings. The therapeutic position I have taken is one of offering myself as a witness from an optimal distance—so that I will neither inappropriately intrude on the self-membrane nor fail to be available if and when the patient is able to make contact. The content of the interpretations has to be sufficiently accurate so that the patient can feel he is in a true "holding" (Winnicott, 1965) environment.

In my experience it is crucial to refrain from making comments that will predictably increase the resistance. The attitude of both analyst and analysand is one of "hovering" (Freud) or "bare" attention (Nyanaponika, 1973). We notice that the resistance centers around issues whose conscious awareness will bring pain. These issues usually have as their central affects anxiety and fear or depression, but also, potentially, great *shame and humiliation*. Raw shame is one of the most potent dissociating forces largely *because it threatens to suddenly lower self-esteem and annihilate the very "sense of self."* Hence the aphorism: "There is no problem so great as the shame of it."

The therapeutic principle of *looking together* and sharing experience has its roots in the mother-infant relationship from the second half of the first year onward. The paradigm consists of the infant's focusing on some spectacle by gazing at or pointing to it, and the mother's responding in some sensitive way to the infant's communication.

In observational studies conducted with children and parents in their natural setting, it has been most impressive to see the intensity of affect—and the amount of "free time"—experienced by parent and child.[10] The affect can be described for the most part as joyful "activity affect" (Schachtel, 1959) and has the quality of being peremptory, and *exclusively* oriented to parent and child. In several families, the fathers complained openly about feeling excluded from this private experience of mother and child, an experience that has the quality of an *exclusively shared private mythology*. A whole body of play, fantasy, and reality becomes interwoven into a system fully known—usually—to one parent and child. *Psychoanalytic therapy is, in part, also a shared mythology* in which the objective truth of the content is secondary to the peremptoriness of its being experienced as mutual, and close to the *subjective sense of truth about one's experience.* Edgar Levenson (1978) has described the psychoanalytic process as one that does not rely only on the truth of the professed content. "Nor does it depend on the therapist's participation with the patient, but rather on a dialectic interaction of these elements." "It is this dialectic between understanding and newness which makes for the core of therapeutic discourse. Metaphor is independent of time and space. It is always true" (p. 96).

The melting down, through analysis, of the sense of shame and its cover-ups allows both analyst and analysand to look at areas that have been dissociated by detachment as these areas surface through dreams,

---

[10]Studies in Ego Development at Albert Einstein College of Medicine, Grant #HD 01155–01. National Institute of Child Health and Human Development.

fantasies, marginal thoughts, and nonobsessional free association. If this new body of experience is not foreclosed by interpretation and "explanation," then "*interpretive pointing*" may be used to enhance the special sense of the therapeutic dyad looking together, as in snorkeling, in subterranean waters. Interpretation and explanation may falsely "wrap up" a dream, for example, before the dream and its associations are afforded an "open state" where it is possible to come back again and again to the dream from new perspectives, and even to redream familiar dreams with new endings. *The therapeutic attitude, then, is one of curiosity and exploration rather than explanation and interpretation.* Explanation and interpretation are often used as "cerebralized" counterresistance—a distancing by the analyst who is threatened by the necessary but finely titrated process of reattachment to a partially detached or "schizoid" person.

What I have noted here about sharing pathways to unconscious material using images and meanings in fantasy and dreams also applies to the exploration of the analysand's "realities" and history—indeed because it is "*his-story,*" *the one and only story he has, one that gives a sense of orientation, identity, time continuity, and drama to his own life.* For myself, if only to keep most hours interesting, I need to have some sense of drama, and of history in its alive current and largely intrapsychic sense. The *analytic expectation* is to share experience in depth, and so our attitude in analytic therapy should strongly project this expectation; otherwise analyst and patient are doing something else with each other and that had best be explored.

It is uncanny how in a good analytic relationship both analyst and analysand find the right "spot" to occupy in the dimensions of closeness vs. distance and attachment vs. detachment.[11] We know intuitively not to move in too quickly, or too intimately, with a suspicious person. For the patient, at first the analyst can be felt as someone who is dangerous, someone who may seduce or disarm a hard-won but extremely isolated fortress of pseudo autonomy. Nevertheless, the patient has come to us for help so that we have the right to inquire into his expectations, his needs, his fears, his shame, his ideal wishes—but always with a sense of what his defensive system can bear. A common question I ask of a depressed or withdrawn patient is when he last felt good or hopeful. Not infrequently, as our contact breaks through the detachment area via the transference

---

[11]"A company of porcupines crowded themselves very close together one cold winter's day so as to profit by one another's warmth, and to save themselves from being frozen to death. But soon they felt one another's quills which induced them to separate again. And now when the need for warmth brought them nearer together, again the second evil arose once more. So that they were driven backwards and forwards from one trouble to the other until they discovered a safe distance at which they could more tolerably exist" (Schopenhauer).

and/or the "real relationship," he may respond with a choked-up feeling or with the shedding of some as yet undifferentiated tears.[12] If this human contact is felt as too threatening, the following analytic session is often distinctly cooler, more distanced, or may even be canceled.

Each participant in the analytic work becomes familiar with the "psychic space" around the self-boundary (ego boundary; Federn [1952]) and then with the boundary itself. The latter is more accurately experienced as a "membrane-around-the-self," a membrane which is semipermeably selective; certain affects and information can flow "in" and "out" in relation to given interpersonal situations. The concepts "self-membrane" and of a membrane around compartments within the self are too complex to discuss in detail in this paper.[13] Suffice it to say that analytic therapy works toward an optimal permeability of such membranes to facilitate the flow of information and affects.

The many therapeutic issues associated with character detachment tend to emerge naturally from an understanding of the phenomenology of attachment and detachment. For example, in the observation of infants and children, one has the experience of being responded to as the "bad stranger" whose presence can evoke near-panic in the six-month-old infant. Analysts who have observed attachment-separation stress behaviors in children are less likely to respond with counter-resistance when these affects are expressed in the adult analytic situation. Similarly, the capacity for empathy with the more primitive nonverbal affects may be more available in analysts who have had experience with infants and children. When one has seen "in the raw" the deep shame, humiliation, and rages of the preschooler, it is easier to recognize the "cover-up" of such affects in adults—a cover-up to protect the patient from a mortification of self-esteem.[14]

In my work with adults, I use both developmental diagnosis (see Freud, 1965; Negera, 1966; Kernberg, 1976; Horner, 1975) and "developmental therapy" with a particular interest in what ego strengths can be engaged for the patient's potential growth in therapy. An example of developmental therapy is seen in the long analysis required to build a "capacity for constancy in relationship." In deprivation or cumulative trauma (Khan, 1974) of infancy and childhood, a capacity for constancy has failed to develop or, if it has developed, it remains highly unstable in relation to the ordinary stresses of life. *The building of a stable constancy of relatedness*

---

[12]An important task of the therapy is the analysand's *learning a well-differentiated vocabulary for his often undifferentiated emotions.* The therapist may sometimes have to offer the vocabulary and the metaphors, as in a "Chinese menu."

[13]See Landis (1970) and Federn (1952) for a searching view of these issues.

[14]In the process of "growing up," disidentification and the mourning of diminishing identifications with parents can stimulate feelings of shame and disloyalty.

with the analyst may require many years with an up and down, "in and out" relationship (Guntrip, 1968). During this long haul, the analyst is tested many times—especially as to his trustworthiness. Each time the patient comes closer to "surrendering" to trust there tends to be a largely fabricated "paranoid attack" which then justifies the patient's moving back to his pretrust and preconstancy position. "Good" and "bad" become all-or-none categories again as is seen in the borderline personality (Kernberg, 1976).

We should not allow the presenting behavioral facade to determine our judgment of the "shape" of a character structure. In both practice and supervision I have seen patients who initially present as shy, inhibited, withdrawn "schizoid" persons turn out to have a rich inner life and capacity for change in analysis. I personally need to find some evidence of "psychic growth buds" that will be available for development in analysis before making the serious commitment to an analytic treatment project.

Two of the psychic strengths I refer to are: (1) a self-observing ego; and (2) a capacity to look to see, to portray and share—by words, dreams, associations, and through the transference—the nature of the patient's "inner psychic world" (Sandler and Rosenblatt, 1962). Obviously many of the therapeutic suggestions presented here apply not only to issues of character detachment but to psychoanalytic work in general.

How one separates or detaches (these are different) is *the* crucial factor to the next stage of interpersonal development. If one has left—or detached—with an inner sense of badness, one brings this "badness" from one situation to another. This phenomenon is seen clearly in the "transferences" from early (original) family life to marital relations or to transference in the narrower technical sense in the analytic situation itself. One brings one's badness and tries to convert the analysis into a "bad relationship." Against this, the forces of the "good-me" and "loving superego" and whatever available "constancy of good relationship" there is all act to facilitate the ongoing analysis in which the analyst "refuses" to treat the patient as if he were "really bad." In effect, the analyst does not follow the patient's attempt to "spoil" the relationship and thus challenges the patient's sense of omnipotent malevolence—a complex that may have resulted from extreme dissociation and detachment in earlier years.

Detachment also functions to protect a frequently hard-won and still fragile *sense of ego autonomy*. This defense stance needs to be explored in depth and with care, since the patient's behavior may present itself as "perversely oppositional," defiant, negativistic, or "wanting to control the therapy" *much as he is used to control attachment vs. detachment and the flow of his affective life.* To surrender some control of the therapy may feel

like a total surrender of autonomy of the self unless this stage of development has gone far enough in its integration with basic trust. The analysand is often found to be hypersensitive to having his "membrane"
invaded by "interpretation," "explanation" from "outside," or even
worse from a superior posture. Thus, psychoanalytic therapy with character detachment involves: (1) validating the patient's attempt to preserve
his not-yet-solid autonomy, and (2) clarifying with the patient how in
almost every important life relationship he suffers now from feeling
imprisoned by the protective fortress he has built to control relationships. The temptation toward regressive resymbiosis and refusion, *may*, in
some cases, be therapeutically warranted on a transitional basis, but must
be monitored very carefully. Almost every patient with whom I have
worked eventually describes the experience of the "fortress," "prison,"
or "shell" in association with a "lack of connection" to another person, a
lonely or isolated state, a lack of nourishment interpersonally—all with
an underlying sense of deep futility.

At this greater depth, we observe clinically that a kind of somnolence, a
deadening, heavy tone sets in, sometimes in relation to all experience,
sometimes selectively, as in Bowlby's case of two-and-a-half-year-old
Laura where the detachment was in relation to the separation from
mother, the person to whom she had been most specifically attached. In
separations from or loss of a beloved person (or part of the self), we see
that the partially adaptive function of detachment is to maintain the
homeostasis in varying degree and *protect the self from being flooded by
painful affect*. It is as if the psyche has the capacity to form or differentiate
out a "membrane" to protect the self. In situations of impending danger
or of loss (actual or sensed), the hypothetical membrane becomes almost
nonpermeable, in effect like the so called schizoid shell, thus cutting off
the input of conscious registration or expression of those affects that are
still preconsciously available with the membrane. In contrast to catharsis,
the increased but selective permeability of the membrane (structural
change) and the flow of affects constitute one of the principal goals of
psychoanalysis.

It is in this area of affect flow that it is most tempting to hypothecate a
sensitively and selectively permeable "membrane-around-the-self." The
"membrane" is, in part, our imaginary construct, but also an expression
of a subjectively felt experience. We will thus forego the temptation to
describe this membrane as if we could see it through a microscope. Yet at
this point further work on the concept of ego or self-boundary and
membrane may be useful in a heuristic sense. Certainly, our experiential
language almost takes it for granted, e.g., "he's getting under my skin," or
"she's coming through to me"—indicating a barrier or "membrane" that
an affect must get "through."

Our language is replete with expressions referring to a person as "hardened" rather than "tender" in relation to certain affects—for example, "hard-nosed" or "hard-hearted" vs. "tender" or "bleeding-heart." These expressions involve a number of functions related but not identical to each other, such as the capacity (1) to *empathize*, (2) to *identify* partially with another, or (3) to be *contaged* by the other's affect. Though each of these phenomena is significantly different, they have one aspect in common—the "permeability" of the "membrane-round-the self." Without sufficient permeability we suffer excessive detachment—a possible advantage if this detachment is selective to negative affects such as a flooding of anxiety from another person. However, in general, all depends on the total personal situation and context, and the balance between attachment and detachment. If I am characteristically "heard-hearted" to a person in need and never allow him partially and temporarily to "get into me," then I will not make a good analyst, friend, or parent. On the other hand, if every child's or patient's anxiety or disappointment becomes "mine" in too great a degree and for too long a time, I will be flooded, "overidentified," and rendered helpless to be a psychoanalyst, or to be helpful in any other way—especially to the extent that the patient and I have become totally the same. The art of living, then, depends on a subtle set of regulatory ego functions which feed back to the self signals of how that self is coping with what has been "taken in" and "expressed out" in the way of information, including its affective charge.

Psychoanalytic therapy aims to explore and increase the awareness of the patient and therapist *especially in the areas of needs and fears.* The need-fear dilemma is not specific to schizophrenia: in some degree it is a universal human problem. If we gradually work into the depth of the patient's defensive structures, we discover that he is a being who *needs* despite the awesome defensive "antineed" detachment structures that have become so synonymous with his very identity. For this reason, to work analytically at this level requires great patience and endurance since the therapeutic alliance is involved in nothing less than a restructuring of the self-identity. Self-consciousness, shame, humiliation, and pride will be the analyst's guides to uncovering hidden and dangerously experienced needs and affects—often associated disparagingly with being childish or babyish.

Authoritarian approaches in analysis—some of which may constitute an induced countertransference response to the patient's withholding—may result in a greater resistance in the form of an obvious "clam-closing-its-shell" reaction, or, even more dangerously, by *pseudo compliance* to an often unconscious sadistic intervention on the part of the therapist. The ego protects the self by responding with the unconscious attitude: "I will get you off my back and at a greater distance by appearing to fulfill the goals you expect of me." This attitude becomes fused with what has been called the "negative therapeutic reaction" since *the patient must now cling to self-sufficiency as his personal sign of autonomy and continuity of the self.* He may go to the extreme of suicide to define a fragile autonomy. The analyst must be most sensitive to the patient's inner struggle between a temptation to fuse symbiotically with the therapist at the one extreme, or to keep him out altogether in his struggle for a sense of prideful autonomy. *When patient and analyst realize in depth that this is part of the continuing human struggle between the polarities of symbiosis and individuation, a greater compassion and a melting away of the humiliation may result.*

As in most psychoanalytic papers, the emphasis here has been on the psychopathologic aspects of detachment. I must reiterate, however, that there are potentially *healthy* aspects of defenses and coping mechanisms involving detachment in the service of developmental progression and differentiation. Especially when we take into account individual differences in sensitivity thresholds and the dizzying amount of input from an urban environment, we realize that *the issue is not of balance whenever the polarities of attachment and detachment have to be reconciled and integrated.* It is in this area that the wisdom of other cultures as well as that of our own can help us attain a greater degree of reconciliation and harmony within the self and in its interpersonal relations.

REFERENCES

Balint, M. (1953), *Primary Love and Psychoanalytic Technique.* New York: Liveright.
Bowlby, J. (1973), *Attachment and Loss,* Vol. 2. New York: Basic Books.
Burgner, M. & Edgcumbe, R. (1972), Some problems in conceptualization of early object relations. In: *The Psychoanalytic Study of the Child,* 27:283–315. New Haven, CT: Yale University Press.
Fairbairn, R. (1952), *Psychoanalytic Studies of the Personality.* London: Tavistock.
Federn, P. (1952), *Ego Psychology and the Psychoses.* New York: Basic Books.
Freud, A. (1965), *Normality and Pathology in Children.* New York: International Universities Press.
Freud, S. (1938), Splitting of the ego in the process of defense. *Standard Edition,* 23:271–278. London: Hogarth Press, 1962.
Guntrip, H. (1968), *Schizoid Phenomena, Object Relations and the Self.* New York: International Universities Press.
Heinicke, C. & Westheimer, I. (1965), *Brief Separations.* New York: International Universities Press.
Horner, A. (1975), Stages and process in the development of object relations. *Internat. Rev. Psychoanal.,* 2:95–107.
Kernberg, O. (1976), *Object Relations Theory and Clinical Psychoanalysis.* New York: Aronson.
Khan, M. (1974), *The Privacy of the Self.* New York: International Universities Press.
Klaus, K. & Kennel, J. (1976), *Maternal-Infant Bonding.* St. Louis, MO: Mosby.
Landis, B. (1970), Ego boundaries. In: *The Structure of Psychoanalytic Theory,* ed. D. Rapaport. *Psychological Issues,* Monogr. 6. New York: International Universities Press.

Levenson, E. (1977), Psychoanalysis—Cure or persuasion. *Interpersonal Psychoanalysis: New Directions,* ed. E. G. Witenberg. New York: Basic Books, p. 96.

Mahler, M., Pine, F. & Bergman, A. (1975), *The Psychologic Birth of the Infant.* New York: Basic Books.

Nagera, H. (1966), *Early Childhood Disturbances: The Infantile Neurosis and the Adult Disturbance.* New York: International Universities Press.

Nyanaponika, T. (1973), *The Heart of Buddhist Meditation.* New York: Samuel Weiser.

Piaget, J. (1954), *The Construction of Reality in the Child.* New York: Basic Books.

Pine, F. (1974), Libidinal object constancy. In: *Psychoanalysis and Contemporary Science.* New York: International Universities Press.

Province, S. & Lipton, R. (1952), *Infants in Institutions: A Comparison of Their Development with Family Reared Infants during the First Year of Life.* New York: International Universities Press.

Sandler, J. & Rosenblatt, B. (1962), The concept of the representational world. In: *The Psychoanalytic Study of the Child,* 17:128–145. New York: International Universities Press.

Schachtel, E. (1959), *Metamorphosis.* New York: Basic Books, pp. 48–49.

Schecter, D. (1968a), Identification and individuation. *J. Amer. Psychoanal. Assn.,* 16:48–80.

———(1968b), The Oedipus complex: Considerations of ego development and parental interaction. *Contemp. Psychoanal.,* 4:111–137.

———(1973), On the emergence of human relatedness. In: *Interpersonal Explorations in Psychoanalysis: New Directions in Theory and Practice,* ed. E. Witenberg. New York: Basic Books.

———(1974), Infant development. In: *American Handbook of Psychiatry,* Vol. 1, ed. S. Arieti. New York: Basic Books.

———(1975a), Of human bonds and bondage. *Contemp. Psychoanal.,* 11:435–452.

———(1975b), Notes on some basic human developmental tasks. *J. Amer. Acad. Psychoanal.,* 3(3):267–276.

———& Corman, H. (1971), Some early developments in parent-child interaction. (Unpublished.)

Sendak, M. (1962), *Pierre: A Cautionary Tale.* New York: Harper & Row.

Stern, D. (1971), A micro-analysis of mother-infant interaction: Behavior regulating social contact between a mother and her 3½-month-old twins. *J. Amer. Acad. Child Psychiat.,* 10:501–518.

Sullivan, H. (1953), *The Interpersonal Theory of Psychiatry.* New York: Norton.

Winnicott, D. W. (1965), *The Maturational Process and the Facilitating Environment.* New York: International Universities Press.

Wolfenstein, M. (1966), How is mourning possible? *The Psychoanalytic Study of the Child.* New York: International Universities Press.

12

INTERPERSONAL PROCESSES, COGNITION, AND THE ANALYSIS OF CHARACTER

JOSEPH BARNETT

[1980]

INTRODUCTION

George Goldstein and Roanne Barnett

Philosopher, theoretician, clinician, and teacher, Joseph Barnett was above all an epistomologist. Throughout the 22-year span of his work, he endeavored to design a metapsychology that would define the larger structural templates of experience while simultaneously elaborating the idiosyncratic thumbprint. This dual consciousness guided his efforts to uncover the overarching characterological and structural issues in each person's life and their representation in the individual situation, that is, the person's predictable and enduring patterns of creative or constricted living.

The centerpiece of Barnett's work is the study of meaning. He rejected the classical doctrine that man is motivated by appetitive drives, asserting instead the position that man's capacity for thought inherently motivates him to seek meaning from his experience. In this way, he was most centrally concerned with what we know about ourselves and the world, and how we come to know it.

Dr. Barnett's work clearly reflects the interpersonal-humanistic tradition as presented by Sullivan, Horney, Fromm, and Thompson. Together they share the view that interpersonal experiences with significant others structure character and shape the basic assumptions we hold about ourselves and others.

George Goldstein, Ph.D. is Faculty and Supervisor, New York University, Postdoctoral Program in Psychotherapy and Psychoanalysis; and Director of Training, Faculty and Supervisor, Westchester Center for the Study of Psychoanalysis and Psychotherapy.

Roanne Barnett, Ph.D. is a trainee in the New York University Postdoctoral Program in Psychotherapy and Psychoanalysis.

In his efforts to communicate the very original and complex intricacies of his thinking, Barnett used words from common everyday parlance in entirely new ways. Anyone reading his work should heed the caveat that this theory-builder revolutionizes language itself, and should be prepared for a challenging endeavor in the Talmudic tradition. This caveat is perhaps most pertinent to his use of the words "cognition", and "cognitive repair."

Barnett defined the term "cognition" as a process by which experience is formulated and organized, referring to the continual ongoing phenomena of "experiential knowing," i.e., the simultaneous and interacting processes of integrating apprehended (or sensate) experience with the comprehended (or syntactic) experience into a self that is personally coherent, meaningful and acceptable to its attendant self-regarding systems.

Barnett continued to break new ground in linking psychopathology to the nature of difficulties in organizing and integrating the sensate and syntactic modes of experience. Difficulties in living, he contended, could be understood as predictable and enduring maladaptive patterns of structuring experience. He termed the amelioration of these difficulties "cognitive repair."

He considered dysfunctional patterns of living as the result of damage to self-esteem and constrictions and distortions in the sense of self. Strongly influenced by the work of family-systems theorists, especially that of his wife Dr. Tess Forrest, he asserted that requirements for family homeostasis in dysfunctional families required "systems of innocence" that evolve from the dictated prohibitions and restrictions on which aspects of experience could be "known," how they could be "known," and the meanings that could be derived therefrom. Like Sullivan's concepts of selective inattention and security operations, the phenomena of "systems of innocence" serve to preserve the self's sense of cohesiveness and significance and regulate an interpersonal reality to accord with the social demands of the "family ideology."

In his now-classic papers on the obsessional character, Barnett elaborates a particular kind of cognitive disorder, theorizing that obstruction to thought by the "implosion of affect" for the purposes of avoiding inferences damaging to self-esteem is central to the obsessional operation. In the tradition of Fromm's "direct relatedness," he recommends a direct approach in treatment by analysis of the internal gaps and distortions due to ambiguous referential systems as the route to the organization and integration of experience and affective freedom for the obsessional patient.

Applying his theoretical position on "cognition" as central to disorders in living, Barnett redefined the central developmental task of adolescence: to emerge from innocent, uncritical acceptance of "family ideologies" and attendant mythologies, to individuate by negotiating a more personal, less restrictive and stereotypic individual identity. This position is akin to Fromm's concept of the necessity to emerge from embeddedness to face the anxieties of true individuation. Barnett felt that failure in this task forestalls a true progression into adulthood and a personally viable identity. In his paper on *Hamlet,* Barnett illustrates how Hamlet's conflict may be understood as a young adult's inability to tolerate the disruptive anxiety attendant upon challenging the "family ideology" and family mythologies.

In his 1980 papers on character and self, Barnett's work coalesces into a cohesive unit. In the article presented here he focuses explicitly on the issues of character and self, dysfunctional character formation ("explosive" and "implosive" disorders) as well as the relationship between narcissism and neurotic dependency. For Barnett the study of character is always an epistemological one, again, a study of the organization and patterning of experience and meaning. Barnett views character as an overarching entity, "the central structural phenomena of mental life." Barnett (1978, 1979) defines self as the recognition, both felt and thought, of one's meaning to the interpersonal environment, to one's inner world, especially in terms of one's roles and functions, which aspects of the self are apprehended, which are comprehended, and which fulfill the individual's systems of innocence are determined by the designs of the person's cognition.

In considering all psychological disorders as synonymous with a disordered sense of self and self-regarding systems, Barnett spearheaded the interpersonal criticism of Kernberg's and Kohut's theories, which established and designated to circumscribed categories individuals with damage to self-esteem.

In his final public presentation, just before his death, Barnett enriched the commonly held interpersonal views of transference/countertransference. He introduced a revolutionary framework for understanding the therapeutic dyad from the perspective of the structural gestalt that each dyad forms. In this new model the way each member of the dyad structures experience will inherently determine how they mutually design their specific therapeutic relationship. For example, Barnett said:

> The obsessional (implosive) analyst may tend to be reticent about and at times even averse to the hysterical patient's emotional expression, relying on logic and literal forms of understanding experience in a way that can be rigid and inflexible. The narcissistic vulnerability of the obsessional analyst may therefore make that analyst excessively oriented towards performance and the need for the hysterical patient's approval and admiration [1988, unfinished work].

Sadly, this paper was never published, existing only in outlined notes from which he spoke.

To know Joe Barnett in one sphere was to know him in another: In the seamless wholeness of his personal and professional life, he influenced a generation of students, supervisees, patients, colleagues, and friends. Exemplifying the interpersonal-humanistic ethic, Joe was always fully mindful of the human condition and its attendant challenges, responsibilities, and possibilities. As his "students," we all learned, in the broadest sense, to be cognizant always of how the social, political, and personal mutually inform the context from which we are each free and responsive to choose *how* to live actively, fully, and creatively; *how* to be of service; *how* to hone and implement our empathic responses to others' efforts and constraints; and *how* to negotiate fiercely and with integrity.

In the consultation room, classroom, and living room alike, Joe's vitality was invigorating. He philosophized and theorized with precisioned elegance and complexity; he engaged passionately with a contagious curiosity and warmth, but missed no opportunity to infect us with his humor, artful silliness and reverence for the ridiculous. Joe was rigorously scholarly and cultured in many areas of endeavor and was acutely sensitized to global as well as personal plights. He held himself to very high standards and expected us to choose and adhere to our own ideals. As professionals we learned the necessity to identify and work with conviction from a theoretical position, to use theory as a framework to continuously enliven and clarify our thoughts and interactions. He used our skills at ping-pong or poker to elucidate how we and our patients could and should creatively hone our apparently most mundane assets into useful interpersonal skills.

Joe had little tolerance for sloppiness of thought or intention, or slavish adherence to any system of beliefs. He held to an optimistic conviction that all conflict is negotiable, urging us to tangle openly and explicitly, with integrity and courage. In short, he encouraged us to live his credo: *Always go for broke.*

Joe would be deeply gratified to find that his inclusion in this volume will permit him to be of enduring service to others and to inform and stimulate ongoing discourse, productivity, and creativity in future interpersonalists.

Post-Freudian psychoanalysis implied a shift from a psychology of drives in which meaning was seen as appetitive and motivations were defined as functions of drives, to a psychology of self and character in which meaning is experiential and both motives and intentionality derive from meaning and the organization of experience. In previous communications, I argued that this shift implicated cognition, conceived as experiential knowing, as the core phenomenon of mental life rather than as an epiphenomenal derivative of drives as envisioned by classical theory. This paper will outline my views on character and self as derivatives of cognition, which I view as the central organizing factor in mental life. In essence, the notion of character or personality represents the general theory of cognition and its organization, while the self can be seen as a special instance of cognitive organization involving the transformation of experience into subjective meaning.

The post-Freudian revisionists of the 1940's, in my opinion, were reconfronting an early problem in psychoanalytic theory development. While this problem had been addressed by others before them and is still being addressed by current revisionists, the post-Freudians offered a more radical solution than had many others who preceded them or who followed them. Freud, in his early work, saw meaning as being derived from actual experience. He interpreted the symptoms of his "hysterical" patients as symbolic expressions of repressed memories of actual childhood seductions. When, later, he discovered that these seductions existed only in the imaginations of these patients, he replaced his original theory with that of the libido theory. Sexual thoughts and wishes created the fantasies, and the sexual drive itself was implicated as the source of meaning of the symptoms.

By this shift, Freud was able to maintain his interest in the sexuality that was so abounding a preoccupation of Victorian Viennese culture, and so inevitably a major content of his patients' mental life. Libido theory, however, radically altered the implicit structure of his approach to meaning. Libido theory heralded the abandonment of the notion that meaning is derived from actual experience with the environment. It located the ultimate source of meaning in the individual's drives, and reduced the concept of motivation to drives, their aims, and defenses against them. Psychoanalytic psychology was locked into viewing the individual as the result of the organization of drive phenomena under the impact of environmental strictures. Not only meaning and motivation, but even personality and psychopathology were reduced to this basic model. Mechanistic and reductionistic though it was, the theory appealed because of its elegance, basic parsimony, and its resemblance to the concrete and highly successful theories of physics and mechanics that dominated the times.

As a direct outgrowth of libido theory, the structural theory of mind was developed, in which the structures of id, ego and superego were postulated to explain the source and eventual distribution of drive phenomena and instinctual energies, and to link all functions of mind to these drive phenomena. Structural theory furthered the commitment to drive explanations by implicitly structuring and institutionalizing the assumptions of drive psychology, and by reinforcing the atomistic approach to personality.

The tension created by this theoretical assumption and its collision with the growing clinical evidence that more holistic forces were at work in the individual has created problems since the earliest days of psychoanalysis, and there were many different attempts to resolve the dilemma, some of which still reappear in contemporary psychoanalytic revisions. The full history of this problem and the many attempts at its resolution is in itself a fascinating intellectual odyssey which unfortunately we do not have time to explore.

The resolutions of the problem offered by Fromm, Horney and Sullivan shared a rejection not only of drive theory, but of structural theory as well. This enabled them not only to readdress the problem of the relationship of meaning to experience, but to focus more on the holistic organizations of experience into structures of self and character which became central to their theories. This reorientation of theory to the organization of experience allowed for a more complex approach to meaning and its relationship to experience, a richer, more diverse understanding of motivation and intentionality, and a broader concept of psychic conflict than was afforded by the vicissitudes of the instincts and their fate in the process of socialization.

It seems to me that the basic issue between classical and post-Freudian theorists was and remains epistemic, and involves this issue of the nature of meaning. Post-Freudian revisions in theory were attempts to redefine and relocate the source of individual meaning to the world of experience, and to the person's cognitive interaction with that world. Fromm (1941), in his position that man is separated from the animals by his capacity for awareness of his own human condition, and his ability to conceive of his own death, exemplifies through generalization this shift of emphasis to a more explicit concern with cognition, and the attempt to shift meaning to experience. Horney (1950), in her concept of basic anxiety which sees the child as feeling isolated and helpless in a world conceived as potentially hostile, clearly derives meaning in relation to the world of experience, and uses such meaning in her development of the dynamics of personality. Horney's concern with an elaboration of a psychology of self, and Sullivan's (1953, 1956) examinations of the self-system illustrate this shift of emphasis to a concern with cognition and an organization of experience that is clearly related to concepts of character and personality not unlimited to the defensive and structural model required by drive theory.

My own concern with cognition derives from my studies of Fromm, Horney and Sullivan, and my belief that they were dealing with an appreciation of cognition that far transcended the usual psychoanalytic interpretation of cognition as being limited to structures of the processes of thinking alone. Interpersonal theory especially, with its operational approach, its concern for the structuring effects of language, its detailed examination of the structure and organization of experience, and its insistence on defining the intrapsychic in terms of interpersonal experience, focused my approach to the central and architectonic nature of cognition in the study of psychoanalytic psychology.

I will begin this outline of my approach to the relationship between cognition and personality with an exploration of the self, both because most theoreticians explicitly or implicitly agree that the self is a cognitive structure and because the self is a concern directly and immediately involved with our patients' perception of their persons and their problems of living.

I view the self as the way the individual experiences his person and his relationship to the inner and outer world. The experience of self is the product of the cognitive apparatus that transforms actual experience into subjective meaning, and arises from the uniquely human capacity to organize experience in two different and interacting modes, the sensate and the syntactic. In previous communications in which I proposed that the designs of knowing and meaning are cognitive templates central to character structure, I indicated that I also view the self as a part of the cognitive system related to character (Barnett 1968, 1978b, 1979, 1980b). I proposed that the self is a cognitive event, a bridging concept between the designs of knowing and meaning on the one hand, and action and behavior on the other. I further observed that the self is designed and limited by the cognitive templates of character.

The self refers to the experience of "I," "me," and "my." It is a system of constructs, implicit and explicit, formed by cognition which I have conceptualized as experiential knowing that includes sensate and syntactic forms existing at all levels of awareness or consciousness. The referent of self is always the person, as subject as well as object. The form and content of the self are provided by the impact of experience with the real world. The structure of the self is designed by the interaction of the person's cognitive system with external experience as well as by the internal organization of that system in the form of character. Our tendency to think of self as a fixed and static entity is related to our awareness of the substance and continuity of our bodies and the memory of the perceived continuity of our experiences in time and space. The self, however, is an holistic experience organized to integrate the constantly changing and growing experiences that arise from our evolving potentials for living and the way we interact with life. Although we tend to conceive of self as relatively monolithic, a conception that satisfies our need for meaning and significance, the self as experience is more fluid and inconsistent than we like to believe. Ideally the experience of self would be constantly growing and changing, reflecting in its dimensions and contradictions our manifold and developing potentials for living and our perceptions of our varied human responses to the constant change and flux of life.

In essence the self is a quasi-fictive rendering of subjective experience and meaning. Drawing on one's historical life experience with the real and significant personal environment, the person constructs a fictive rendition in the attempt to integrate outer reality with the sense of personal existence and significance. The extremely varied, conflicting, and contradictory aspects of one's person and one's interaction with the complexities of living are difficult to organize into a coherent and consistent system. It is a task we respond to with a range of construction varying from the one extreme of the most conventionalized stereotypes to the other extreme of fantastic and idiosyncratic constructs which burst the bounds of reality. From a psychological point of view, the self is the person's major artistic and creative expression of his life and subjective experience. The wisdom and functional adequacy of the self involves the degree to which it reflects and integrates the person's sources of vitality and aliveness, the extent to which it is responsive to his potentials for living and to the complexities and ambiguities of life. The danger of the self involves the fact that an organized system of this sort can easily live our lives for us, and we can become constrained and confined to a sterile existence by the very system we erect in our search for meaning.

I find it convenient to divide the self experience into phenomenal aspects which I call the operational self and the representational self. This is obviously an heuristic and arbitrary division of what is an holistic experience of our person and our relationship to the world. The distinction is not absolute because static representations may be constructed about actions and operations, and actional concepts may be constructed from static representations. The utility of the distinction between operational self and representational self is that it focuses attention and distinguishes between constructs formed about the self as agent and self as essence. The tension between the operational self and the representational self is often the source of great ambiguity and confusion in living, and frequently defines the focal point of disorders of living.

The operational self corresponds roughly to James's (1892) notion of the self as subject, and to Sullivan's (1953) concept of the self-system. The operational self involves the perceptions and constructions about the person as actor or agent. It includes the organization of perceptions of one's ability to act, make choices, initiate or react to the environment and the ongoing process of living. The operational self implies both will and intentionality. It is the organization of what is conceivable to the individual of his own action and behavior, and of his functional roles with the environment. As the "I" of the experience of self, the operational self has its origins in the earliest sensate perceptions during infancy of one's actions in response to inner and outer sensations and perceptions. The operational self involves the growing sense of one's actional impact on the environment. It evolves into patterns created by the response of the environment to the child and by the sensations experienced by the child in the course of his actions and reactions. While Sullivan emphasized the structuring affects of anxiety, and the creation of an operational sense of self related to the tendency to avoid anxiety, which he called the self-system, other factors have been implicated in the development of the operational self. Schachtel (1959) discussed the existence of what he called activity affects, tension states which are pleasurable experiences orienting the child towards action. I consider these activity affects central to the development of the person's perception and organization of the operational self. Recent research by Stern (1977) and others has substantiated such a view of the patterning of the operational self by microanalytic observations on the impact of mother–infant play and interchange on the development in the child of patterns of interpersonal communication, a sense of the nature and timing of dialogic interaction, the development of expectational sets in relation to action and interaction, and even the development of affects and their expression. Yogman (1977), R. K. Barnett (1979) and others have extended these microanalytic observations in father-infant interactions as well, providing us with evidence of the earliest patterning of the operational self by experience with significant others.

The representational self corresponds roughly to James's (1892) notion of the self as object, Sullivan's (1953) conception of the personified self, and Horney's (1950) self-concepts. As the "me" and "my" of experience, the representational self encompasses constructs about the perceived substantive aspects of the person, about the parts, qualities, nature and essence of the person perceived as the object of mental activity. It is the representational self, existing at different levels of cognitive organization and levels of awareness, that we usually refer to as self-images, self-concepts, self-representations, etc. The representational self involves the creation of referential systems that become the static, objectified, and eventually ideological reflections of one's perceived meaning and significance, as well as one's experience of others as seen through the filter of one's own perceived meanings. The representational self defines individual meaning in terms of static constructs and representations derived from the person's organization of experience with the real world. The constructs of the representational self, positive and negative, have special significance in that they become the source and reservoir of the dialectic of meaning which results in the person's self-regarding systems, the ultimate source of self-esteem and self-contempt.

The individual's self-regarding systems are a natural outgrowth of the complexities and ambiguities of the self as a product of the individual's cognitive system. The formulation of constructs about one's person inevitably creates a polarization of experience, in that it creates an implicit contrast with a construct perceived as its polar opposite. Both Sullivan and Horney implied as much in their explorations of the self. Sullivan's concept of the "good me" and "bad me," personifications of actional possibilities according to the gradient of anxiety evoked because of past experience with significant others, and Horney's observations about idealized and despised aspects of self, relating to the attempt to actualize grandiose images and concepts derived from past experience, both imply the polarization I believe is inevitable in self-construct formation. Since neither the environment nor the individual are neutral about the terms of one's polarized constructs, preferred and non-preferred constructs of the experience of self are designed. The evolving fictions and ideological premises of one's experience determine the judgments and evaluations of the self which are a central aspect to the self-regarding systems.

The dialogue of internal meaning about self not only reflects this tension between preferred and non-preferred constructs of the self, but involves also the ambiguity that often exists between constructs of the operational self and the representations of self as object. It is possible, as Sullivan pointed out, to construe one's actions and operations with the environment in a way that implies congruence with representations of self even when they are incongruent. It is equally possible to create representations which imply congruence with behaviors and operations which are in fact incompatible with existing self-concepts. The coexistence of incompatible behaviors and concepts leads to stress about the perceived unity and integrity of the self, and to conflict about self exposure, shame and self-contempt.

The development of self-regarding systems that structure self-esteem and self-contempt and determine the parameters of the internal dialogue of meaning, stimulates the evolution of two modes of self-expression, the presentational and private modes of self experience. Each mode includes elements of the operational self and the representational self which are organized according to the individual's perception of which aspects of self are most acceptable. The presentational mode and the private mode reflect the dominant fictional or ideological structure of the experience of self, its preferred and non-preferred aspects, and the attempt to organize that structure into a system of content and process. The presentational and private modes of self experience directly reflect, as Forrest (1978) has observed, the roles and functions the individual has had in his social and familial experience and the impact these roles and functions have on his sense of personal meaning. The presentational self includes those aspects of self which the person identifies with the roles and functions he has learned to accept as the dominant view of self that makes him meaningful to others. It reflects the structure of the person's perceived significance to the interpersonal world. The private mode is the counterpoint to the presentational mode, involving those aspects of self withheld because they might negate one's significance to others.

The problem of authenticity in the experience of self is a recurrent and complicated issue in the study of self. Various authors have proposed a concept of a real self, an authentic self as opposed to a false self, pseudo-self, or actual self. From our clinical experience, we can see where this tendency derives. Social and interpersonal factors, psychodynamics and psychopathology do warp and distort the person's sense of self. The person who, during the course of analysis, moves towards experiencing himself with a broader and more human repertoire of potentials for living than he was able to tolerate before, can be said to be experiencing himself in a more authentic way; a real self rather than a pseudo-self can be said to be emerging. It is probably more valid, though, to speak of authenticity of our moment-to-moment responses to living than to speak of a real self. The concept of a real self is problematic because it is idealistic, not existent, and tends to be ideological. A more central issue in any discussion of authenticity of self is the congruence of self-constructs with the person's capacities, talents, behaviors, values, way of living, etc., as well as the tension and ambiguities that exist between action and conception. It is difficult to conceive of an existent real self, first because the self is of necessity a limited and fictionalized view of a highly complex group of experiences, secondly because a real self would have to include the unfolding of potentials for living in the context of ongoing and even future experience, and finally because the very notion of a single self, true or false, arises out of our need for meaning and unity of experience. The idea of a single self reflects the attempts to organize what is, in effect, the variety of selves that characterize most people's lives, which have varying degrees of consistency with each other and varying degrees of congruence and incongruence with our actional relations to others. The capability of living a rich, full and varied life depends on the person's capacity to develop a sense of self that is not too narrowed by the twin forces of the social pressures of his past experience and his own cognitive organization of that experience.

My orientation is clearly towards the self as experience. It presupposes a shift from a psychology of instincts in which meaning is appetitive, derived from motivations which are functions of drives, to a psychology of knowing in which meaning is directly derived from experience, and in which intentions and motives stem from meaning. Post-Freudians, myself among them, prefer a psychology of self integrally interwoven with a psychology of personality or character to a drive psychology. We do not consider a psychology of self merely a second psychology for selected conditions, or an epiphenomenal appendage to a drive psychology. Post-Freudian theorists, and I include in this term all those who reject both libido theory and the structural theory of id, ego, and superego which supports and institutionalizes drive theory and its assumptions, believe that all the classical syndromes of the disorders of living are understood more accurately and treated more effectively from a perspective of self and character. My own conviction is that such a perspective is essentially a cognitive one, and needs further explication of the cognitive and epistemic issues implicit in self and character. To accept the view proposed by recent theorists that a theory of self is required by a new group of disorders, the narcissistic or borderline personalities (Kohut, 1971, 1977; Kernberg, 1975), would, in my opinion, truncate the significance of self, character and cognition. For, in fact, we find in clinical practice that the notion of psychological disorder is synonymous with a disordered sense of self and disturbed self-regarding systems. Dysfunctional patterns of living, whether of hysteric, obsessional, impulse neurotic, paranoid or depressive nature, are without exception outcomes of damage to self-esteem and of a constricted and distorted sense of self. The study of the self, and the analysis of character, make untenable a division of pathology into transference neuroses in which distortions of meaning are libidinal and appetitive, and narcissistic neuroses in which distortions of meaning are self and experience related. It seems unlikely to me that two theories with contradictory implicit premises about meaning and motivation can comfortably coexist as explanatory systems. The study of both self and character indicates, I believe, that the central issues of mental life and of psychopathology are cognitive, having to do with the organization of experience and its fate in the process of socialization. What is called for is the reorientation of our concerns and our theories of therapy so that these issues are explicated as central rather than the peripheral phenomena they are envisioned to be by classicalist models of theory (Barnett, 1966a, 1980b).

I view the self, then, as a special instance of the organization of cognition, involving the architectonics of subjective experience and personal meaning which provides the psychological matrix and impetus for intentionality and motivation. The self is designed and confined by the cognitive templates of character, by the restrictive systems of knowing and meaning created by the impact of living, and by the systems of innocence established to protect the individual's sense of cohesiveness and significance. This position is based on an interpretation of character which views it as a central phenomenon of mental life rather than an epiphenomenon of ego serving defensive or at best adaptational functions. I propose that character is the general organization of cognition and meaning while self is a special instance reflecting the subjective organization of cognition and personal meanings. I would now like to sketch for you the relationship between self and character especially as we see it in the clinical situation, an outline of prominent themes in my understanding of the origin, organization and structure of the self experience as it is designed and influenced by the cognitive templates of different character structures.

I have suggested that the neuroses in essence are cognitive disorders (Barnett, 1966a, 1968, 1978, 1979), defined cognition as experiential knowing, derived from the human capacity to structure experience simultaneously in two interacting but distinct modes, the sensate and the syntactic. Sensate processes result in the apprehension of experience, commonly called feelings, while syntactic processes result in the comprehension of experience, commonly referred to as thought. Adequate systems of knowing involve a harmonious interchange between the sensate and syntactic modes of experience.

I have defined character as the central structural phenomenon of mental life whose design and formal attributes arise from the organization of experience in a person's life, and are reflected in his behavioral and cognitive operations. Character functions to determine the organization of ongoing experience, its perception and interpretation, the designs of meaning, of expectation and anticipation and the behavioral tendencies and interpersonal operations of the individual in relation to self, others and the inanimate world. Ideally, the state of cognition in character organization would be an expanding interchange between levels representing both sensate and syntactic structure, each enriching, complementing and renewing the other, and each dependent on the other for optimal functioning. This ideal model is that of an open-ended system in homeostasis with the environment, restricted only by the inherent limitations of the human organism.

In normal living, affective experience has both external and internal importance to the personality. Affect is used expressively for reaction and communication, and intrapsychically as data for thought and syntactic organization of experience. Affect thus normally gives rise to expression and impression. Expression involves the direct presyntactic communication of affects. Impression refers to the perception and storage of sensate data of experience which become important sources of experience for syntactic organization and comprehension.

Dysfunctional character organizations, the dynamic roots of neurotic living, have consistent areas of "not knowing" or innocence which function as predictable systems. These systems of innocence imply historically and dynamically created areas of difficulty in cognitive organization. Their effect is to block the interchange between apprehension and comprehension, to create closure of cognition, and to restrict opportunities for growth. Knowing is interfered with at various specific levels of cognition, and the creative interplay between apprehension and comprehension is limited by the confines of a rigid and dysfunctional template.

In the dysfunctional character formations affective experience is used either explosively or implosively and disorders normal cognitive organization. Explosion of affect is a cognitive dynamism in which a forceful ejection or voiding of apprehended experience takes place before adequate structuring or thoughtful integration of experience can occur. Implosion of affect is a cognitive dynamism in which affect is forced inward on the cognitive processes and disorganizes them. Both explosion and implosion interfere with normal cognitive ordering of experience, but differently. In affective explosion, there is an emptying of the apprehended data of experience before adequate syntactic structuring and comprehension can take place. Implosion of affect, on the other hand, disorganizes the very processes necessary for adequate organization, with the result that apprehended data is contained but left simply as raw data. These dynamisms are reflected in characteristic ways in the dysfunctional characters which give rise to neurotic living.

I have proposed that two basic types of dysfunctional character can be defined structurally, the explosive disorders and the implosive disorders. Explosion of affect is the dominant cognitive dynamism in the hysterical disorders, the acting-out personalities and the impulse disorders. Affective implosion characterizes the obsessional disorders, the paranoid character disorders and the depressive personality.

The utility of such an understanding of the dysfunctional character organizations is that it bears directly on issues of cognition central to the issues of neurosis, that it concerns itself with the epistemics of experience including the experience of self, and that it opens the way to a theory of therapy explicitly concerned with the psychoanalytic enterprise as an exercise in personal epistemology (Barnett, 1966b, 1972, 1978, 1979, 1980a).

The development and characteristics of self in those disorders of living I call the implosive disorders (i.e., the obsessional, the paranoid and the depressive character organizations) are organized around a central dysfunction in which systems of innocence about self are maintained dynamically to avoid further damage to self-esteem or confrontation with self-contempt. Because of the nature of the person's past experience, and of its effect on the organization of experience (described elsewhere at greater length), implosion of affects is utilized to create dysfunctions in interpersonal inference-making which prevent the syntactic organization and comprehension of self, others, and relationships in specific areas determined by past experience with significant others. The threat is that such syntactic organization of experience might lead to perceptions of self that might challenge their literal view of their competence and expose their underlying and implicit sense of self-contempt and lack of significance (Barnett, 1966a).

The operational self of the patient suffering from an implosive disorder of living is severely constricted by the danger of interpersonal behaviors or transactions which might precipitate self-contempt by revealing non-preferred or dissociated aspects of self to oneself or to others. Their selective inhibition of activity in areas in which they need to maintain innocence leads to passivity which guards against the possibility of self-exposure and shame, prominent aspects of the dynamics and experience of these patients. Because of the interrelatedness of many aspects of intimate interpersonal integrations, irradiation both of guarding and inhibition and the resulting passivity may occur to the point that there appears to be no effective operational self in interpersonal situations other than that cued by the significant other in the relationship. Withdrawal, distantiation, and withholding patterns are all related to this inhibition of the operational self. In the most severe situations, an actional or operational self is only constructed in impersonal areas like business or the patient's profession in seeming contrast to the lack of actional constructs in intimate situations.

The sense of "I" as actor and agent in interpersonal situations is usually relegated to what I have called the secret life of these patients. Feelings, thought, fantasies, and even actions which involve shame and fears of exposure are maintained in the private mode of self-experience, disowned as aspects of self and unavailable for adequate comprehension of the range of one's human responsivity.

The representational self of the implosive patient has a fixity, rigidity and stereotypy that belies its significance as a true reflection of an ongoing process of self-experience. As I have indicated, there is a dysfunction in the inferential processes that might organize syntactic comprehension of experience, and the representational self of these patients is often derived from the use of preferred labels from the past rather than ongoing constructions about self-experience. These labels reflect the interpersonal demands which were the conditions of acceptability to significant others in the past around which the earliest concepts of acceptability are organized. Being good, right, etc. are related, in effect, to role perceptions of the past, ignoring the realities of the patient's ongoing interaction with life.

Implosive patients show the widest discrepancies between their operational self and their representational self especially in intimate interpersonal relations. The need to maintain innocence of their intentions as well as the need to fictionalize self-representation in terms of the conditions of the past conspire to divorce action from conception in the most extreme manner. This gulf is perpetuated by a cognitive system organized to maintain obscurity, vagueness and lack of awareness especially in the area of self-experience. These discrepancies, as I have noted before, are of great importance to the therapeutic situation and to the problem of the development of effective insight in the patient, indicating the areas of cognitive repair essential before effective integration of insight can occur. The dichotomy between operational self and representational self in these patients also serves as a clue to the understanding and reaching of the private mode of self-experience which indicates the specific design of the patient's past experiences and the referential systems created by his family which are often obscured in their presentation.

Implosive characters all have nuclear problems of damage to self-esteem and the sense of self, not as accessory facts to supposedly central libidinal or Oedipal pathology, but as central issues in their organization of experience and their dysfunctional living. Covert yet central problems of narcissistic damage are the core of these neuroses and issues of narcissism are central to the organization of their experiences of self and others. The implosive character, in my opinion, shows a typical pattern in his use of narcissism in the structure of his personality (Barnett, 1971). I have described this typical relationship between narcissism and dependency as one in which the implosive character uses overt dependency in the service of his covert narcissism. The ambiguous referential systems of his past enable him to define love as service, and to be openly dependent in his covert search for approval and narcissistic repair. The formal restrictions in his sense of self, the areas of innocence, the need to maintain ambiguity and confusion about self in relation to others establishes an extensive vagueness about self especially in situations implying relative degrees of intimacy. Such patients often show increasing reliance on others for "self" definition as a substitute for the sense of self and approval as a substitute for self-esteem. The increment of such behaviors especially in situations where self-esteem is damaged even in the impersonal areas of living can lead to full time preoccupation with narcissistic issues. In my opinion, implosive characters are often incorrectly called "narcissistic personalities" because of this preponderance of narcissistic themes.

The development and characteristics of self in those disorders of living I call the explosive disorders (the hysteric, the acting-out personalities and the impulse neurotics) are similarly organized around the cognitive disorders at the core of these character organizations (Barnett, 1971). The patient with an explosive disorder typically expels affective experience before it is adequately structured syntactically. Hyperemotionality or acting-out is used to void apprehended aspects of experience and consequently the impressions which provide the experiential data for refined syntaxis. The early history of such patients regularly reveals an affective overload in areas such as aggression or sexuality which results in a fear of the cognitive implications of affects and severe feelings of helplessness and isolation. The premature voidance of affectivity and lack of organization do not allow for the differentiation, nuances and ordering of the meaning of experience, and as a result the hysteric's comprehension of experience is simple and imprecise. Expelled and undigested affective experience is often used to form the overgeneralizations, hyperbolic constructs and crude formulations that characterize the hysteric's transitory comprehension of experience, unrefined by the effect of impression.

In terms of self, the hysteric has suffered profound anaclitic damage. Affective overload has disturbed the basic dependent support and trust the child needs to adequately structure and organize experiences of self and others as separate and interacting entities. The resulting fused self-image leads to attempts to repair the anaclitic damage by the development of a surface narcissism geared to capturing dependent contact with others. In the explosive character organizations, overt narcissism is used in the service of underlying, covert and often denied dependency needs. The counterphobic quality of many explosive characters is related to the fact that their sense of self involves a presentational mode of narcissism and exhibitionism and a private mode of the more covert dependency needs of their fused self-image.

Patients with explosive disorders show a much greater latitude in the development of an operational self than do those with the implosive disorders. Indeed, they often seem addicted to affective expression and action. Among their greatest assets are their empathic sense of others, their expressive abilities, and their ability to chance action and commitment in living. In contrast to the inhibition, caution and circumspection of the implosive characters, one often gets the impression of recklessness or thoughtlessness in the actional and behavioral proclivities of the explosive characters.

It is in the area of the representational self that the crudities of the cognitive systems of the explosive characters take their greatest toll. Representations of self and others are hyperbolic and idealized, accounting for the rapid shifts between adoring idealization and hateful contempt and cynicism, both of self and others. These swings are not related to adequate self-constructs but to constructs reflecting their search for fusion and dependent contact. These patients believe that what they feel must be right. This breakdown between sensate experience and syntactic organization prevents adequate self-representation and mars the authenticity of self-experience.

You will undoubtedly have noticed, in this outline of my approach to the relationship between character and self, that my discussions of narcissism and (neurotic) dependency relate them at all times systemically to one another, and, indeed, imply different dynamic balances between narcissism and dependency in different dysfunctional character types. I have found this to be so important an observation clinically, both in the understanding of individual dynamics and in the clarification of interpersonal and transactional dynamics, that I would like to sketch my approach to characterological patterns of narcissism and dependency, leaving a more complete examination for another paper.

From a perspective that makes cognition and the organization of experience central to personality development, narcissism and (neurotic) dependency are inevitable accompaniments of dysfunctional character organizations and damage to the sense of self and self-esteem. In the everyday experience of psychoanalytic therapy, analysts constantly deal with organizations of self in which patterns of pathological dependency and narcissism are prominent. By and large, our theories have tended to isolate these patterns from each other, and to deal with them separately, implying they arise from discrete lines of development relatively unrelated to each other. This theoretical tendency has become especially marked in the work of recent theoreticians like Kohut and Kernberg who see narcissistic disorders as disorders of self and neurotic dependency disorders as transference neuroses. They imply, therefore, that narcissism and dependency not only have unrelated sources of origin, but, indeed, are to be understood by different theories of the source of meaning and motivation, narcissism being self and experience related while dependency is drive and instinct related. Above and elsewhere (Barnett, 1980b) I have enlarged on my objections to this approach. Let me say here that I find this approach to theorizing both untenable and rather patchwork.

My observation is that narcissism and neurotic dependency always occur together and are systemically related to each other in pathology of the self, i.e., in all the dysfunctional character types. I have observed that narcissism is a pathological system arising from damage to self and self-esteem (Barnett, 1980b). Similarly, I believe that neurotic dependency is present in all neuroses as an attempt to solve problems of self-esteem and damage to the sense of self. Narcissism and dependency both reflect damage to the self structured by early experience. Both imply damage to the self in its potential for the development of autonomy and the creative evolution of the sense of uniqueness and completeness that might result from each individual's confrontation with life. Narcissism and dependency are aborted forms of the cognitive experience of self and involve the sacrifice and subversion of authentic self experience. Dependency sacrifices autonomy for care while narcissism sacrifices autonomy for approval. Dependency appeals through need for helplessness while narcissism appeals through performance. Both incorrectly identify approval with self-esteem, and both create operational systems inevitably bankrupt and evocative of still further damage to the self.

Where there is damage to the self, the options of attempting to repair the damage by dependent fusion or narcissistic performance are open to the developing individual. Experiential factors determine the use of dependency and narcissism and their interrelationship dynamically. Performance and need become polarized operational constructs at different levels of awareness in the person's attempts to achieve interpersonal security and a spurious sense of self contingent on others. In the presence of damage to self, approval is sought by utilizing both narcissism and dependency in different relationships to each other as flawed substitutes for a sense of significance.

In an earlier paper (Barnett, 1971) I described in detail the interpersonal and interactional dynamics that arose from systems of narcissism and dependency as they were seen in marriages between male obsessional patients and female hysterics. I found that, in the obsessional, dependency was overt and used in the service of more covert and central narcissistic demands in intimate interpersonal situations. Often this was revered in impersonal areas of living. The hidden theme of the obsessional lay in his covert damage to self. Dependency became the tool for repairing narcissistic damage in personal living. The hysteric, in contrast, utilizes overt narcissism and exhibitionism in the service of more covert anaclitic damage. Surface narcissism is used to fill dependent needs for contact and care which are the hidden theme of the hysteric.

I have found that these dynamic systems are highly characteristic of the developing structure of personality in the implosive and explosive characters and lead to dynamic interactional systems that are highly predictable and characteristic. For me the systemic relationships of narcissism and dependency have provided an invaluable bridge between the psychodynamics of the individual and the dynamics of marital and familial dysfunctions. Narcissism and dependency provide an important guide in understanding the clash of subjectivities and the difficulties in communicating and relating that occur between people in their search for intimacy and interpersonal security. Above all, though, these systems aid in understanding the individual's organization of experience and its dynamic impact on the experience of self in the different character types.

In summary, then, I have outlined a view in which cognition and the organization of experience is the core of the development of personality and the root of the disorders of living that concern psychoanalysis. The concept of character becomes the general theory of cognition reflecting the design of cognitive templates which organize the experience of self, others and the inanimate world. Self is a special instance of cognition, reflecting man's capacity for the transformation of experience into personal subjective meaning, and providing the bridge between the organization of experience and action. As a subsystem of character, self is designed and confined by the cognitive templates of character structure, and always exists in intimate integration with character, its integrity and deformations. Narcissism and neurotic dependency are seen as inevitable accompaniments of dysfunctional character organizations and damage to the sense of self and self-esteem. They appear in all neurotic structures, and are systemically related to each other. Their relationship to each other provides important clues to the understanding of interpersonal and interactional dynamics in living.

REFERENCES

Barnett, J. (1966a), On cognitive disorders in the obsessional. *Contemp. Psychoanal.*, 2:122–134.

——(1966b), Cognitive repair in the treatment of the obsessional neuroses. In: *Proceedings of the IV World Congress of Psychiatry*, Exerpta Medica International. Congress Series No. 150.

——(1968), Cognition, thought and affect in the organization of experience. In: *Science and Psychoanalysis, Vol. 12*, ed. J. Massermann, pp. 127–147.

——(1971), Narcissism and dependency in the obsessional-hysteric marriage. *Family Process*, 10:75–83.

——(1972), Therapeutic intervention in the dysfunctional thought processes of the obsessional. *Amer. J. Psychother.*, 26:338–351.

——(1978), Insight and therapeutic change. *Contemp. Psychoanal.*, 14:534–544.

——(1979), Character, cognition and therapeutic process. *Amer. J. Psychoanal.*, 39:291–301.

——(1980a), Cognitive repair in the treatment of the neuroses. *J. Amer. Acad. Psychoanal.*, 8:39–55.

——(1980b), Self and character. *J. Amer. Acad. Psychoanal.*, 8:337–352.

Barnett, R. K. (1980), The father's role in early infancy: A case study of paternal paralanguage. Unpublished doctoral dissertation, Yeshiva University.

Forest, T. (1978), A synthesis of individual theory and therapy with family concepts. *Psychoanal. Rev.*, 65:507–521.

Fromm, E. (1941), *Escape From Freedom*. New York: Holt, Rinehart and Winston.

Horney, K. (1950), *Neuroses and Human Growth*. New York: Norton.

James, W. (1892), *Psychology: Brief Course*. New York: Henry Holt.

Kernberg, O. (1975), *Borderline Conditions and Pathological Narcissism*. New York: Aronson.

Kohut, H. (1971), *The Analysis of the Self*. New York: International Universities Press.

——(1977), *The Restoration of the Self*. New York: International Universities Press.

Schachtel, F. G. (1959), *Metamorphosis*. New York: Basic Books.

Stern, D. (1977), *The First Relationship: Mother and Infant*. Cambridge, MA: Harvard University Press.

Sullivan, H. S. (1953), *Interpersonal Theory of Psychiatry*. New York: Norton.

——(1956), *Clinical Studies in Psychiatry*, ed. H. Perry. New York: Norton.

Yogman, M. W. (1977), The goals and structure of face to face interaction between infants and fathers. Presented to Society for Research in Child Development, New Orleans, LA.

13

COGNITION IN PSYCHOANALYSIS

SILVANO ARIETI

[1980]

INTRODUCTION

Edward R. Clemmens

There is a special quality to Silvano Arieti's style that sets it apart from most psychoanalytic writing. I was again struck by it as I reread "Cognition in Psychoanalysis," written two years before his death.

I feel privileged to have witnessed the unfolding of his writing, his talent, his intellect, and his creativity throughout his life, having missed only his childhood. My admiration for him began as soon as we met, long before psychiatry and psychoanalysis had even begun to influence our thoughts.

Silvano was different from the other medical students whose group he belonged to, when I joined them. Some of the others seemed equally bright. They were, however, mainly focused on the tasks at hand, memorizing anatomy and other such subjects. Silvano talked about art, literature, philosophy, and poetry. He quoted Dante, Petrarca, and Boccaccio; Latin classics, and modern Italian authors such as Alessandro Manzoni and Gabriele D'Annunzio; and French writers and philosophers such as Henri Bergson, all by heart. He held firm opinions that were surprisingly mature. Cultural achievements were paramount to his interest, and their pursuit was what mattered most to him. He lived in a world of ideas, constantly searching for more knowledge and deeper understanding of the creative human mind.

Within the next few years it became clear to him that psychiatry was to be his chosen field. Such a pursuit was far more remarkable than contemporary American readers could possibly imagine. Our medical school education in

---

Edward R. Clemmens, M.D. is a Training and Supervising Analyst, American Institute of Psychoanalysts; and a Fellow, American Academy of Psychoanalysis.

the field consisted of a combined neurology and psychiatry course that neglected psychiatry almost completely. Dynamic psychiatry was hardly mentioned and, when it was, it was with a mixture of hostility, ridicule, and contempt.

Being forced to leave Italy was a blessing in disguise. Silvano found in America, his adopted country, the emotional and intellectual climate, and the training opportunities that allowed him to grow unimpeded. He synthesized from then on the best of two heterogeneous worlds, the richness of his classical educational background and the openness that he found on these shores. His strong sense of self, his powerful individuality, kept distinguishing him throughout his career.

Silvano's style never adopted the dry, stilted, pseudolearned jargon in which much of academic psychiatric writing is couched. He expressed his ideas in the manner of a poet, and whenever possible, he used the beauty of symbols as the bridge to understanding. He never wavered in his belief that the fate of mankind will depend upon the continued development of what is most uniquely human, those qualities and those achievements that set man apart from his biological beginnings. A psychodynamic theory based on instincts did not appeal to him. He felt that such a theory omitted, by stressing man's most ordinary qualities, the best that man is capable of. He did not share Freud's pessimism that led inexorably to the postulate of a death instinct. To Silvano, Freud's error began with the uncalled for assumption that humans are best understood by studying their prehuman traits that continue to linger. Silvano's outlook, of course, is shared by many of us so-called neo-Freudians. But what set him apart, however, was his conviction that the most sublime achievements, the peak of performances, the almost divine qualities that some humans are capable of, are the unique characteristics of our breed. His own thirst for knowledge, his own unrelenting search to *conoscere* (the Italian term that is rooted in the Latin *cognitio*), made the cognitive viewpoint impossible to disregard, even obvious and mandatory. He was ahead of his time in advocating it. I believe that, as has happened with other innovators, a lack of understanding by contemporaries in positions of institutional power may have resulted. He was, I am sure, not sufficiently appreciated, in his time. Even now that cognitive analysis has become widely accepted, it is considered to be superficial in the writings of some authors and fanciful hyperintellectualization by others.

An author's style, of course, reveals the essence of its creator, his values, and his character structure. It can even supply an attentive reader with clues of a more subtle kind, such as formative influences during the author's earlier life. The following passage in the Arieti paper that follows offers yet another angle: "For instance, when I speak to you in English, I do not attend to my knowledge of Italian. As a matter of fact, I try not to let my Italian interfere with my English."

It would seem that Silvano was aiming for a degree of separateness, short of repression, that is neither achievable nor desirable. In its stated aim it unintentionally acknowledged the existence of a problem area for him. I see it in a different way.

Clearly, his paper is written in perfect English, as is most, if not all, of his literary output. It contains no grammatical errors nor awkward sentence structures. Yet, for me it is strongly reminiscent of the manner in which Silvano expressed himself in Italian all his life. He may not have been "attending to his knowledge of Italian," yet it shines through, nevertheless. Such an observation may be understood from a psycholinguistic perspective, and this introduction is not the place for such an in-depth discussion. I do suspect, however, that what I shall call "his flavor of Latinate foreignness" may have contributed to the reserved manner in which many colleagues greeted him and his achievements. He never became "one of us" within the in-group.

The paper chosen for publication in this volume, while representative, cannot do justice to the entirety of his work. Such a shortcoming is unavoidable however, and must not become a source of criticism. Silvano Arieti wrote prodigiously for many years. I listened to his new ideas as they emerged, and discussed them with him during our Thursday lunches. Some of them reached their written version years later. I was always fascinated by the power and constant flow of Silvano's imagination. He used to invite me to debate his ideas and I was glad to comply. We often disagreed, as we had since we first met. Our friendship was secure and it certainly was not based on agreement or on resemblance.

There often was a whimsical note to our discussions. In the early days of our New York City meetings, we repeatedly debated whether the interpersonal or the intrapsychic schools of psychoanalysis were closer to the truth. Our discussions were akin to fencing matches, while wearing face masks and padded body armor. We both knew that the either/or formulation of the issue rendered it useless. Rather, our arguments were meant to be parodies of the struggle going on between warring factions among our teachers. A remnant of those days exists even today. The same old doubts about whether Silvano Arieti truly belongs to the school of Interpersonal psychoanalysis are still being aired. I agree that these doubts are justified, since in my view he never belonged to any school, nor did he wish to. He was an avid student and a dedicated teacher. He had ambitions, but they did not include the desire to become a leader with an enthusiastic following. He wanted to be heard, read, discussed, and appreciated for his contributions, for being one more voice to move humanity forward.

In a paper published in 1965 in Volume 8 of *Science and Psychoanalysis*, edited by Masserman, I wrote, "Cognition is or has been, up to now, the Cinderella of psychoanalysis and psychiatry. No other field of the psyche has been so consistently neglected by clinicians and theoreticians alike. Isolated studies and manifestations of interest have not so far developed into a definite trend" (Arieti, 1965). Since then the attitude of the profession has changed, but, until recent years, only to a modest degree. For a person like me, who wrote his first paper on cognition in the year 1947,

Journal of the American Academy of Psychoanalysis, 8:3–23. Keynote address at the 23rd Annual Meeting of the American Academy of Psychoanalysis, New York, May 11, 1979.

these 32 years of waiting have been a taxing experience, but not a "waiting for Godot." Now cognition has become a growing stream of study and concern. And yet, if some colleagues who have not been interested in this subject were to ask me to define cognition and then hear my answer, they would feel like Molière's famous character, Mr. Jourdain, who, when his teacher explained what prose was, said, "I spoke prose all my life without even knowing it." Similarly, even those of us psychoanalysts who have not been interested in cognition have done cognitive psychoanalysis every day, during every session, because cognition is the study of ideas and their precursors, that is, the study of the development, formation, content, interconnections, and dynamic effect of ideas. It is through ideas that we communicate with our patients; it is by hearing the content of their ideas that we get to know them and to know what ideas do to them. It is through ideas that we bring about improvement and cure. In the present paper, cognition will not be discussed as a medium by which we get to know and represent reality—this is the usual representation made by academic psychologists—but as a major component of our inner reality and as a dynamic force. Time limitations will compel me to make a cursory presentation and a selection of topics which may be arbitrary.

Under the influence of classic psychoanalysis, many psychoanalysts have stressed only the primitive—the bodily needs and instinctual or primitive behavior which can exist without a cognitive counterpart or with a very limited one. Simple levels of physiopsychological organization, such as states of hunger, thirst, fatigue, need for sleep, and a certain degree of temperature, sexual urge, or relatively simple emotions, such as fear about one's physical survival, are undoubtedly powerful dynamic forces. They do not include, however, the motivational factors that are possible only at preconceptual levels of development.

Freud stressed how we tend to suppress and repress ideas which elicit anxiety. But we psychiatrists and psychoanalysts have suppressed or repressed the whole field of ideas, that is, cognition. We have repressed it apparently because it is anxiety provoking. As a matter of fact, as we shall see later, there would be very little anxiety in the human being without ideas or precursors of ideas. But psychoanalysts have for a long time preferred to think that cognition deals with those so-called conflict-free areas and therefore does not pertain to psychoanalysis. The contention of cognitive psychoanalysts is that very few conflicts, and only elementary ones, would exist in the human being if he were not able to think, to formulate ideas, old or new, to assimilate them, make them part of himself, face and compare them, distort them, attribute them to others, or, finally, repress them.

When I stated that cognition has been neglected, some could have pointed out to me that that is not really so. At least three giants,

Freud himself, Jean Piaget, and Heinz Werner, have been very much interested in cognition. This is true, but let us see what kind of impact the contributions to cognition of these three giants have made on psychoanalysis.

One of Freud's great breakthroughs was his discovery of the primary process and the description of the primary and secondary processes. Freud, however, did not maintain a great interest in the primary process as a mode of cognition, but only as a carrier of unconscious motivation stemming from an instinctual source. Inasmuch as motivational theory in the Freudian system came to be interpreted in the function of the libido theory, the primary process came to be studied not in a framework of cognition, but in a framework of energetics. Primary and secondary processes came to be considered primarily not as two different ways of thinking, but as two different ways of dealing with cathexes. In the primary process the cathexis was described as free. In other words, cathectic quantities of energy are easily shifted from some objects to others. Inasmuch as this shifting may easily occur from realistic and appropriate objects to unrealistic and inappropriate ones, the primary process becomes an irrational mode of functioning.

These points of view leave many unexplored aspects, especially those which pertain more closely to cognition. Cognition is relegated to being a medium, and is not considered as a source of conscious or unconscious motivation.

Piaget's contributions are very significant, especially in child psychology. But they have not made much impact on psychoanalytic therapy, mainly because they are difficult to integrate with a psychodynamic view of the human being. Piaget's works reveal very well the process of cognitive maturation and adaptation to environmental reality and disclose the various steps by which the child increases his understanding and mastery of the world. Although they are important, they do not represent intrapsychic life in its structural and psychodynamic aspects. They neglect affect as much as classic psychoanalytic studies neglect cognition, and do not deal with motivation, unconscious processes, and conflicts of forces. The cognitive functions, as described by Piaget, seem really autonomous and conflict-free, as the ego psychologists have classified them. All attempts up to the present to absorb Piaget's contributions into the core of classic psychoanalysis—including the attempt made by Odier (1956)—have, in my opinion, not gone very far. The only contributions of Piaget that could be reconciled with classic psychoanalysis are those he made very early in his career when he was still under the influence of the psychoanalytic school (Piaget, 1919). For instance, his concept of the child's egocentrism is related to the psychoanalytic concept of the child's feeling of omnipotence.

The contributions of Heinz Werner (1948) are perhaps more pertinent to psychiatric studies because, in following a comparative developmental approach, they take into consideration pathological conditions. However, like the works of Piaget, they do not make significant use of the concepts of the unconscious and unconscious motivation.

When my first writings on cognition appeared, from 1947 to 1955, such studies were looked at askance in America, whether they dealt with psychological structure or content (Arieti, 1947, 1948, 1953, 1955). And yet in France, Lévi-Strauss (1949, 1951) was very well received for his structural approach, and in America, too, Chomsky (1957) introduced structuralism to linguistics. In the 40's and in the 50's, psychology, under the influence of behaviorism, was concerned mainly with overt behavior; classic psychoanalysis focused on energetics and instinctual precognitive life; and neo-Freudian, cultural psychoanalysis was concerned with the study of conflicts without considering their cognitive origin. In France in the meantime, Lacan (1966) started his cognitive studies of inner life and stressed the importance of the signifier in conscious and unconscious life. By signifier (in French, *signifiant*), he meant language or the word, whatever gives a meaning to things. Unfortunately, his works are written in such a difficult style as to discourage many readers.

OTHERNESS AND INWARDNESS

Another reason that has induced many psychoanalysts to neglect cognition has been the assumption that a cognitive approach would neglect infancy and early childhood, a period of life during which there is little cognition and which, in some respects, can be called precognitive. It is a period during which sensations and elementary perceptions prevail. The child lives at what Piaget called a sensorimotor level, regulated mostly by the simple stimulus-response mechanism. In spite of this poverty of cognitive processes, many people rightly point out that at this level the baby and his mother are already capable of establishing a bond of love, with attachment, empathy, and mutual concern. Isn't this bond of love, or the lack of it, or its vicissitudes, of fundamental importance for the subsequent life? A dialogue of love has already started in the first few hours of life. A large number of clues and signals are exchanged between the few-day-old baby and his mother. What is more meaningful than the eye-to-eye language, the body contact between mother and baby, contact established by sucking at the breast and by the embrace? What is more full of meaning than the reciprocal smile between the baby and his mother? The beauty of the embrace and the contact with the body of the mother cannot be spoiled even when we use our arid scientific language and call it an activation of sensorimotor systems in the infant (Harlow and Harlow, 1965). A cognitive approach does not deny the importance of this early stage of human life. However, the following considerations have to be made:

The dialogue of love between mother and baby is unequal. Even though the mother may not speak to the child, she touches him, feeds him, holds him, rocks him, smiles at him, sings to him, and she attributes an affective-cognitive meaning to these actions. For her, each gesture and action has a meaning. She does embrace her child with the warmth and love of her adulthood. When we see that beautiful scene, mother and baby together, and we call it a "dialogue" of love, we attribute to it our meanings and our words, our word about words—we call it a *dialogue*. Happy the baby who, in the smile on the face of his mother, intuitively perceives in a precognitive way a reflection of his own smile. But this precognitive intuition will not develop into a real and bilateral bond of love unless cognitive developments follow. This exchange between mother and child is a superb beginning; but no matter how superb and beautiful, in the human infant it would remain at a level not superior to that occurring in animal forms unless one of the two partners is a human adult, equipped with cognitive power, and unless the mother sowed cognitive seeds so that the primitive embrace does not remain primitive but becomes an embrace later capable of including other members of the family, the whole group of people with whom the child has significant contacts, and eventually possibly humankind. But how can the maternal embrace become a potentially worldwide embrace? By the gradual and subsequent acquisition of cognitive and symbolic forms. Language and concepts, mediated through language, and emotions made possible by the acquisition of language, will expand, deepen, transform the life of the child and give rise to a universe of ideas, mutual understandings, interpersonal ties, loves. The gradual independence from mother is accompanied by a gradual immersion in the big world. Thus whatever pain is involved in the gradual separateness from mother is compensated for by the opening and joy of the world, which is gradually better understood and savored. But it must be a world from which mother is not absent. Mother is still there, symbol of the concrete precognitive attachment and as representative and intermediary of the world of incoming symbols. The openness to the big world has its earliest beginning when the child is approximately nine months old.

Mother becomes increasingly absent, but to the increasing absence of mother I shall return later. Now let us give another look at these early eight to nine months of life. In these early months, actually as soon as he is born, the baby is more or less receptive to some exchanges with the *other*. The other at first is only the mother, who becomes instantly the forerunner and representative of all future others: family members, people, mankind. So the first other is the person who is experienced the least as an other. Even those of us who do not believe the child considers himself part of mother, do agree that the first Thou is the least other. It is through this relatedness to mother that the child starts to develop the I–Thou relation, described by Martin Buber (1953). This relatedness is the prototype of subsequent meaningful interpersonal relations, leading to attachment, affection, friendship, intimacy, and love. Martin Buber also describes another encounter of the individual, the I–It, the encounter with the inanimate world, be it that of a simple object or of a solar system. Buber rightly stresses the superiority of the I–Thou relation over the I–It.

Martin Buber is the philosopher of what I call *otherness*, the relation with the other, which later was further explored by many authors, especially by George Herbert Mead and Harry Stack Sullivan.

Buber's contribution is very important. Nevertheless, it has limitations. As a philosophical or psychological entity the human being cannot be defined exclusively in terms of the formulas "I–Thou" and "I–It." Although Buber has made it clear that by reaching out to a fellow man, a person reaches into himself, and that in reaching out to others one reaches oneself, this formulation is vague. The "I," or self, needs a special consideration, a more profound treatment, which is not included in the concept of otherness. The "I," or self, is a human being, too, but is not just an other. In reaching myself, I have an attitude different from the one I have in reaching others. The attitude toward oneself is based on introspection, or self-awareness, which other animal species have only to a rudimentary degree. It is only with the human being that this attitude or mental set expands to an enormous degree. Otherness requires openness to the world. Introspection and self-awareness require openness to oneself, that attitude or mental set that I call *inwardness*. Although in his otherness the human being is by far superior to, and extremely more complicated than, other animal species, in the beginning and first stages of otherness the human being is not completely dissimilar from other animals. Of course, he changes dramatically later when he is able to act, to embrace, to touch, to love, and to hate with words, too. Inwardness unfolds later and would not develop at all unless at least a rudimentary otherness already existed. Inwardness makes us reach for ourselves, inside, opens to us our inner life. I enter into a special dialogue with a special person, me, I face myself, speak to myself, and read myself. I am not an object to me. I have a special encounter—"I–I"—and what I can discover can be unexpectedly new; a whole universe opens up to me, my own universe. But this inner universe consists of cognitive structures with cognitive content. If not for cognition, I could not have an inner life, or perhaps I could have only a very limited one. Moreover, if I want to discover my unconscious, I must do so in a cognitive way. For what I have repressed from consciousness is predominantly cognitive in nature; that is, I repress ideas, attitudes, mental dispositions, and in most cases the emotions derived from them. Many cognitive forms have a double entity, they consist of what seems a psychological bifurcation. One branch of this bifurcation is interpersonal, reaching the other with a word, an idea, a complicated relation. The other branch is intrapsychic, and makes it possible to retain such an idea, attitude, disposition, within ourselves. When I acquire a new cognitive form, let us say a new word or a new concept, not only is it my otherness which expands but also my inward-ness. Not only do I have a new way to reach others, or new understanding to give to others, but to myself. That new word or new concept, and the emotions which accompany the new concept, will enrich myself, too, will become from now on part of my inner life.

IMAGERY

At this point I wish to give a bird's eye view of the development of cognition from babyhood to adulthood, as far as inner life is concerned. In the limited time at my disposal, I will be able to discuss the develop-ment of cognitive forms and of their content in a very succinct way. I shall try to show how they are necessary for the origin of emotions and psychodynamic mechanisms. When we psychoanalysts interested in cog-nition stress the importance of ideas and systems of ideas, we do not minimize the importance of affective life, or of motivation, conscious or unconscious. On the contrary, we stress a fact which is very seldom acknowledged, namely, that at a human level most emotions would not exist without a cognitive substratum. The expansion of the neocortex and, consequently, of our cognitive functions has permitted an expan-sion of our affective life also. In a classic paper, published in 1937, Papez demonstrated that several parts of the rhinencephalon and archipallium are not used for olfactory functions in the human being, but for the experience of emotion. In spite of the diminished importance of olfac-tion, these areas have expanded, not decreased, in man and have become associated with vast neocortical areas.

It is at approximately nine months of age that the "second birth" of the child occurs. This is the time when the child realizes that mother be-comes more and more frequently absent. He gradually learns to under-stand language and to talk, but he acquires another faculty, which at first develops much more rapidly than language: imagery. The very first stage of internalization, that is, of inner life and inwardness, occurs through images. For simplification's sake we shall take into consideration only visual images. Brodmann's area 19 in the occipital lobe now becomes myelinized and capable of functioning. Visual sensations and perceptions which were mediated in area 17 and 18 have left memory traces that assume the form of representation, that is, of images. The image is now an internal quasi-reproduction of a perception that does not require the corresponding external stimulus in order to be evoked. The image is indeed the earliest and one of the most important foundations of human symbolism. By symbol we mean something that stands for something else that is not present. Whereas previous forms of cognition and learning permitted an understanding based on the immediately given or experienced, from now on cognition will rely also on what is absent and inferred. Mother is now more and more frequently absent. But the child can endure her absence. Her image is with him; it stands for her. The image is based on the memory traces of previous perceptions of the mother. The mother acquires a psychic reality that is not tied to her physical presence.

Image formation is actually the basis for all the following higher mental processes. It enables the child not only to reevoke what is not present, but to retain an affective disposition for the absent object. For instance, the image of the mother may evoke the feelings that the child experiences toward her. If we adopt the terminology generally used in reference to computers, we can say that now the psyche or the brain is capable of analogic codification. The image thus becomes a substitute for the external object. It is actually an inner object, although it is not well organized. It is the most primitive of the inner objects if, because of their sensori-motor character, we exclude motor engrams from the category of inner objects. When the image's affective associations are pleasant, the evoking of the image reinforces the child's longing or appetite for the corresponding external object. The image thus has a motivational influence in leading the child to search out the actual object, which in its external reality is still more gratifying than the image. The opposite is true when the image's affective associations are unpleasant: the child is motivated not to exchange the unpleasant inner object for the corresponding external one, which is even more unpleasant.

Imagery soon constitutes the foundation of inner psychic reality. It helps the individual not only to understand the world better, but also to create a surrogate for it. Moreover, whatever is known or experienced tends to become a part of the individual who knows and experiences. Thus, cognition can no longer be considered only a hierarchy of mechanisms, but also an enduring psychological content that retains the power to affect its possessor, now and in the future.

The child who has reached the level of imagery is now capable of experiencing not only such simple emotions as tension, fear, rage, and satisfaction, as he did in the first year of life, but also anxiety, anger, wish, perhaps in a rudimentary form even love and sadness, and, finally, security. Anxiety is the emotional reaction to the expectation of danger, which is mediated through cognitive media. The danger is not immediate, nor is it always well defined. Its expectation is not the result of a simple perception or signal. At subsequent ages, the danger is represented by complicated sets of cognitive constructs. At the age level that we are discussing now, it is sustained by images. It generally refers to a danger connected with the important people in the child's life, mother and father, who may punish or withdraw tenderness and affection. Anger, at this age, is also rage sustained by images. Wish is also an emotional disposition, which is evoked by the image of a pleasant object. The image motivates the individual to replace the image with the real object satisfaction. Sadness can be felt only at a rudimentary level at this stage, if by sadness we mean an experience similar to the one the sad or depressed adult undergoes. At this level, sadness is an unpleasant feeling evoked by the image of the loss of the wished object and by the experience of displeasure caused by the absence of the wished object. As I described in the mentioned paper, written in 1947, this is the stage when the child becomes capable of anticipating the future and is no longer capable only of expecting imminent events. This is also the stage when the baby becomes able to experience security, or the first forerunners of what will be security. As Sullivan (1953) was the first to point out, security is different from satisfaction. Satisfaction occurs when all the bodily needs, like food, sleep, rest, warmth, and contact with the body of mother, are satisfied. No cognition is necessary for the experience of satisfaction, but it is for the experience of security. Security does not consist only of removal of unpleasant emotions or removal of uncertainty, but also of pleasant anticipation, a feeling of well-being, a trust in people and things to come. Security is experienced by the year-old child not only by his contacts with his mother, but by the feeling that, if she is absent, she will return. The inner image of his mother, which he always carries inside himself, gives him this feeling of trust. Many other things could be said about images, imagery, and imagination. I shall limit myself to saying that imagery emerges not only as the first or most primitive process of reproducing, or substituting for, the real, but also is the first and most primitive process of creating the unreal. The French philosopher, Gaston Bachelard, has stressed this point repeatedly in his books (1960, 1971). It is true that the image does not reproduce reality faithfully; it emerges as an innovation, a state of becoming, a force of transcendence, and it is the beginning of human creativity (Arieti, 1976). Unfortunately, we cannot explore this subject, but must pass on to the next stage of cognitive development, represented by the endocept or amorphous cognition.

THE ENDOCEPT

The endocept is a mental construct representative of a level intermediary between the image and the word. At this level, there is a primitive organization of memory traces, images, and motor engrams. This organization results in a construct that does not tend to reproduce reality, as it appears in perceptions or images: it remains nonrepresentational. The endocept, in a certain way, transcends the image, but inasmuch as it is not representational, it is not easily recognizable. On the other hand, it is not a motor engram that leads to prompt action. Nor can it be transformed into a verbal expression; it remains at a preverbal level. Although it has an emotional component, most of the time it does not expand into a clearly felt emotion.

The endocept is not, of course, a concept. It cannot be shared. We may consider it a disposition to feel, to act, to think that occurs after simpler mental activity has been inhibited. It is an interrelation of feelings and residues of former experiences which has not yet crystallized into a concept. The awareness of this construct is vague, uncertain, and partial. Relative to the image, the endocept involves considerable cognitive expansion; but this expansion occurs at the expense of the subjective awareness, which is decreased in intensity. The endocept is at times experienced as an "atmosphere," an intention, a holistic experience that cannot be divided into parts or words—something similar to what Freud called "oceanic feeling." At other times, there is no sharp demarcation between endoceptual, subliminal experiences, and some vague primitive experiences. On still other occasions, strong but not verbalizable emotions accompany endocepts.

For the evidence of the existence of endocepts and for their importance in adult life, dreams, and creativity, the audience is referred elsewhere (Arieti, 1967, 1976). It is more than likely that it is the right hemisphere that is mediating endoceptual activity.

MOVING TOWARD CONCEPTUAL THINKING

At this point, I would have to open up an important area of cognition which includes the acquisition of language and the various stages of preconceptual thinking leading to the formation of the mature concept. This is the stage in which, in addition to the analogic codification of imagery and the diffuse grouping of the endocept, the psyche or the brain becomes capable of digital codification, mediated chiefly by the left hemisphere. Entire libraries have been written on these subjects. From the acquisition of language (naming things) to a logical organization of concepts, various substages follow one another so rapidly and overlap in so many multiple ways that it is very difficult to retrace and individualize them. These intermediary stages are more pronounced and more easily recognizable in pathological conditions.

Some of them appear in the most fleeting way in ontogenesis (Arieti, 1967), and some of them reappear in schizophrenia (Arieti, 1974). In other writings (1967, 1970), I have described how the acquisition of language and concepts is necessary for the experience of high-level emotions, like sadness, depression, hate, love, or joy.

In studying preconceptual stages of thinking, we view a vast cognitive realm which extends from the primitive cognition of the primary process to the elaborate one of the secondary process and Aristotelian logic. Unfortunately, I cannot deal here with this vast subject. I shall make only a few remarks. During these stages the child tends to explore more and more the external world, but also himself. The randomness of the cognitive experiences is more and more superseded by the gradual organization of inner constructs. These inner constructs at first consist of the forms we have already mentioned: images, endocepts, and preconceptual forms. Later they consist also of simple concepts, and finally of complicated concepts with all their conscious and unconscious ramifications.

THE IMAGE OF MOTHER AND THE SELF-IMAGE

These constructs continuously exchange some of their components and increase in differentiation, rank, and order. A large number of them, however, retain the enduring mark of their individuality. Some of them have powerful effects and have an intense life of their own, even if at the stage of our knowledge we cannot give them an anatomic location or a neurophysiological interpretation. They may be considered the very inhabitants of inner reality. The two most important ones in the preschool age, and the only two to which I shall devote a few words, are the image of mother and the self-image. At this point the word "image" is used with a different meaning. It is no longer exclusively used to signify an attempted reproduction of a perception, but a complicated cluster of cognitive components. For instance, the image of the mother is a conglomeration of what the child feels and knows about her.

In normal circumstances, the mother as an inner object will consist of a group of agreeable images: as the giver, the helper, the assuager of hunger, thirst, cold, loneliness, immobility, and any other discomfort. She becomes the prototype of the good inner object. At the same time she will become, as we have already mentioned, the representative of the "Thou." Any other fellow human being, in his essential human qualities, will be modeled after her.

Much more difficult to study in early childhood is the self-image. At the precognitive sensori-motor level, the primordial self probably consists of a bundle of relatively simple relations between feelings, kinesthetic sensations, perceptions, motor activity, and a partial integration of these elements. At the image-level, the child who is raised in normal circumstances learns to experience himself not exclusively as a cluster of feelings and of self-initiated movements, but also as a body-image and as an entity having many kinds of relations with other images, especially those of the parents. Inasmuch as the child cannot see his own face, his own visual image will be faceless—as, indeed, he will tend to see himself in dreams throughout his life. He wishes, however, to be in appearance, gestures, and actions like people toward whom he has a pleasant attitude or by whom he feels protected and gratified. The wish tends to be experienced as reality, and he believes that he is or is about to become like the others or as powerful as the others. As the child grows, his self-image will consist less and less of analogic images and preconceptual cognition, and more and more of concepts related to the self.

CONCEPTUAL LIFE

Struggling rapidly through preconceptual stages, the child finally reaches the conceptual level. As Vygotsky (1962) has illustrated, conceptual thinking starts early in life, but it is in adolescence that it acquires prominence.

Whereas psychiatrists and psychoanalysts study primitive and preconceptual types of thinking from the points of view of both form and content, they generally study concepts only in relation to their content. The study of conceptual forms remains almost exclusively an object of study for academic psychologists. I shall follow this tradition, and I shall discuss concepts only from the point of view of content.

In a large part of psychiatric, psychoanalytic, and psychological literature concepts are considered static, purely intellectual entities, separate from human emotions and unimportant in psychodynamic studies. I am among those who cannot adhere to this point of view. Concepts and organized clusters of concepts become depositories of emotions and also originators of new emotions. They have a great deal to do with the conflicts of man, his achievements and his frustrations, his states of happiness or despair, of anxiety or of security. They become the repositories of intangible feelings and values. Not only does every concept have an emotional counterpart, but concepts are necessary for high emotions. In the course of reaching adulthood, emotional and conceptual processes become more and more intimately interconnected. It is impossible to separate the two. They form a circular process. The emotional accompaniment of a cognitive process becomes the propelling drive not only toward action but also toward further cognitive processes. Only emotions can stimulate man to overcome the hardship of some cognitive processes and lead to complicated symbolic, interpersonal, and abstract processes. On the other hand, only cognitive processes can give origin to, and extend indefinitely, the realm of emotions (Arieti, 1967). Between known conceptual meanings there are gaps of potential meanings and consequently of potential emotions. Perhaps it is more accurate to say that clusters of meanings are islands in an uncharted ocean of potential meanings and emotions. Unstable clusters produce conflictful waves of anxiety, sorrow, and anger. A perennial effort is made to diminish the cognitive dissonance (Festinger, 1957) and to form new clusters which either do not make waves or repress the wave-making clusters. A perennial effort is made to diminish the contrast between the concepts which echo the objectivity of the universe and those which echo the inner subjectivity—the subjectivity which shifts between harmony and turmoil, craving and satisfaction.

From a psychiatric and psychoanalytic point of view, the greatest importance of concepts resides in the fact that to a large extent they come to constitute the self-image. When this development occurs, the previous self-images are not completely obliterated. They remain throughout the life of the individual in the forms of minor components of the adult self-image or as repressed or suppressed forms. In adolescence, however, concepts accrue to constitute the major part of the self-image. Such concepts as inner worth, personal significance, mental outlook, more mature evaluations of appraisals reflected from others, attitudes toward ideals, aspirations, capacity to receive and give acceptance, affection, and love are integral parts of the self and of the self-image, together with the emotions that accompany these concepts. Like other concepts, the concepts and emotions which constitute the self are generally not consistent with one another, in spite of a prolonged attempt made by the individual to organize them logically.

The motivation of the human being varies according to the various levels of development. When higher levels emerge, motivations originated at lower levels do not cease to exist. At a very elementary sensorimotor level, the motivation consists of obtaining immediate pleasure and avoidance of immediate displeasure by gratification of bodily needs. When imagery emerges, either phylogenetically or ontogenetically, the individual becomes capable of wishing something that is not present and is motivated toward the fulfillment of his wishes. Let us remember that no wish is possible without a cognitive component, perhaps one of the most primitive, the image. The child will continue to be wish-motivated as he moves on to more advanced stages of primary cognition, such as the prelogical stage. As I have already mentioned, although the motivation can always be understood as a search for (or as an attempt to retain) pleasure and avoid unpleasure, gratification of the self or of the self-image becomes the main motivational factor concerned with danger throughout his life: immediate danger, which elicits fear, and a more distant or symbolic danger, which elicits anxiety. However, whereas at earlier levels of development this danger is experienced as a threat to the physical self, at higher levels it is many times experienced as a threat to an acceptable image of the self. To reduce the emotional factors which accompany complicated cognitive processes to the status of cover-up of primitive instinctual drives is a reductionistic assessment of the human psyche; it is forcing a return to a presymbolic or prehuman level. Even feelings, sensations, bodily needs, which theoretically stand on their biological processes, become involved with systems of symbolism which give them special meaning and involve them in intricate networks of motivation. Let us take as an example the sexual need. It is obvious that sexual life cannot be considered only from a sensuous or instinctive point of view. Sexual gratification or deprivation become involved with such concepts as being accepted or rejected, desirable or undesirable, loved or unloved, lovable or unlovable, capable or incapable, potent or impotent, normal or abnormal. Thus sexual gratification and deprivation become phenomena that affect the whole self-image.

The self is a system of interrelated cognitive items and of the emotions to which they give origin. The value and identity of these items are defined not only by their history but by their place or distribution in the system. The historical identity, although extremely important, does not coincide with the present identity. The way I am today cannot totally be subsumed by my past. In other words, what counts is not only the sequence of historical events but their integration and cognitive transformation. Each of us to some extent is created by the acts of cognition which we initiate or at least in which we participate. We must study how each item is distributed and integrated with the others. Preexisting structures, or schemata, are brought to bear upon the present. Also schemata concerning the future are brought to bear upon the present, so that our present day may be brightened or darkened by the vision of tomorrow. Since the realm of cognitive symbolism is potentially infinite and consequently the distribution of these cognitive elements can vary in an infinite number of ways, complete or absolute knowledge of the psyche and sure predictability are impossible. What are possible, however, are presumable knowledge and the assessment of probability.

In other writings I have shown the importance of cognitive life in schizophrenia. I have shown how the preschizophrenic, in a period of life which precedes the psychotic break, generally during adolescence or young adulthood, finds himself threatened on all sides, as if he were in a jungle (Arieti, 1974). It is not a jungle where ferocious animals are to be found, but a jungle of concepts that remain unconscious until shortly before the onset of the psychosis, or the phase that I have called the prepsychotic panic. The threat is again not to physical survival, but to the self-image. The dangers are concept-feelings, such as those of being unwanted, unloved, inadequate, unacceptable, totally dependent on others, inferior, awkward, clumsy, not belonging, peculiar, different, rejected, humiliated, guilty, unable to find one's own way among the different paths of life, disgraced, discriminated against, kept at a distance, suspected, and so forth. Some of these concepts were conscious even in earlier periods of life. What had remained unconscious were their full significance, their ramifications and connections, especially with similar concepts about the self, originated in early childhood. When these constellations of concepts are interconnected and become vividly conscious, they are experienced as unbearable and undergo drastic changes. At this point, the patient undergoes a conceptual transformation of cosmic magnitude. He either withdraws from the world or becomes possessed by a system of unusual beliefs which makes him see the world in a different way, he has to make a drastic shift; he has to adopt a different type of cognition, the cognition of the primary process, the cognition of the dream. And then, no longer will he be besieged by the jungle of concepts which hurt his inner self, no longer will he consider himself inadequate, worthless, and deserving of contempt. The inner danger has now been transformed into a danger which comes from others. Inwardness is projected into otherness. I cannot possibly talk about schizophrenic cognition in the time at my disposal. But I shall mention only how the patient, at a certain period of his psychotic transformation, enters into the world of metaphor.

A patient thinks his wife is putting poison in his food. He really believes his wife is poisoning his life, but he cannot accept that belief. If she disturbs his life, he may have something to do with the marital difficulties. Another patient has an olfactory hallucination. He smells a bad odor that emanates from his body. We can be fairly sure that he attributes to his body what he thinks of himself. He has a rotten personality, one which stinks. It is easier for him to blame his body than his character. Another patient, while he was in a teenage camp, believed that at night people were going into his closet and drawers and changing his clothes by putting female clothes in their place. He was still concerned with his identity, especially gender and sex identity. Was he really a man? Another patient believes that a mysterious, unidentified person from another planet controls his thoughts. But this man is a symbol of the patient's father, toward whom he felt so emotionally distant, as if he were on another planet—this father, however, whom the patient experienced as wanting to control his ideas and the direction he wanted to give to his life. When another patient tells us that invisible rays pierce him and cause him harm, he refers to the hidden, or hard to detect, ways with which society has treated and harmed him.

The patient uses what is for us metaphorical language. From what he tells us, we can indeed learn some hidden truths, as we would learn from a poet. But is the patient a poet? He is not. The big discrepancy between him and the poet lies in the difference I described in the book, *Creativity*: the magic synthesis between the cognition of the primary process of the schizophrenic and the cognition of the tertiary process of the creative person (Arieti, 1976). The patient is not at all aware of the metaphorical meaning of his delusions; he accepts them literally. The metaphors are for him metamorphoses. For him it is literally true that his wife poisons his food, that a bad odor emanates from his body, that a man controls his thoughts from a distant planet, that invisible rays go through his body. He is like a dreamer who, while he is dreaming, thinks the dream is true. The dream is true, of course; not just as an act of life, but also in its symbolic content. It is as true as the poetry which, in its metaphorical revelations, discloses to us ways and feelings deeper than those usually attached to a daily reality. It is one of our tasks to guide this pseudopoet, the patient, to return to the reality of the secondary process; but it must be a reality which is less anxiety provoking and, hopefully, not prosaic.

I regret that lack of time does not permit me to discuss further either schizophrenic cognition or creative cognition. Also for lack of time, I must omit discussing the importance of cognition in depression, as Bemporad and I have illustrated (Arieti and Bemporad, 1978). I must overlook Barnett's (1966, 1968, 1972) studies on obsessive neurosis and I cannot even open the extremely important and vast topic of how culture provides the individual with innumerable basic concepts which lead to growth as well as to pathological conflicts. Before concluding, however, I want to refer again to an important issue to which I have alluded in passing throughout my presentation: the relation between cognition and the unconscious. It is a basic tenet of the cognitive school of psychoanalysis that the unconscious and unconscious motivation include much more than infantile strivings. They include also a great deal of inner life, built in childhood, adolescence, and adulthood with cognitive forms.

Because of the enormous expansion of the neopallic areas, the human being is the first entity, at least in the history of our solar system, to be confronted with an infinite array of symbols and of emotions to which they give origin. We would not be able to bear this tremendous burden unless we had relief mechanisms. Other species have only the mechanism of non-attending or of reducing to tacit knowledge what they do not use at the moment. We, too, have the mechanism of non-attending. For instance, when I speak to you in English, I do not attend to my knowledge of Italian. As a matter of fact, I try not to let my Italian interfere with my English. But this is not equivalent to making conscious material unconscious, or transforming it into dynamically different forms. In other words, non-attending is not a mechanism of repression. But we do repress. As a relief mechanism, we do have the mechanism of repression, first described by Freud. Whatever disturbs one's cherished self-image tends to be modified, reevaluated, denied, or removed from consciousness. Whatever might make the individual appear to himself unworthy, guilty, inadequate, sadistic, vindictive, inconsistent with his ideas or ideals, escapist, or not living up to his ideals tends eventually to be repressed. Indeed, some of these evaluations of the self remain conscious; but even so, what is eliminated from consciousness is much more than the individual realizes. Psychoanalytic practice reveals how many of these cognitive constructs about oneself, and how many of their ramifications, are kept either in a state of unconsciousness or in dynamically acceptable or less unacceptable cognitive transformations.

Repression of the main motivation (protecting the self-image) is often achieved with the help of psychological mechanisms that detour consciousness toward other avenues of thought and behavior. Intricate cognitive configurations lead the patient to feelings, ideas, and strategic forms of behavior that make the self-image acceptable or at least less unacceptable. At times any form of self-criticism is repressed, and even benevolent criticism from others is resisted with awkward cognitive strategies.

We may thus conclude that we human beings are confronted not only by the infinite external cosmos, but by the infinite cognition which reflects the cosmos, and the infinite cognition that we internalize, and the infinite cognition that we repress. The self remains a unity, a giant enriched and battered by all sides. We psychoanalysts must maintain a humble attitude, because no matter how much we explore and bring to consciousness, what we will clarify will be only a part of the psyche, the whole of which we shall never know. But we shall accept this limitation of our goals without a sense of defeat because cognition teaches us that the human being is *Homo symbolicus*, for which a small part becomes a symbol that stands for the whole. The proper symbol may be a little spark which sheds an intense light and guides us to a vast understanding and to the depths of our hearts.

REFERENCES

Arieti, S. (1947), The processes of expectation and anticipation. *J. Nerv. & Mental Dis.*, 106:471–481.

—— (1948), Special logic of schizophrenic and other types of autistic thought. *Psychiatry*, 11:325–335. [Reprinted in Arieti, 1978, pp. 23–45.]

—— (1953), Some aspects of language in schizophrenia. Read at Clark University, Worcester, MA, on November 25. Clark University Press.

—— (1955), *Interpretation of Schizophrenia*, 1st ed. New York: Brunner.

—— (1965), Contributions to cognition from psychoanalytic theory. In: *Science and Psychoanalysis, Vol. 3*, ed. J. Masserman. New York: Grune & Stratton.

—— (1967), *The Intrapsychic Self. Feeling, Cognition and Creativity in Health and Mental Illness.* New York: Basic Books.

—— (1970), The structural and psychodynamic role of cognition in the human psyche. In: *The World Biennial of Psychiatry and Psychotherapy, Vol. 1*, ed. S. Arieti. New York: Basic Books.

—— (1974), *Interpretation of Schizophrenia*, 2nd ed. (rev. & expanded). New York: Basic Books.

—— (1976), *Creativity: The Magic Synthesis.* New York: Basic Books.

—— (1978), *On Schizophrenia, Phobias, Depression, Psychotherapy and the Farther Shores of Psychiatry: Selected Papers.* New York: Brunner/Mazel.

—— & Bemporad, J. (1978), *Severe and Mild Depression: The Psychotherapeutic Approach.* New York: Basic Books.

Bachelard, G. (1960), *The Poetics of Reverie.* Boston: Beacon.

——(1971), *On Poetic Imagination and Reverie.* Indianapolis, IN: Bobbs-Merrill.

Barnett, J. (1966), On cognitive disorders in the obsessional. *Contemp. Psychoanal.*, 2:122–134.

—— (1968), Cognition, thought and affect in the organization of experience. In: *Science and Psychoanalysis*, ed. J. Masserman. New York: Grune & Stratton.

—— (1972), Therapeutic intervention in the dysfunctional thought processes of the obsessional. *Amer. J. Psychother.*, 26:338–351.

Buber, M. (1953), *I and Thou.* Edinburgh: Clark.

Chomsky, N. (1957), *Syntax Structures.* The Hague: Mouton.

Festinger, L. (1957), *A Theory of Cognitive Dissonance.* Stanford, CA: Stanford University Press.

Harlow, H. F. & Harlow, M. K. (1965), The affective systems. In: *Behavior in Nonhuman Primates, Vol. 2*, ed. A. M. Schrier, H. F. Harlow & X. X. Stollnitz. New York: Academic Press.

Lacan, J. (1966), *Ecrits.* Paris: Editions du Seuil.

Lévi-Strauss, J. (1949), L'efficacité symbolique. *Rev. Hist. Relig.* (January–March).

—— (1951), Language and the analysis of social laws. *Amer. Anthropol.*, 53:155–163.

Odier, C. (1956), *Anxiety and Magic Thinking.* New York: International Universities Press.

Papez, J. W. (1937), A proposed mechanism of emotion. *Arch. Neurol. Psychiat.*, 38:725–743.

Piaget, J. (1919), La psychanalyse dans ses rapports avec la psychologie de l'enfant. *Bull. Soc. Alfred Binet de Paris*, 20.

Sullivan, H. S. (1953), *Conceptions of Modern Psychiatry.* New York: Norton.

Vygotsky, L. S. (1962), *Thought and Language.* Cambridge, MA: M.I.T. Press.

Werner, H. (1948), *Comparative Psychology of Mental Development.* Chicago: Follet.

14

PSYCHOTHERAPY WITH ADOLESCENTS: THE ART OF INTERPRETATION

JOHN L. SCHIMEL

[1986]

INTRODUCTION

Amnon Issacharoff

Reading this paper—an outstanding piece from a body of writing by Jack Schimel on clinical issues in the treatment of adolescents—was for me a revisit with a familiar presence. Candor, a laconic style of delivery, and humor were common threads in his way of being a therapist, a friend, a speaker, or a writer. All of these qualities are displayed here.

A young colleague, listening to one of Schimel's always witty professional deliveries, once wondered if he could ever measure up to Schimel's ebullient vitality and penetrating insights. I was reminded of Schimel's (1972) tongue-in-cheek remark in a footnote to one of his papers: "Generally speaking, there are three types of psychoanalysts: hysterics, obsessionals, and compensated paranoids. The former stress love and the uncovering of feelings; the obsessionals write the papers with the longest bibliographies; and the compensated paranoids are the liveliest, most troublesome and innovative" (p. 4). I could guess where Schimel would have placed himself.

Schimel always understood that wit was a double-edged sword. His "pungent, sharp, incisive speech—at times unkind" could humiliate or intimidate, could become the "whip of the oppressor" (Schimel, 1978, p. 373), as well as build rapport or generate insights. But Schimel wielded the weapon of wit expertly, and his patients, like most of us, loved him for it. This I gather from his writings as well as from a recent conversation with one of his patients, a young actor (whose mother has been my patient for some years):

Amnon Issacharoff, M.D. is a Training and Supervising Analyst, William Alanson White Institute.

"His wit was fast—always related to what was going on, always surprising. I laughed a lot," he said. In his use of humor, Schimel was what the young actor–patient described as a "situation comedian" more than a stand-up comic delivering one-liners. His humorous twist came from the conversation, the issue at hand, and it was typically delivered in a dead-pan style. And as his patient recounted, Schimel shared in the pleasure: "I remember him laughing a lot. It was very nice to make him laugh."

But not all was fun and games. The patient found the work of the sessions intense: "The discussions could take unexpected turns, it was unpredictable. I had no idea which way we would go. I would come with one idea and it ended in something completely different, always interesting." Humor, for Schimel, was not only a way of building rapport; it was part of an arsenal of methods in the art of interpretation, a common feature of which was indirection. As the young actor recalls, "He was very clever. I could never quite tell what he was working on. We talked about air conditioning, his hat collection, or some of the people whose photographs were on the wall. Often it was not until after I left his wonderful office that a thought that seemed important would come to my mind. It was like the work had slipped in, in a subtle way." Or, in Schimel's (1986) words, "The laconic or analogic form of the psychotherapist's interpretation does not spell out the psychodynamics for the patient but leaves work to do" (p. 185).

When the therapeutic alliance was well established, as with this patient, Schimel was capable not only of subtle analogies, but of dogged confrontations. In this patient's words: "He reminded me of Humphrey Bogart, close to the vest. At times I wouldn't know if I would be confronted or if he would make me laugh. He could be quite disagreeable in arguing over some issue. Sometimes he wouldn't believe me no matter what and he would win. He was pretty stubborn when his mind was made up. I couldn't fight him."

Schimel's distinctive technique derives from Sullivan's notion of "directed associations"—an active therapeutic engagement in which the patient is directed from the general to the particular. This respect for the material that emerges from the patient's everyday experiences, past and present, cultivates an atmosphere of on-going collaboration between the therapist and the patient. The continuous use of examples for clarification fosters consensual validation, a pillar of the interpersonal technique. In Schimel's hands, perhaps paradoxically, the use of "directed associations" generated a productive dynamic of indirection. Confrontations without explanations and evolving interpretations occur in a collaborative frame that is not completed or dictated by the therapist. Schimel's distinctive playfulness was, for him, essential for a successful therapeutic engagement with the adolescent patient, and I believe that he would have extended this requisite to the treatment situation in any age category.

Perhaps it was his range of therapeutic devices that allowed Schimel to finesse what Gitelson (1973) calls "the empathic problem" with adolescents. Schimel did not concern himself with the difficulties of matching adaptation of the patient-therapist dyad. The range of his techniques, which were not limited to the doggedly intellectual, allowed him to deal successfully with a range of adolescent patients. True, his was a private practice with affluent and generally bright patients. It is not clear if he lamented these limitations.

In fact, he relished the special challenges posed by gifted adolescents. But in all cases he relied on his wit, humoring his young patients and provoking them to look themselves in the mirror and not to take themselves too seriously.

When Schimel describes his uniquely crafted interpretive technique with adolescents, he stresses—with a clear and acknowledged debt to Sullivan—the connection between the self-knowledge derived from interpretation and the style and form of the communications between patient and therapist. Cognizant of that connection, he fashions a gradual build-up of rapport to facilitate the interpretative task, both over time and moment to moment, during each session. In the paper chosen for this volume, Schimel emphasizes the preinterpretative groundwork that is a common ground of sound clinical practice among psychoanalysts—the establishment of rapport, or positive transference, that must precede work that is necessarily painful to the patient.

Schimel's way of establishing that communicative rapport is noteworthy for its empathic quality. During this stage, there is a continuous monitoring of the state of the therapeutic alliance, while confrontation, clarification, and close attention to "other people in the room" prepare the ground for future understanding. And unlike many analysts who work with adolescents, Schimel always made himself acquainted with some of those other people—the patients' parents—directly and personally. Long years of trial and error taught him the need to achieve rapport with both the parents and the patient (Schimel, 1973), for he was convinced that the family situation was a reality that envelops the autonomous maturational needs of the adolescent. Other practitioner-authors with a family orientation have remarked on the need to respect the adolescent's feelings of loyalty towards the family, even when obscured by what seems to be an entrenched rebellious stance. Rapport with the family also helps to place in context a long-recognized tendency of adolescent patients to remember and emphasize the polar opposite of the habitual family experience, the exception rather than the rule.

Schimel's description of his pre-interpretative work—careful listening interspersed with confronting inquiry or request for clarifications—may fall under the rubric of interpretation for some, and so may the counterprojective maneuver to defuse the build-up of resistance. But the theoretical umbrella covering these activities matters less than their outcome. Who is to tell whether the seemingly temporary relief afforded by the small miracle of minds meeting in shared feeling and thought—we may call it consensual validation or the affirmation of a budding and struggling identity—can be transformed into working self-knowledge within analytic canons. Perhaps this building-by-blocks seems more appropriate with younger souls emerging from chrysalis-like states, but I have seen those same souls timidly gazing from behind adult masks.

Schimel (1973) describes the adolescents he treated in his office as of "high intelligence, affluence, middle to upper social class ambiance, one or two vocationally accomplished parents, some prior orientation to psychoanalytic psychotherapy, and at least a modicum of hope for the future." This description fits a good part of private psychoanalytic practices with all ages. The potential contributions from child psychoanalysis to techniques of adult therapy have been widely acknowledged, and this debt should include adolescent psychotherapy as well. Schimel's writings in the field of adolescent psychiatry over thirty years—his 160 publications include one book and 30 book chapters and numerous articles on adolescent issues—bear the same useful implications for the adolescent characteristics that remain, for better or for worse, latent or manifest, in all of us.

In the many years we shared the sometimes exciting and sometimes boring meetings of the Council of Fellows of the William Alanson White Institute, we all expected and welcomed the sudden "motion to adjourn" that was uniquely Schimel's prerogative to thrust upon us to cool us off or rescue us from obsessive ritualistic behavior. I can hear it now.

The notion of interpretation in psychoanalytic theory and practice is close to its dictionary definition: an explanation of that which is obscure (*Webster's Second International Dictionary*). Freud (1900), in *The Interpretation of Dreams*, presented the thesis that explanations (interpretations) of unconscious material result in their being uncovered. This, along with the remembering of early traumatic events and forbidden wishes, leads to recovery. In his study, Freud did not dwell on the style or manner of interpretations—or, for that matter, with the style or manner in which the dreamers' words and affect were reported. In some instances, only a summary of the dream was offered. Such matters also were not emphasized as the study of psychodynamics became more sophisticated and the fate of interpretations was presumed to be related to resistance and transference.

Many of the debates of the time dealt with the meaning of the dream, other symbols, symbolic behaviors, and notions of their correct interpretation, as in the commentaries of Stekel (1943). An early exception, however, was the work of Aichhorn (1925) in *Wayward Youth*. His writings are of particular interest to us since he dealt with adolescence and left glowing testimony to the importance of knowing how to relate to and talk with adolescents. Adler, whose social concerns led him to be one of the first to become involved in child guidance and schools, also noted the importance of the form as well as the content of communications with the young (see the summary and references provided by Ansbacher and Ansbacher, 1956, pp. 384–410).

What was to be interpreted was also an issue. This is a primary concern for many. For the early Freud (1900), the vicissitudes of instincts and

---

Annals of the American Academy for Adolescent Psychiatry, Volume 13: Developmental and Clinical Studies. Chicago: University of Chicago Press, pp. 178–187.

intrapsychic phenomena were central. Reich (1933) stressed the importance of the psychoanalysis of the character defenses, customary modes
of feeling and relating, as a prerequisite to the analysis of the intrapsychic. Sullivan (1954) focused on the psychoanalysis of interpersonal
factors from both historical and current perspectives. He stressed the
importance of the form as well as the substance of the communications of
both patient and therapist and offered numerous suggestions regarding
the function of various modes of interacting with patients.

TRANSFERENCE-COUNTERTRANSFERENCE IN ADOLESCENT PSYCHOTHERAPY

A therapist is concerned with acquiring skill in understanding: what
the patient is telling him or her; how the patient is affecting him; how the
patient sees and experiences him; what the patient expects from him
both consciously and unconsciously; what has happened to the patient in
the past and what is happening to him in the present; and how the patient
feels from moment to moment during the interview. The psychotherapist
who works with adolescents also must develop skills in understanding
certain pertinent but less immediately relevant matters—such as the
genetics of the situation; the psychodynamics involved. He also needs to
gauge accurately the effect on the patient of further listening (not necessarily beneficial), of his talking, and of other behavior.

For example: An adolescent patient complains bitterly about the fact
that her parents disapprove of her boyfriend. They are unfair, and,
anyway, she is old enough to choose her own friends. She does not like
their friends either, but she does not try to choose their friends for them.

What do we know from this prototypical encounter between adolescent and therapist? We know that the patient is demanding that the
therapist ally himself with her against her parents, that she sees him as an
adult authority to whom she can appeal, and that she expects or hopes for
sympathy and agreement. This is not the first such encounter with her
parents, nor will it be the last. Sooner or later the therapist will walk a
tightrope on this and other matters. At some point, the patient will be at
least tempted to leave treatment—a prospect more easily contemplated
than leaving her home or her boyfriend.

The therapist observes and feels her near-panic state, recognizing her
massive denial of her own doubts about the boyfriend. He knows that her
mother's remark, "There is more to a relationship than sex," has inten-
sified the rage, self-doubt, and self-loathing in his patient. He inwardly
weighs further silence against another form of intervention. He inter-
venes with a counterprojective maneuver. This is a term that Havens
(1976) uses to describe a type of intervention, recommended by Sullivan,

when the patient is already in or is likely to be propelled into a highly defended position. The action is moved out, away from the protagonists (therapist and patient) to more or less hypothetical third persons:

T: It is unfortunate that your parents interfered.

P: They mess into everything.

T: Lots of times, when that happens, young women marry out of spite or defiance. [The therapist has attempted to introduce the subject of young women and their parents, rather than this particular young woman—a counterprojective technique.]

P: I know what you're up to. You're just like them, only sneakier. You know I have doubts about John, but that's my problem. I have doubts about everything and everybody. John's different. He's OK. He's nice to me. He's everything a girl could want—lots of the girls want him. But he loves me.

T: You sound like a tigress defending her young.

P: Pretty fancy interpretation. But you're right; I feel fierce.

The following hour, the patient complains bitterly about the way one of her teachers has been treating her and her girlfriend; it is unfair and unjust:

T: This sounds like a rerun of the last hour.

P: What do you mean?

T: It's the same story, just a different cast of characters.

P: You're awful, but it sounds right. It's true that I'm angry a lot of the time and I'm always defending myself or my friends. But I don't get the connection. What are you up to? It's got nothing to do with me and John. What I said is still true. My mother is a bitch and John is OK. All right, you're right. I'm always angry, and here I am mad again with you this time. But what does it mean? I don't get the connection. What does it mean?

T: It means that there are parallel processes at work.

P: (laughs) You're smart today.

[At the end of the hour, as she is leaving, she again turns to the therapist and demands:]

P: All right. It's raining and I lost my umbrella today. What does that mean?

T: I see you're itching to have a go at me, too, but it probably means that you don't carry an umbrella when it's not raining.

P: (laughs) You're very smart today.

What has been happening and what is relevant to the art of interpretation? We must reconsider the notion of interpretation as an explanation of that which is obscure. No interpretation, in that sense, occurred. Something did occur, however, that will make the acceptance of future explanations more likely; a preparation for future interpretations.

Confrontation with the adolescent patient has occurred. Technically, confrontation is the bringing of some aspect of the patient to attention, without explanation. This was done repeatedly. Among the matters confronted, without explanation, were the fact of the patient's own doubts about her boyfriend and other matters, her pattern of rages, her preoccupation with justice and injustice, her clinging and demanding (infantile) behavior, and, perhaps especially, her utilization of denial in dealing with conflictual intrapsychic and/or interpersonal material.

The excerpts illustrate a process of clarification rather than explanation; an exercise in consensual validation between therapist and patient. There is a subtle collusion between patient and therapist. They are playing a game. The patient repeatedly tries to convert the psychotherapist to open support of her position. The therapist refuses. She counters with a defiant challenge to engage him in an argument. The psychotherapist sidesteps this challenge. The patient applauds him. The psychotherapist has introduced a note of playfulness forgotten by the patient, a relationship that her neurosis has precluded previously. The art of the psychotherapeutic encounter lies precisely in such matters.

The therapeutic encounter can be conceptualized as an engagement between two people in which one or the other may operate, from time to time, in a regressed fashion, expressed as resistance or transference manifestations. But this is not quite adequate for our review of the excerpted materials. Sullivan's (1954) notion of "the other people in the room" is more helpful. Here is the adolescent (or is it the infant?) warring with authority in the person of the therapist, screaming a challenge: "What does it mean?" He is the authority, pontificating: "It is unfortunate that your parents interfered." There is also the adolescent who is thoughtful and, one might say, mature, remarking, "It's true; I am angry a lot of the time and I'm always defending myself or my friends." There is the psychotherapist who is less an authority than a thoughtful listener: "You sound like a tigress defending her young." And, there is the adolescent who is an irreverent peer, competitive, and at times, admiring: "Pretty fancy interpretation," and "You're smart today." Here, she is responding to the psychotherapist as competitor who obviously enjoys both her challenges to his authority and his own one-upmanship in those situations.

So we have many people in the room, alternating rapidly, even kaleidoscopically. The pair that bear the main therapeutic burden consists of the thoughtful psychotherapist and the thoughtful patient. The psychotherapist must also utilize his alter ego, expressing authority or competitiveness as indicated. The patient is burdened by her clinging, dependent, demanding infant and rebellious defiant adolescent impulses. While there may be occasional indications for the psychotherapist to exercise his authority or even, on rare occasions, to attempt to discipline his patient, his goal should always be to foster the collaboration of the two thoughtful people in the room.

The interpretation, or, rather, the introduction of an interpretation with adolescent (or other) patients before such a therapeutic alliance is established, often leads to an impasse. The therapist may be completely convinced of the correctness of his interpretation, but the interpretation seems wrong, useless, meaningless to the patient, and, in any event, painful. The resistance interpretation, consoling as it may be to the psychotherapist, simply adds insult to injury for the adolescent patient. Such unresolved confrontations may result in regression to an infantile emotional level manifested by primitive expressions of rage, tearfulness, fearful clinging, or other symptomatic behaviors. Such situations may result from various interventions, including inappropriate silences and premature and other frightening interpretations. Although there may be, as a consequence, the production of suppressed and/or repressed material, the situation approximates that described in Freud's (1910) article on "wild" psychoanalysis. The therapist may be pleased with the deep material uncovered, but it may be experienced as a calamity by the patient.

Greenson (1978) has noted that the procedures of psychoanalysis may seem odd, artificial, and irrational to the patient. This is particularly true for many adolescent patients. I have noted elsewhere (Schimel, 1974) the negative therapeutic responses of adolescent patients to strictures against the answering of even innocuous questions, the requests of patients for orientation to the psychotherapeutic process, and the exchange of greetings and pleasantries. I have also noted the importance of the choice of language, the function of the element of surprise, and the timing of interventions. Greenson further notes, "Facility in selecting the right word or language is similar to what one observes in story tellers, humorists, or satirists. I am stressing verbal dexterity rather than literary ability." F. Alexander (1964) once remarked that, in psychotherapy, "what you plan to do depends upon how good an actor you are." He referred not to pretending but to the degree that thoughts and emotions can be communicated meaningfully and with traction for patients. This is the art of interpretation—an essential element in the art of healing.

But let us return to our patient, now in a later stage of her treatment. She has become aware of her continuing tendency to integrate situations with others, including a subsequent boyfriend, in a manner in which any frustration of her wishes moves her to attack. She is now aware of her vigilance to any signs of vulnerability in herself to which others may respond with criticism or attack—as well as vigilance to areas of vulnerability in others whom she might attack when frustrated. She knows now that she tends to be blind to defects in others (denial) when things are going well. She knows that at those times her friends can do no wrong; her enemies can do no right. She has some appreciation, in a nontechnical sense, that her world is one of good or bad, black or white (splitting, if you will), and that this is a reflection of an early childlike cognitive and developmental level, a narcissistic orientation. At times, however, she is despairing in contemplating the repetition of infantile patterns.

P: I'm much better than I used to be, sometimes for days on end. I'm getting pretty good marks in school, too. But I still fly off the handle—and sometimes for no reason. OK, OK, I know there's always a reason. You've told me so often enough. But it feels like there's no reason. Like uncontrollable. I know, I know; you always want an example. Well, last night Mother walked into my room and I blew. I blew it. Ranting and raving. She hadn't done anything.

T: Black and white again. She's all right; you're all wrong.

P: Well, she's supposed to knock first. But I don't always blow when she comes in without knocking. She's hopeless, the original Snoopy.

T: So, something was different this time.

P: One plus one equals two. Sure. Yes, something was different. I was supposed to be studying and I was daydreaming—about Bill, I suppose. But she couldn't read my mind. Maybe I reacted as though she had. You once told me that children sometimes believe that their mothers can read their minds. But what if she did read my mind; what's to be ashamed of? It's the matter of intolerance again. I'm getting tired of it. I'm afraid of everybody and what they think of me. And I always imagine the worst. I'm just as bad. Sometimes I feel I don't really have a good word for anybody, at least not for very long. I should be more loving. I'm the most intolerant person in the world.

T: Congratulations.

P: You mean grandiose again! The most intolerant person in the world! OK, but what do I do? This whole thing stinks. I have to do something. What can I do?

T: You already have your own solution.

P: What's that?

T: You know: to become all-wise, all-knowing, all-loving.

P: The same shit again. That's what I expect from others. That's what I expect from myself.

DISCUSSION

The foregoing excerpts were selected to illustrate an ongoing collaboration between patient and psychotherapist in which the interventions are more or less jargon free, even laconic, and in which there are elements of surprise for the patient in the twisting of perspective that permit the appearance of new dimensions of problem areas. Confrontation as a technique is continued. It may be apparent that interpretations—in the sense of explanations of that which is obscure—have been made and have been integrated. Ongoing interpretations are made as the material evolves, once the groundwork has been sufficient to permit collaborative use by patient and therapist. In this context, it may be seen that the psychotherapist's remark, "Black and white again. She's all right; you're all wrong," served to explain what had been obscure. The remark, in addition, served to focus the patient's attention in a particular direction. I believe that the matter of directed associations, Sullivan's (1954) term, is a matter for continual scrutiny by the psychotherapist. I do not believe that there is an escape hatch for the therapist in the notion of free association. Patients find direction in any event. I believe that the issue is one of heightened consciousness on the part of the psychotherapist of the effect of his interventions or presumed noninterventions. Freud once suggested that, when the patient became capable of free association, it was a signal that the therapy was completed.

The laconic or analogic form of the psychotherapist's interpretation does not spell out the psychodynamics for the patient but leaves work to do. The same reasoning applies to his humorous "congratulations" to the patient as a way of bringing to her awareness the grandiose posture she struck with her statement, "I'm the most intolerant person in the world." This matter of leaving work for the patient to do fosters the feeling of the two working together. Similar considerations apply to the use of anecdotes, humor, aphorisms, information giving about childhood modes of perception, and average expectable reactions of people in our culture generally. The patient is offered a conceptual tool, a generalized explanation that she can apply to one or, one hopes, to many situations in which she regularly finds herself.

This is a far different and more dynamic matter than the psychotherapeutic notion of waiting for the material to emerge. I believe that, for the alert psychotherapist, the material is always there. The question is one of timing and appropriate formulation. There is no safety in psychotherapeutic waiting, particularly with adolescent patients. This is not to obviate the exercise of respectful and prolonged listening when appropriate.

No solutions to the patient's problems have been or are currently offered, nor will they be. In fact, the circularity and interdigitations of the neurotic processes are constantly being explored and exposed. Meanwhile, the process of growth achieves a kind of inexorable momentum that is reflected in the content of the excerpts. The foregoing is not meant to preclude the possibility of offering information, coaching, or advice when indicated.

One note: Sullivan (1954) wrote that the supply of interpretations is always greater than the need. I hope this discussion has succeeded in suggesting that there are more important matters than the truth of interpretations. There is the crucial matter of laying the groundwork for interpretations and for the development of a collaborative working relationship with the patient generally. When this is successful, the patient has integrated, in part, the image of the thoughtful psychotherapist. In the final excerpt the patient repeatedly demonstrates that she is listening to herself with the third ear of the psychotherapist. She says, for example, "OK, OK, I know there's always a reason . . . ." Call this an observing ego, if you will.

CONCLUSIONS

The analogy of the psychotherapist to the chess player may be a useful one in considering the art of interpretation. Intervention may well be made when the therapist knows the patient reasonably well, with a foreknowledge of future interventions. This follows if our theories of personality and therapy have validity. The psychotherapist need be in no hurry with interpretations. They have to be made in stages as they become applicable and usable. They may have to be made in bits and pieces, endlessly repeated and extended to meet new situations as they arise. They must grow as the patient grows in order to be relevant to progressive developmental stages and the problems that attend them. While being prepared for surprises and detours, the psychotherapist nevertheless may have a clear appreciation of the route that the therapist and the patient must traverse. Human growth and development are relatively predictable and assured when the hindrances are progressively attenuated by the collaborative work of patient and therapist.

REFERENCES

Adler, A. (1956), In: *The Individual Psychology of Alfred Adler,* ed. H. L. Ansbacher & R. R. Ansbacher. New York: Basic Books.

Aichhorn, A. (1925), *Wayward Youth.* New York: Viking Press, 1974.

Alexander, F. (1964). In: *The Newsletter of the American Academy of Psychoanalysis,* 8, quoted by M. Grotjahn, p. 6.

Ansbacher, H. L. & Ansbacher, R. R., eds. (1956), *The Individual Psychology of Alfred Adler.* New York: Basic Books.

Freud, S. (1900), *The Interpretation of Dreams.* New York: Modern Library, 1938.

—— (1910), Observations on "wild" psychoanalysis. *Collected Papers 2.* London: Hogarth Press, pp. 297–304, 1933.

Greenson, R. R. (1978), *Explorations in Psychoanalysis.* New York: International Universities Press.

Grotjahn, M. (1957), *Beyond Laughter.* New York: McGraw-Hill.

Havens, L. (1976), *Participant Observation.* New York: Aronson.

Reich, W. (1933), *Character-Analysis.* New York: Orgone Institute, 1945.

Schimel, J. L. (1974), Two alliances in the treatment of adolescents: Towards a working alliance with parents and a therapeutic alliance with the adolescent. *J. Amer. Acad. Psychoanal.,* 2:243–253.

Stekel, W. (1943), *The Interpretation of Dreams.* New York: Liveright.

Sullivan, H. S. (1954), *The Psychiatric Interview.* New York: Norton.

INTRODUCTION REFERENCES

Chapter 2

Freud, S. (1907), Psychoanalysis and the establishment of facts in legal proceedings. *Standard Edition*, 9:103–114. London: Hogarth Press, 1959.

Fromm-Reichmann, F. (1939), Transference problems in schizophrenics. *Psychoanal. Quart.*, 8:117–128.

———(1950), *Principles of Intensive Psychotherapy*. Chicago: University of Chicago Press.

———(1959), *Psychoanalysis and Psychotherapy: Selected Papers*, ed. D. M. Bullard & E. V. Weigert. Chicago: University of Chicago Press.

Racker, H. (1968), *Transference and Countertransference*. New York: International Universities Press.

Santyana, G. (1894), O world though choosest not. In: *A Bibliographical Checklist*, ed. H. J. Saatkamp & J. Jones. Bowling Green, OH: Philosophy Documentation Center, Bowling Green State University, 1982.

Sullivan, H. S. (1940), *Conceptions of Modern Psychiatry*. Washington, DC: William Alanson White Psychiatric Foundation.

Thompson, C. (1964), *Interpersonal Psychoanalysis*, ed. M. R. Green. New York: Basic Books.

Winnicott, D. W. (1945), *Through Paediatrics to Psycho-Analysis*. London: Hogarth Press.

Chapter 4

Green, M., ed. (1964), *Interpersonal Psychoanalysis: The Selected Writings of Clara Thompson*. New York: Basic Books.

Thompson, C. (1950), *Psychoanalysis: Evolution and Development*. New York: Hermitage House.

Chapter 5

Crowley, R. (1964), The analyst's motivation to help. *Contemp. Psychoanal.*, 1:30–37.

——— (1975a), Harry Stack Sullivan: The complete bibliography. *Contemp. Psychoanal.*, 11:83–99.

——— (1975b), Farewell to innocence. *Contemp. Psychoanal.*, 11:382–387.

——— (1983), Difficulties in the teaching of interpersonal psychoanalysis. *Contemp. Psychoanal.*, 19:130–133.

Chapter 6

Blatt, S. J. (1990), Interperson relatedness and self-definition: Two personality configurations and their implications for psychopathology and psychotherapy. In: *Repression and Dissociation*, ed. J. L. Singer. Chicago: University of Chicago Press, pp. 299–336.

Freud, S. (1895), Project for a scientific psychology. *Standard Edition*, 1:295–397. London: Hogarth Press, 1966.

Harlow, H. F. (1953), Mice, monkeys, men and motives. *Psychoanal. Rev.*, 60:23–32.

Hartmann, H. (1958), *Ego Psychology and the Problem of Adaptation*. New York: International Universities Press.

Hebb, D. O. (1956), The motivating effects of exteroceptive stimulation. *J. Ment. Sci.*, 105:235.

Holt, R. (1964), Imagery: The return of the ostracized. *Amer. Psycholog.*, 19:254.

——— (1976), Drive or wish? A reconsideration of the psychoanalytic theory of motivation. In: *Psychology Versus Metapsychology*, ed. M. Gill & P. Holtzman. *Psychological Issues*, Monogr. 36. New York: International Universities Press.

Klein, G. S. (1967), Peremptory ideation: Structure and force in motivated ideas. In: *Motivation and Thought*, ed. R. R. Holt. *Psychological Issues*, Monogr. 18. New York: International Universities Press, pp. 78–128.

Piaget, J. (1962), *Play, Dreams, Imitation in Children.* New York: Norton.

Rapaport, D. (1960), On the psychoanalytic theory of motivation. In: *Nebraska Symposium on Motivation,* ed. M. R. Jones. Lincoln: University of Nebraska Press.

Schachtel, E. G. (1959), *Metamorphosis.* New York: Basic Books.

—— (1966), *Experiential Foundations of Rorschach's Test.* New York: Basic Books.

Schafer, R. (1976), Emotion in the language of action. In: *Psychology Versus Metapsychology,* ed. M. Gill & P. Holzman. *Psychological Issues,* Monogr. 36. New York: International Universities Press.

Singer, D. G. & Singer, J. L. (1990), *The Child's World of Make-Believe.* Cambridge, MA: Harvard University Press.

Singer, J. L. & Bonanno, G. (1990), Personality and private experience: Individual variations in consciousness and in attention to subjective phenomena. In: *Handbook of Personality,* ed. L. Perrin. New York: Guilford, pp. 419–444.

Spurgeon, C. (1935), *Shakespeare's Imagery and What It Tells Us.* Cambridge: Cambridge University Press.

Tolman, E. C. (1949), *Purposive Behavior in Animals and Men.* Berkeley: University of California Press.

Tomkins, S. S. (1962, 1963, 1991), *Affect, Imagery, Consciousness* (3 vols). New York: Springer.

Werner, H. (1948), *Comparative Psychology of Mental Development,* rev. ed. New York: International Universities Press.

White, R. W. (1959), Motivation reconsidered: The concept of competence. *Psycholog. Rev.,* 66:291–333.

Chapter 7

Sullivan, H. S. (1953), *The Interpersonal Theory of Psychiatry* New York: Norton.

Tauber, E. S. & Green, M. R. (1959), *Prelogical Experience: An Inquiry into Dreams and Other Creative Processes.* New York: Basic Books.

Chapter 8

Fromm, E. (1941), *Escape from Freedom.* New York: Avon Books, 1965.

——(1947), *Man for Himself.* Greenwich, CT: Fawcett Premier Books.

——(1955), *The Sane Society.* Greenwich, CT: Fawcett Premier Books.

——(1956), *The Art of Loving.* New York: Bantam Books, 1970.

——(1962), *Beyond the Chains of Illusion.* New York: Simon & Schuster.

——(1966), *You Shall Be As Gods.* Greenwich, CT: Fawcett Premier Books.

——(1976), *To Have or To Be.* New York: Harper & Row, 1981.

——(1992), *The Revision of Psychoanalysis.* Boulder, CO: Westview Press.

Chapter 9

Crowley, R. (1975), Bone and Sullivan. *Contemp. Psychoanal.,* 11:66–74.

Chapter 11

Becker, E. (1964), *Revolution in Psychiatry.* New York: Free Press.

Crowley, R. M. (1971), Notes on Sullivan's approach to the science of man. *Contemp. Psychoanal.,* 8:64–71.

Schecter, D. E. (1968), Identification and individuation. *J. Amer. Psychoanal. Assn.,* 16:48–80.

——(1971), Two of Sullivan's conceptions. *Contemp. Psychoanal.,* 8:71–75.

——(1973), On the emergence of human relatedness. In: *Interpersonal Explorations in Psychoanalysis,* ed. E. G. Witenberg. New York: Basic Books, pp. 17–39.

——(1974), Infant development. In: *American Handbook of Psychiatry* (2nd ed.), ed. S. Arieti. New York: Basic Books, pp. 264–283.

——(1978a), Attachment, detachment, and psychoanalytic therapy. In: *Interpersonal Psychoanalysis: New Directions*, ed. E. G. Witenberg. New York: Gardner Press, pp. 81–104.

——(1978b), Malevolent transformation: Some clinical and developmental notes. *Contemp. Psychoanal.*, 14:414–418.

——(1980), Early developmental roots of anxiety. *J. Amer. Acad. Psychoanal.*, 8:539–554.

——(1981), Contributions of Erich Fromm. *Contemp. Psychoanal.*, 17:468–480.

——(1983), Notes on the development of creativity. *Contemp. Psychoanal.*, 19:193–199.

Sullivan, H. S. (1953), *The Interpersonal Theory of Psychiatry*. New York: Norton.

Chapter 12

Barnett, J. (1966a), On cognitive disorders in the obsessional. *Contemp. Psychoanal.*, 2:122–134.

——(1966b), Cognitive repair in the treatment of the obsessional neuroses. *Proc. IVth World Congr. Psychiat.*, 150:752–757.

——(1966c), A structural analysis of theories in psychoanalysis. *Psychoanalyt. Rev.*, 53:85–98.

——(1971a), Sex and the obsessive-compulsive person. *Medical Aspects Human Sexual.*, 5.

——(1971b), Dependency conflicts in the young adult. *Psychoanalyt. Rev.*, 58:111–125.

——(1971c), Narcissism and dependence in the obsessional-hysteric marriage. *Family Process*, 10:75–83.

——(1972), Therapeutic intervention in the dysfunctional thought processes of the obsessional. *Amer. J. Psychother.*, 26:338–351.

——(1973a), Sexuality in the obsessional neuroses. In: *Interpersonal Explorations in Psychoanalysis*, ed. E. Witenberg. New York: Basic Books, pp. 180–195.

——(1973b), On ideology and the psychodynamics of the ideologue. *J. Amer. Acad. Psychoanal.*, 1:381–395.

——(1973c), Adolescence and ideology. *Newsletter, Society for Adolescent Psychiatry.*

——(1975), Hamlet and the family ideology. *J. Amer. Acad. Psychoanal.*, 3:405–417.

——(1978), On the dynamics of interpersonal isolation. *J. Amer. Acad. Psychoanal.*, 6:59–70.

——(1979) Character, cognition and therapeutic process. *Amer. J. Psychoanal.*, 39:13–20.

——(1980a), Self and character. *J. Amer. Acad. Psychoanal.*, 8:337–352.

——(1980b), Interpersonal processes, cognition and an analysis of character. *Contemp. Psychoanal.*, 16:397–416.

——(1988), The interplay of patient/therapist character structures on cognition, thought and affect in the therapeutic process. [Title by the authors from Dr. Barnett's notes.] Paper presented to the Manhattan Institute for Psychoanalysis.

Fromm, E. (1947), *Man for Himself*. Greenwich, CT: Fawcett.

Sullivan, H. S. (1953), *The Interpersonal Theory of Psychiatry*. NY: Norton.

Chapter 14

Gitelson, M. (1973), *Psychoanalysis: Science and Profession*. New York: International Universities Press.

Schimel, J. L. (1972), The power theme in the obsessional. *Contemp. Psychoanal.*, 9:1–15.

—— (1973), Esoteric identification processes in adolescence and beyond. *J. Amer. Acad. Psychoanal.*, 1:403–415.

—— (1978), The function of wit and humor in psychoanalysis. *J. Amer. Acad. Psychoanal.*, 6:369–379.

—— (1986), Psychotherapy with adolescents: The art of interpretation. *Annals of the American Academy for Adolescent Psychiatry*, 13:178–187. Chicago: University of Chicago Press.

INDEX